Perennials for Cutting

Perennials for Cutting

JOHN JEFFREYS

With line drawings by Yvonne Skargon

FABER AND FABER
3 Queen Square London

First published in 1977
by Faber and Faber Limited
3 Queen Square London WC1
Printed in Great Britain by
Latimer Trend & Company Ltd Plymouth

British Library Cataloguing in Publication Data

Jeffreys, John
  Perennials for cutting.
    1. Flower gardening   2. Flower arrangement
    3. Perennials
    I. Title
    635.9'32'024745   SB406

    ISBN 0-571-10916-0

TO GRACE G. WYLIE

Contents

List of Illustrations   *page* 9
Introduction   11

PART ONE

Ways and Means   15
Some Notes on Cultivation   27
Cutting the Flowers and Caring for Them   33

PART TWO

Alphabetical List of Selected Perennials   39
Alphabetical List of Selected Hardy Perennial Grasses   190
Selective Lists of Perennials for Cutting   194
Some Sources of Supply   209
Index   212

List of Illustrations

Section of a border showing 'right-angled' planting	*page* 17
Aquilegia	54
Astrantia	64
Crocosmia	86
Dicentia	95
Eryngium	104
Fritillaria	108
Gentiana	111
Hosta	122
Lilium henryi	134
Mimulus	144
Physalis	159
Pulmonaria	163
Scabiosa	172
Stachys	179
Trollius	184
Viola	188

Introduction

Hardy perennials give a wealth of choice among cut flower subjects, some of which are very long-lasting and full of character, beauty and fragrance. The range is much wider than many gardeners and some growers realize. It is the lunatic system of marketing cut blooms that sharply curtails the varieties florists are able to offer, for growers can only supply the market with those capable of withstanding long journeys and delays in transit. Where such journeys are avoided the enterprising florist may offer treble the usual variety of cut flowers, but few are able to make such satisfactory arrangements. This book is not concerned with the commercial aspects of cut flower growing and supply, however, but rather the emphasis has been laid on ways and means open to amateur gardeners and allotment holders for supplying their own household needs if they are willing to experiment and, in some cases, compromise.

I am very much concerned with the problems of those who are eager to have their own supply of flowers for cutting but whose space for growing them is restricted. There are those who have very little in the way of a garden but are still keen to cut their flowers for indoor decoration and I have suggested ways in which they can achieve their aim. This book is for all who are anxious to cultivate their own cut flower plants, whether their gardens are restricted to a few square yards or to a plot of half an acre or more, but I hope my advice will be of particular help to the former, for there the need is often the greatest. Formal flower arranging is not within the scope of my text, but flower arrangers should find here something fresh to consider in their endless search for new material.

The Hardy Plant Society is affiliated to the National Association of Flower Arrangement Societies of Great Britain (NAFAS). This pioneering society is devoted to hardy perennials: its exhibits at the various agricultural and rose shows, together with members' displays at the Royal Horticultural Society's London shows, often come as a revelation to those hitherto concerned with more ephemeral or run-of-the-mill plants. The Hardy Plant Society welcomes to its membership all who are interested in perennial plants. The Secretary, Miss B. White of 10 St. Barnabas Road, Emmer Green, Reading, Berkshire, is always pleased to advise on the Society's aims and membership.

PART ONE

Ways and Means

It is well to bear in mind that, while many perennials will give a very good account of themselves in the first year, some even flowering for an extended period, the real quality of bloom which is so desirable in cut flowers will often be found only in plants that have been well grown for two or three seasons. There are some exceptions both sides of this generalization, but a little patience will be rewarded with an abundance and reliability that is the hallmark of well grown perennials.

Small Gardens

It is possible to grow cut flowers for the house in a small garden, without spoiling the garden in the process, but it entails a careful and well thought out selection of suitable plants.

The basic need to select plants appropriate to their site, as opposed to random choice based on a passing whim, cannot be over-emphasized. The planting of, for example, nepeta in un-treated clay loam is fraught with troubles. Such planting would be wasteful, but the foolish would blame the plant. Nepeta then becomes a poor, short-lived perennial. Planted in a poor, light soil in the full eye of the sun this same plant becomes a good, rewarding and quite long-lived perennial.

Selection goes deeper than this, however. Experience has clearly shown that some perennials benefit from some cutting during their flowering season. By such means the more free-flowering plants are not allowed to overtax their root systems. Such cutting can stimulate the growth of roots long before the onset of winter sees them becoming apparently dormant. Three or four good perennials in this category that immediately come to mind are *Achillea fili-pendulina*, catananche, erigeron and sidalcea. All these improve as hardy perennials for being cut when in flower, and catananche and sidalcea in particular benefit greatly by having their flowering stems cut right back as soon as the main flush of flowering is over, in about mid-September. This promotion of root vigour keeps these generous perennials long-lived.

With certain varieties of *Armeria maritima* the flowering period may be extended by weeks, or even months, by the removal of old flower heads or by judicious cutting, taking care not to cut those still in bud. Some mimulus may even be lightly trimmed over after flowering in June if a heavy downpour has thrashed all the blooms on to the soil, yet by August they will be in full flower once again. Exactly the same may happen with that incredibly prolific trio of campanula—*portenschlagiana, carpatica*, and *rotundifolia*, and this without unduly harming or straining the plants' reserves. These all have a fibrous mat of roots feeding over a wide area, whereas the earlier mentioned catananche and sidalcea are far more fleshy and compact of root and would be weakened by the inducement of a second flowering. Thus a study of plants' roots will be seen to be fundamental to all gardening.

The following method of growing cut flower perennials in a small garden takes selection into account, but here the emphasis is on planting with precision.

The small garden's border or island bed does not easily accommodate both border perennials and cut flower plants without some compromise being made. In such confined spaces one cannot acceptably and conventionally plant for a long succession of flowering without the resulting gaps becoming too noticeable for comfort. So a new approach to planting must be considered by those who insist upon having both garden flowers and blooms for the house. The conventional and longitudinal view of the border must here be dispensed with to a certain extent. In a border or bed devoted to herbaceous perennials the indispensable 'backbone' planting may be carried out as usual. Into this planned design tapestry may be woven slender threads of cut flower subjects *planted at right angles* to the main view of the small garden. As these

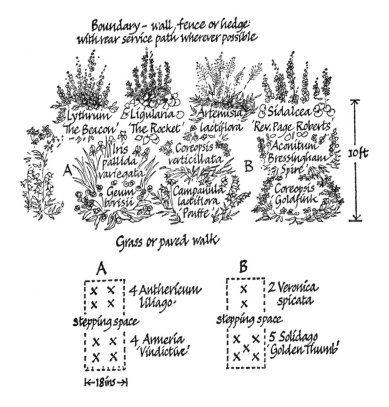

Boundary - wall, fence or hedge:
with rear service path wherever possible

Lythrum   &Ligularia⭘   Artemisia   &Sidalcea
'The Beacon'   'The Rocket'   &lactiflora   'Rev. Page Roberts'
Iris   Coreopsis   Aconitum
pallida   verticillata   Bressingham
variegata   B   Spire
Geum   Campanula   Coreopsis
borisii   lactiflora   Goldfink
Pouffe

10ft

Grass or paved walk

A

x x | 4 Anthericum
x x | liliago·
stepping space

x x | 4 Armeria
x x | 'Vindictive'

|←18ins→|

B

x | 2 Veronica
x | spicata
stepping space

x x | 5 Solidago
x x | 'Golden Thumb'

plants occupy only a narrow space, the gaps caused by removing the blooms will be far less noticeable when the garden is being looked at from the usual position.

This 'right-angled' planting of cut flower subjects can be very successful if the gardener first considers with great care both the siting and the appropriate grouping of those subjects notable for their attractive foliage as well as for their abundant flowers. Thus, even at the very front of the border, the evergreen grassy hummocks of *Armeria maritima* remain attractive when all their flowers have been picked. At the other end of the season, the dwarf asters remain pleasing when well grown, and are green throughout the summer, and these may be used to separate the summer-flowering frontal subjects. It is of course important that the number of such summer-green plants be sensibly restricted. If three such dwarf asters is the most suitable number, these are better planted one behind the other, at right angles to the edge of the border, rather than in a row parallel to the edge.

Some of the 'backbone' plants may have some of their flowers cut for the house without spoiling the garden outlook. Of the taller subjects a few stems of *Artemisia lactiflora*, lythrum and veronica may not be unduly missed and such as these can thus be used as dual purpose plants. Among the middle ranks the asters of *amellus* parentage, hemorocallis, and achillea have sufficiently fine leaves and abundant flowers to bear such treatment. This brings us back directly to the essential need to select with care.

In extremely small gardens such compromises are, on the whole better not made at all. Here space is usually far too precious to be dissipated by half-hearted measures and common sense insists that the better place for flowers is in the garden rather than in the house. But exemptions to this rule can be made, and careful selection and some precise right-angled planting will do much to preserve the garden and yet supply the house with some decorative flowers. Preference should be given to shallow-rooting, easy-growing subjects which require very little space. Even the tiniest garden can give a good supply of the sweetly scented alpine forms of dianthus, alpine campanulas and the prolific *Gentiana septemfida*. Many will prefer these delicate flowers in small bowls to the more ostentatious occupants of larger vases.

Larger Gardens

Where the garden is more than, say, a quarter of an acre (0·1 hectare), then at least three ways of growing cut flower subjects for the house come to mind.

Firstly the garden can be planted up along the lines just indicated to make it appear even larger. Here the border or island bed of herbaceous perennials may be of sufficient size to incorporate the planting of selected cut flower plants without any noticeable sacrifice of quality—especially if the principle of right-angled planting is carefully allowed. Obviously, the larger the border the more simple the problem becomes, so long as the guiding precepts of common sense are observed.

Even in a garden of reasonable size, only well behaved cut flower plants can be admitted to the border. This is of paramount importance. To plant, for instance, such a mischievous-rooted subject as physalis in a border would be very foolish. The couch-like roots of physalis spread in good border soil at an alarming rate, and are by no means readily curbed. This is a plant for a confined site or a well-nurtured tub. Likewise, even where space saving is not the major consideration, freely self-seeding subjects should not be admitted unless timely cutting down is assured. In the notes devoted to the plants, perennials fit by their good behaviour for inclusion in the border are clearly indicated. Obviously the owners of small gardens should restrict their selection to such troublefree plants as are suitable, and eschew the flowery temptations of those with rampageous roots and untidy habits. Further, such selection must take into account the plants' foliage, the merits of which should never be overlooked or taken for granted.

The second method of growing cut flower perennials in the larger garden has its advantages. A separate bed can be thoroughly prepared and cunningly screened by other plantings. Sometimes this might be close to the house so that one is not tempted, in one's weaker moments, to pillage the pride of the border! Alternatively such a bed could be concealed near the vegetable garden, when this is masked off from the select realm of hardy perennials in island beds.

In such a segregated flower bed a wide variety of plants can be grown, so long as space permits and the art of selection is exercised. Here I agree with the old practice of growing plants in blocks or in rows, leaving ample room for air, light, easy access and cultivation. The growing of plants in rows has much to commend it and is probably better than the block system. Plants arranged in rows may receive plenty of the air vital to their health, and away from all baneful influences a sturdiness and tidiness of habit will be promoted. Such rows may be simply supported, where necessary, by parallel lines of sticks and soft wire, or cord, so placed as not to interfere with cutting or prove dangerous when stooping. Planting in rows also gives a ready means of segregating the slow-growing from the more boisterous plants, thus avoiding a highly undesirable tangling of growth which can be so tedious and time-consuming to separate, even with scissors.

Planting in rows makes cutting, hoeing, weeding and watering simpler. Segregation in rows also readily widens the variety of plants one may grow. Half such a bed could be prepared to grow plants relishing sun and light and comparatively dry soil, such as anthemis and achillea. The remaining half would receive a little shade from the other, and here one could suitably enrich the soil with humus and install sub-irrigation to grow such subjects as astilbe and primula. It is a simple matter to provide a gradation of nutriment and moisture to suit individual plants' needs when they are grown in rows separated by ample paths.

The third way of growing perennials for cutting is in the time-honoured kitchen garden. While many will still grow their cut flowers in regimental rows for the good reasons just explained, there is a most rewarding alternative and that is the decorative method of growing cut flower plants and vegetables together, not only to provide food and decoration for the house but as a more creative form of productive gardening which will give double satisfaction. The vegetable garden may provide dramatic material for decoration. The globe artichoke, with its deeply cut leaves and heads of purple flowers, is undeniably ornamental, while the ferny foliage of asparagus is indispensable to the flower arranger.

Many cut flower subjects do not make good border plants. Such as pyrethrum and gaillardia are extremely generous plants giving long-lasting cut blooms, but their habit leaves much to be desired and their cultural needs are best dealt with in a vegetable plot.

A NEW KITCHEN GARDEN

Many vegetables are decorative, and some are very distinctive in form. A group of tall and slender sweetcorn, or maize, could well form a centrepiece in an island bed devoted to vegetables and cut flower plants. Frontal subjects in such a bed would include group plantings of carrots, dwarf curly kale, parsley and dwarf french beans. Among these, groups of cut flower subjects would be selected and planted for their soil preferences, height, habit and so forth. So long as sufficient space is left between all groups of plants, such a dual purpose bed may be both highly productive and attractive. The vegetable and cut flower subjects will, of course, be segregated in groups, not 'dotted' indiscriminately, and spaced to allow for the lifting of the vegetables and the cutting of the flowers.

Some of the dwarf beans have a very long season, as well as being attractive of habit and leaf, and highly decorative with their pendulous pods of green, blue and purple. A group of fennel makes a splendid light green or plum-purple backcloth to many flowering plants throughout the entire summer, besides being edible in every part, while the grassy-leaved salsify with its mid-summer blue flowers is a fine dual purpose plant. Gaps caused by the culling of vegetables could be filled with catch crops.

Such an ornamental way of growing vegetables and cut flower subjects together calls for a knowledge of their roots and an ability and willingness to prepare the soil accordingly. The fleshy fangs of fennel demand the same soil conditions as those of *Achillea Filipendulina*, which are both fleshy and fibrous, so these may be planted as neighbours to give good results. The stately sweetcorn must have its head in sunshine but its roots demand an abundance of summer moisture. One can take advantage of this by planting moisture (and shade) loving cut flower plants in its lee. Phlox can look magnificent in such company, as can astilbe.

Planning and planting up a mixed bed along these lines can thus add zest to gardening for those who find the growing of vegetables something of a dull but necessary routine. Should slugs become a nuisance then they can be partly repelled by interplantings of garlic, and the encouragement of visiting toads and hedgehogs.

Allotments

Those who have allotments will rightly grow their cut flower plants in blocks or rows. Where the soil is unduly heavy or badly drained in winter, many plants can be grown on broad ridges, while such as lythrum and astilbe can be grown in the valleys. Shade-loving plants can be grown behind a screen of runner beans or artichokes. By using a little ingenuity and imagination a wide range of hardy perennials giving cut flowers can be successfully grown. Again, the selection is governed by the soil of the allotment, and the laws of spacing still hold good.

Soil conditions and treatment, with special reference to vegetable gardens and allotments, are discussed in Chapter 2.

No Garden, but a Terrace, Courtyard or Patio

Those with no garden and perhaps only a terrace, courtyard or patio, can often overcome such a daunting handicap by constructing a raised bed in which to grow selected plants. Provided this is not in heavy shade, a remarkable variety of comparatively shallow-rooted subjects can be successfully raised. A depth of 2 ft (60 cm) is desirable to give good long-term value, yet even half this depth can be put to good use. Large tubs or deep, lined boxes can similarly be pressed into service. In such confined spaces above paving or concrete, a few inches of coarse drainage material is all that is required at the base, and this can be topped with gravel to prevent the downward seepage of the soil clogging the drainage. The selection of plants must be directly governed by the nature of the soil provided, and by the amount of shade present.

In a shady courtyard such a raised bed could be utilized to telling effect by converting it into a moisture bed, using a humus-rich soil or a polythene lining sheet perforated at the base. Here a beautiful array of astilbe and primula may flourish and brighten the shade, though one might then think it would be a shame to use such plants for cutting!

There may well be those who grow a plentiful supply of flowers for cutting in their allotments but who have virtually no garden at home. For them it is worth noting that a drab backyard may be enlivened by the use of a wide variety of seasonal cut flowers. If they are placed in large containers, such as earthenware pots, and sheltered from direct sunlight and from destructive winds and draughts, they will often have an outdoor life of weeks, as opposed to days only when they are indoors. If the containers are large enough to hold several gallons of water they will be sufficiently heavy to take spread out cut blooms without any fear of wind blowing them over. Containers with removable linings can be permanently fixed to walls or countersunk into paving material. Water in containers for outdoor use should be changed or topped up as frequently as possible.

Such use of cut flowers for outdoor, rather than indoor, decoration can give much scope to the imagination and is well worth consideration by the town dweller who may well have an allotment but no garden to speak of.

Selection

The importance of careful selection cannot be over-stressed. It will ensure that the gardener will not fill his precious domain with a surfeit of mid-summer flowering plants and will pay special attention to those valuable subjects with a long flowering season. These may be regarded as the backbone to the more ephemeral plantings: good examples are lythrum, *Artemisia lactiflora, Polygonum amplexicaule* and *Campanula portenschlagiana.* Also to be highly rated are those perennials such as euphorbia, pulmonaria and tellima which flower very early in the season and vernonia, echinacea and aconitum which flower very late: at these times florists' prices are at their highest and, because of natural scarcity, choice in the shops is severely restricted. Some flowers, for instance cimicifuga, tiarella and alpine subjects, may never be found in flower shops, either because they are not widely grown commercially or because they are unreliable 'travellers' and this is where the amateur can score over his professional counterpart.

In addition to the perennials that have a long season in bloom in the garden, the ones that last a long time in water are obviously especially valuable to those who buy their flowers, and here again the gardener is fortunate for, with careful planning, he can provide for the house a succession of the more fleeting beauties.

Also valuable and high on the gardener's list are the scented flowers. Besides the more obvious border phlox and dianthus, there are some beautiful herbs that are all too often overlooked. Many of these will grow well in a meagre sun-baked soil. The common marjoram, *Origanum vulgare*, gives a wealth of flowers for cutting throughout the summer. The lemon-scented balm, *Melissa officinalis*, adds a delicious freshness when a few of its leafy stems are added to a vase of flowers and, for good measure, the leaves of the variegated form are shot with gold. Both the green and the bronzy-red forms of fennel, *Foeniculum vulgare*, are redolent of aniseed, the filigree foliage makes a splendid background for cut flowers and the small umbels of yellow flowers are decorative and long-lasting both in garden and vase.

I usually cut down most of the perennials in the island beds in my garden in the latter half of October and it is surprising how many odd blooms one can then amass for the house. A customary visit from a professional grower during the first week of November is usually greeted with an array of around forty different kind of flowers in the house, from this source alone.

It is not only flowers that may be gleaned in this way, but also a fine selection of leaves, ranging in colour from green, blue and yellow through to orange, red and purple. All these are useful and valuable for decoration in the house and are beautiful to look at on cheerless November days. Then one may, at leisure, examine both leaves and flowers, learning to appreciate both to the full and in the minutest detail. With each passing year I am more convinced of the vital importance of foliage, whether in the garden or in a vase. Leaves should be given at least as much consideration as flowers, for a good balance of the two is always highly desirable, especially indoors when a vase of bald-stemmed flowers can be greatly enhanced by the inclusion of some foliage.

When considering foliage, the gardener and the flower arranger should also look to the ivies where a dozen forms, embracing a range of fine variegations including green and gold, are available. Stems of these are long-lasting and provide a delightful contrast in many types of flower decoration. Many growers of hardy plants offer them in their catalogues under *Hedera helix*. Ivies are far too good and useful to ignore and they could, to great advantage, be far more widely grown in both small and large gardens. Their ever-green and varied leaves give double value, both in the garden where they provide winter attraction and indoors where they have a prolonged vase life.

There is also plenty of scope for finding new material among the generally diminutive hardy perennials collectively classed as alpines. Many of these look very charming in shallow bowls, even if their life there is limited to only a few days. The alpine forms of aster, alyssum, phlox, arabis and erodium, gentians galore and sprigs of variegated thyme, together with a wide range of dianthus and campanula, can be used to great advantage. I have long cut these for indoor arrangements, though I have a natural reluctance to deprive the rarer and more choice plants of their blooms and one's cutting must be very selective.

Often it is only when flowers are in a vase that the gardener really appreciates their marvellous construction. They are seldom still in the garden and it is surprising how the smallest movement can deceive the eye. A patch of London pride in the garden is an airy cloud of pink, but a few sprays studied in the stillness of their vase reveal the delicacy of each tiny bicoloured and speckled bloom in all its exquisitely fine proportion. This in turn causes one to marvel at their resistance to the wind and to understand the reason why so many fragile flowers are borne on pliant stems.

Protection

In the garden a few cloches are valuable at the beginning and end of the flowering season. In early spring, cloches placed around such perennials as narcissi and peonies will ward off the cold winds and induce an earlier flowering. Cloches placed over smaller subjects such as trollius and caltha will similarly ensure an earlier blooming. At the other end of the season a cloche over *Helleborus niger* might induce this to flower sufficiently early to merit its common name of Christmas Rose, and will in any event prevent the valuable blooms from being spoiled by rain.

Similar protection may be given to the dwarf, very late-flowering asters and chrysanthemums, thereby protecting the flowers from frost damage, and prolonging their cutting season. One may then have unspoiled blooms of dwarf asters and sprays of the Otley Korean chrysanthemums in November, and sometimes in early December.

By using polythene, one may also give protection to a very tall subject such as *Vernonia crinita*, which often bears its purple heads of flowers right through November. These may be sadly marred by harsh autumn frost and their blooms thus be wasted, if they are not given the protection of a simply improvised polythene 'umbrella'.

Such protective gardening devices are harmless to the plants, but I do not favour inducing an unnatural second flowering towards the end of the year. This tests the roots too much for my liking, at a time when they have to prepare themselves for the onset of winter. It is essential for longevity that perennials have their accustomed long 'rest' from flowering and setting seed. Many gardeners seem unaware that certain perennials' roots often carry on working after flowering. Some, such as the tall veronicas, form new buds months before any new growth is visible. To interfere, therefore, with a plant's rhythm of life for the sake of a few extra blooms is a gamble best not undertaken by an honest ignoramus, while the true gardener is content to leave well alone, perhaps devoting his time to the profounder study of plants' roots!

Cloches should, therefore, be used with discretion and, in larger gardens, are better banished from the border altogether and consigned to the vegetable garden. The odd small group of winter-flowering heaths in the border will more than compensate for the loss of a few late blooms in the harsher months.

Some Notes on Cultivation

Soil Preparation

The annual dressing of lime indulged in by many gardeners is no-thing short of lunacy. This practice is the cause of much scab on potatoes and of chlorosis, or yellowing of foliage, among cut flower subjects. The usual recommended dressing of 8 or more ounces to the square yard (224 grams to the square metre) is quite ridiculous for most purposes. Such a heavy dressing is, however, of some use when treating very heavy or clay soils for the first time. The chemical action of lime upon clay breaks up those intractable clods over the winter and by spring the soil will be so well flocculated as to produce a fine tilth when it is raked. This enables some planting of lime-tolerant subjects to take place, but the remedy is not long-lasting.

Lime certainly has many valid uses in the vegetable garden, in encouraging the earthworm, in breaking down organic matter to supply a vital source of humus, and in warding off such evils as clubroot in cabbages, but only sour or very acid soils call for a heavy dressing of lime to bring them back to a more useful neu-trality. Such soils are seldom found in established kitchen gardens and allotments, and heavy dressings of lime are seldom advisable or desirable unless the gardener is certain of its correct usage.

Fortunately, most hardy perennials are tolerant of a little lime, and many are indifferent to a slightly acid soil. Some, such as most dianthus, and scabiosa, relish some lime. A few perennials hate it and these demand an acid soil in which to thrive. These points of preference are noted later when the individual plants are discussed.

Clay loams are full of plant nutriments, but these are often imprisoned in a solid mass totally unfavourable to the fine feeding roots of many plants. As just indicated, lime is useful in the first instance in helping to break up this airless mass, with the great assistance of a winter's wetness and weathering. But even though a spring raking will then produce a good tilth, any walking on the soil afterwards will re-compact the clay back into its former undesirable state. Such loam does not respond permanently to chemical treatment unless the spring raking down is immediately followed by a liberal incorporation of grit, sharp sand and sedge peat.

Such clay loams *left roughly dug* over the winter months will generally break down very well, making the use of lime an unnecessary expense. After raking down in spring, one should then spread up to a 9-in (22·5-cm) layer of grit and sharp sand. This should then be worked well into the soil by taking deep but narrow bites with the spade. The dug plot should then be covered with a similar layer of sedge peat and any short, chopped straw, and this too thoroughly incorporated with a second digging. Later a careful forking over of the plot might well reveal a need for further grit or sharp sand, and if this is the case the job must not be shirked if permanent improvement is one's aim. This fundamental work is well worth the effort, for grit is curiously immortal. Such a treatment, working with the weather, is of enduring worth, transforming a sticky, hard-digging mass into one holding more air, and thereafter never a penance to dig.

In such an improved clay loam one can grow an immense variety of perennial plants, and vegetables. Speaking from hard-won experience, I would prefer to have a garden with such a soil than one with a very light soil.

At the other end of the soil scale, dry, light loams need more regular attention. These are greatly improved by incorporating large quantities of compost and peat to counter any tendency to too much dryness in summer. In such soils this mulch should be incorporated deeply in order to encourage the roots of plants to probe downwards in their search for moisture and nutriment. If the soil is a river silt, the addition of some grit to the top layers will prevent the topsoil being panned by heavy rains. The precious water will thus not be wasted by running off the surface, but will penetrate the soil. With an increase of humus the earthworm population will increase. If the light soil is mulched each year, the tireless earthworms will carry down some of this mulch during their journeyings, so maintaining a constant supply deep in the soil for the bacteria to convert into vital humus.

Pests and Diseases

The hardy perennials described in this book seldom succumb to the unwelcome attentions of pests and diseases, though of course this is especially so where the grower is a good gardener. It is best to ensure at the outset that the soil is well worked and thoroughly cleansed, and if subjects are then chosen sensibly to suit the soil and aspect the plants will flourish, the roots being content. A flourishing plant can and will resist marauding insect pests and infections far better than one condemned to suffer from bad planting in an unsympathetic soil and site. With this principle firmly fixed in the good gardener's mind, these perennials will be accounted among the most trouble-free garden plants. It is obvious that a sun loving plant will languish when consigned to deep shade and is thereby constitutionally but needlessly weakened. The fault here lies with the gardener, not with the plant.

Soil not cleansed of alien refuse is often the cause of disappointment and plant wastage. Here will be found at least a trio of undesirables in the slug, wireworm and chafer-grub. These unwelcome pests are often present in the plots attached to new houses, and in old and long-neglected gardens. The former will conceal builders' rubble and litter while the latter's often ill-conceived and overgrown crazy paving and rockeries will harbour a host of weeds and pests.

If the cut flower plot is to be part of the allotment, then the prevalent mania for dosing the soil with liberal and repeated applications of lime might well have discouraged such pests as snails, slugs and wireworm, but this dosage might restrict the variety of choice to lime loving perennials such as scabious and dianthus, and even induce chlorosis in such as salvias. Fortunately many hardy perennials of merit like or tolerate a limy soil.

The visitations of hedgehogs, toads and ladybirds should be welcome and encouraged. Whilst you sleep, the hedgehog will scour the ground between the plants for slugs overlooked by the toad. The ladybird thrives on a feast of milky gluttonous aphides. The hover-fly and the dainty, diaphanous-green lacewing are similarly the gardener's friends and should be valued for their part in the control of the virus-disease-bearing aphids. The wise gardener will study the common insects so that friend can readily be distinguished from foe. The belief that chemicals alone provide the answer to all garden problems is a dangerous and short-sighted one, especially where the amateur is concerned. It is useless to annihilate enemies if one is left without friends! Uncontrolled slugs will despoil many plants, but in particular their vile nocturnal attentions are often turned to the new buds of delphiniums, campanulas, aubrieta and dianthus. Timely protection for such as these should not be overlooked in the autumn. Slugs are at their most destructive in spring and autumn and will often find a sanctuary underground where the bloated white chafer-grub has eaten out a cavity in the larger root portions of plants. Another underground spoiler is the leather-jacketed offspring of the cranc fly. Starlings have a wonderful instinct for leather-jackets, and their vigorous attentions to patches of grass almost invariably indicate the presence of the drab-looking grubs. There are specific remedies available for all these undesirable underground biters and where the preparation of the ground has been less than thorough, such specifics, when applied strictly according to the manufacturer's directions, may be most helpful.

Many of the common pests are slow moving. The many-legged and useful centipede is a nimble mover but the often-confused millipede is a comparative crawler. Among the slow-moving villains are aphids in general, cutworms, chafer-grubs, slugs and snails, and the froth-surrounded froghopper or spittle bug. The well known earwigs are the exception and are mostly a nuisance in wet summers, when trapping remains the best form of control.

Plant diseases often baffle professional researchers, and the advice to amateurs must therefore be both brief and brutal. Infected plants, with deformed or unnatural growth, should be lifted and burned and the site thoroughly cleansed. Disease is best avoided by insistence on buying in good quality stock from a reputable source and by planting in clean and suitable soil where a free circulation of fresh air is assured, the plants being sensibly spaced out in the sun or shade they prefer. Stock obtained from a reliable nursery-man gives one a good start: properly propagated perennials have a vigour and constitution not possessed by those subjected to very intensive propagation under artificial conditions, where the emphasis has been on commerce rather than quality.

Virus diseases cannot be satisfactorily countered, but the common curse of mildew among such as the Michaelmas daisies is now more readily controlled by selecting varieties that are known to be less prone to the disease, by keeping the stock vigorous and young by regular division, by good spacing of the plants and by spraying with Benlate (benomyl) early in the season. Mildews are often found on plants consigned to damp and dismal sites in over-crowded conditions, a clear rebuke to the neglectful gardener. No matter whether the plants are grown in garden, allotment or cold greenhouse, the same rules of cleanliness and common sense hold good.

Weeds

Many of the more robust perennials can hold their own against the encroachment of all but the most vigorous and strangulating weeds, but to allow this battle to ensue is both wasteful and unwise. Weeds consume soil nutriments at the expense of other plants, and as they are hosts to pests and diseases, their eradication is sufficient reward for persistence. Yet again, time is of the essence, and the removal and destruction of weeds before they have gone to seed is an obvious injunction. In small plots, systematic hand weeding is the most thorough and virtuous method, while larger areas call for the hoe to keep down the annual crop of weeds. Perennial weeds such as docks and thistles will entail deep digging with a fork to cleanse the ground of every vestige of their hideous and fecund roots. The horror of bindweed may also be mastered by much care and labour and, if need be, the precise application of a suitable hormone weed-killer.

To sum up, garden cleanliness or good husbandry remains the finest counter to pests and diseases. Air and space about the plants is a prime requirement and these vital gaps must be kept free of weeds, which act as hosts to pests and diseases. All fallen leaves and garden refuse should be burned or properly composted, if room permits, for the same reasons. Where good husbandry prevails the grower is well rewarded by the healthy plant's response and the use of chemicals for pest or disease control becomes the exception rather than the rule.

Cutting the Flowers and Caring for Them

The amateur can sometimes produce finer cut flowers than the professional grower. The former is often forced to cut flowers in spite of the weather, rather than with the weather, in order to meet market requirements, while the amateur can afford to wait until favourable conditions prevail. Obviously flowers cut in the midday heat of summer or the drying winds of spring may well flag unless immediately steeped in water. Many flowers are very difficult to revive after being subjected to such wilting and those which do will often have a briefer span of life in a vase than those cut and immediately put into water.

Cutting with scissors is usual for the smaller and softer-stemmed flowers, but a pair of light, sharp secateurs is essential for cutting the woodier and tougher stems of flowers like Michaelmas daisies. Those with a knack born of long experience may pick by hand the flowers of such as heuchera and armeria, but scissors are to be preferred.

In general, summer cutting is best done in the evening, a time when the wind often abates for a few hours. This particularly applies to flowers such as campanula, geum and delphinium, which have fragile petals, but the firm-headed achillea and sedum can be cut at any time of day. Some of the more fragile subjects are best stood overnight up to their necks in water.

The best stage at which to cut varies. Poppies and delphiniums are best cut while still in bud, but this practice would cause aquilegias to flag sadly. Catananche and erigeron should be fully open before being cut, while aquilegias, phlox and peonies should be cut while at the halfway stage of flowering. Such requirements are best learned from experience, but the notes devoted to the individual

B   33

plants include such advice where this is necessary. These small refinements in cutting can often lengthen the flowers' vase life by a week.

To obtain the maximum indoor life from cut flowers, a brief study of their stems is always helpful. Cut stems react to drastic surgery by immediately beginning to seal up, so the sooner they are put in water the better. It is essential that the stems are able to absorb as much water as possible. The cutting of thick stems is always best done diagonally, for thus a greater area of stem is exposed to absorb water. Ideally it should be carried out with the stems under water. The oblique cut also prevents the ends of the stems being blocked by resting on the base of the vase, something which should always be avoided. With some flowers it is necessary, in order to prolong their life, to remove an inch of the stems daily and reset them in fresh water. Stems should be re-cut under water, otherwise the sealing process will cause an airlock which prevents the full absorption of water.

If the stems are hard the base should be crushed or slit by some 2 in (5 cm) with a sharp knife. Hollow-stemmed subjects may be filled with water, using a small funnel, and with the large stems of hollyhocks and delphiniums any form of wick can be used as a plug to keep air out and let water in: this works wonders. Poppy stems and other milk exuders should have their ends charred in a candle flame to stop the flow which would impede the stems' ability to take in water.

Fresh cut blooms should, as a general practice, always be given a deep drink for several hours in a cool, dim and draught-proof place away from all domestic fumes such as gas. The deeper the stems are first immersed in water, the longer the flowers will last when placed in the vase or other container. Water in containers should be topped up daily and changed where necessary. Some flowers, such as the rudbeckias, drink prodigious quantities of water and their water is best changed every two or three days in addition to the regular topping up. Rainwater, collected in clean containers, rather than in dubious waterbutts, is wonderful for promoting longevity and well worth collecting.

There are some exceptions to the rule that cut flowers be immediately placed in cold water. The leaf stalks of hosta must be stood in an inch of hot water and, after being allowed to cool off, only then placed in an ample depth of cold water. They should then have a vase life of two weeks. *Papaver orientale* is another whose stems should first receive a soaking in hot water, and this when the flowers are still just in bud. When the blooms have faded and dropped the stems bearing the seed vessels may be hung up, dried and coloured for winter decoration, thus giving these poppies a dual decorative life.

No stem leaves should be allowed within the vase, as these would quickly foul the water. In this connection, the addition of two or three drops of household bleach to the water will be an effective bactericide, thus ensuring a longer life for the flowers. This is particularly effective with such as dahlias and chrysanthemums: the bleach will prevent the water from becoming slimy and foul-smelling. Be careful, however, not too much as this will kill the leaves and eventually the flowers too.

Remembering that leaves should not come into direct contact with the water, the removal of other foliage should be done with restraint and never be overdone, for leaves perform many functions vital to the plant's life and longevity. If a plant is unreasonably robbed of its leaves, it will undoubtedly suffer. If leaves are picked for their ornamental value, they are nearly always better for an initial thorough submergence in water, though this does not, of course, apply to any soft or woolly leaves.

Cut flowers should not be subjected to strong sunlight or currents of hot dry air from central heating. Flowers left in a warm room overnight will droop and, where possible, containers should always be moved to a cool place. Tired blooms can often be revived by immersing their stems deeply in warm water and in centrally heated rooms they will greatly benefit from an occasional mist spray with tepid water.

Remember above all that the stems of cut flowers should never be in contact with the base of the container. Many cut flowers cannot drink, and therefore will not last, if the cut ends of the stems are thus obstructed. The time-honoured practice of giving a bunch of flowers in a vase a fractional upward lift to ensure that all are free to drink is a good habit to acquire, but needless to say, one cannot do this with a formal arrangement, so special care must be taken at the outset to ensure that the stems are correctly placed in the container.

PART TWO

Alphabetical List of Selected Perennials

Acanthus (Bear's Breeches)   *Acanthaceae*

Acanthus mollis and *A. spinosus* are both more fleshy than fibrous of root. These roots, in time, probe to considerable depths, and while acanthus will grow in almost any soil a light, deeply worked loam is to be preferred. In rich loams the plants expand steadily to occupy considerable space. Correct siting at the outset is advisable, as moving mature plants is a laborious task. It is often impossible to dig out cleanly either of these long-lived perennials, and any piece left in the ground will sprout anew.

Both *A. mollis* and *A. spinosus* grow sturdily and erect, and are distinctive for their deeply cut, deep green leaves and hooded flowers. *A. mollis latifolius* grows to 3½ ft (105 cm). The leaves are broad and basally very large, and the purple-hooded, white flowers are borne in stiff spikes between early July and the end of August. *A. spinosus* will grow to 4½ ft (1·3 m) in good deep soil. The very dark green leaves are deeply dissected and spine-tipped, but by no means as prickly as they appear. The rigid stems of purple-hooded, white flowers, each guarded by a sharp spine on the hood, last many weeks between July and September. The spikes of both forms are tightly packed and commendably scornful of the highest winds. Even after flowering they are decorative, with their hard, elongated, acorn-like brown seed vessels.

These drought-resistant perennials are distinctive from head to foot. The highly ornamental basal leaves and the sharply outlined flower spikes present a fine and balanced pyramid of growth. Neither species should be used as back row plants in a border, as here much of their merit is wasted. A planting at the end of a border or, better still, in some isolation among paving, shows their architectural features to more advantage. Aptly sited in a large border they can be sternly majestic. If grown for cut flower purposes, both are fine plants for the kitchen garden or a dry sunny corner.

Acanthus will grow in partial shade but is better in full sun. Plants are readily raised from seed, or even more quickly from root cuttings. Both species may be regarded as being fully hardy and perennial in all but cold, winter-wet clays. Grown in rows in the kitchen garden, the plants should be spaced 2 ft (60 cm) apart and left undisturbed for several years, according to their rate of expansion.

Achillea (Yarrow, Milfoil, Sneezewort) *Compositae*

Achillea filipendulina, (or *A. eupatorium*) has two fine cultivars in 'Gold Plate' and 'Parker's Variety'. Both these 4–5-ft (1·2–1·5-m) plants have deeply cut, aromatic, green foliage and sturdy stems topped with large, densely packed heads, or corymbs, of golden-yellow flowers solid to the touch. The flowers of 'Gold Plate' are more domed than those of the rarer 'Parker's Variety'. Both flower for some three months between early July and late September. The flowers are very long-lasting when cut, and if hung upside down and dried will hold their colour for many months. The 3-ft (90-cm) 'Coronation Gold' is a smaller version. This splendid hybrid is equally long-flowering and a sturdy grower. All three are admirably suitable for the border and staking is never necessary.

Achillea × 'King Edward' and *A. tomentosa* are two dwarf forms bearing yellow plates of flowers at about 6 in (15 cm). These are both grey-leaved, especially the woolly-leaved *A. tomentosa*. Both look well planted at the front of a sunny border where the drainage is sharp, or in a raised bed among alpines. They also last very well as cut flowers.

Achillea 'Taygetea' and *A.* 'Clypeolata' are also grey-leaved. The former grows to a little over 2 ft (60 cm) and bears its yellow heads of flowers between late June and early September. *A.* 'Clypeolata' has more silvery and ferny foliage but is more lax in habit at 18 in

(45 cm). A hybrid of these two is *A.* × 'Moonshine', growing to about 18 in (45 cm). This has aromatic, silvery foliage and pale yellow heads of unfading flowers between May and July. They also make fine, long-lasting cut flowers for the house. All these achilleas can be used in borders as dual purpose plants, and are probably all the better for some cutting.

Achillea decolorans 'W. B. Child' grows to 2 ft (60 cm) and gives a profusion of pure white flowers in May and June. This is a fine plant for the kitchen garden. Another best in the kitchen garden is *A. millefolium* 'Cerise Queen'. This forms a lax bush of nearly 2 ft (60 cm). The green leaves are prettily and very finely cut. The rosy cerise heads of flowers come in late June and throughout July and last well when cut, but the plant's habit is lax and somewhat untidy.

All these achilleas have fibrous roots and are truly perennial when planted in well drained soils, preferably in full sun. This particularly applies to the grey- or silver-leaved forms.

More tolerant of heavier soils and some shade are *A. ptarmica* 'The Pearl' and *A. p.* 'Perry's White'. The roots of these are couch-like, and must be curbed by an annual spading off, or by planting in a confined area. *A. p.* 'The Pearl' grows to 2½ ft (75 cm) and gives a wealth of small, pure white double blooms between late June and the end of September. These are beautifully proportioned and decorative. *A. p.* 'Perry's White' is very similar but a week or two earlier to bloom. In ordinary garden soil these very fine white-flowered perennials need no support, but rich loams produce too lush and topheavy a growth, and too rampant a root spread. Cutting is good for the plants, and detached laterals look charming in small table bowls. Unlike the yellow-flowered achilleas, these do relish a little humus in the soil and, where the soil is poor, a light annual dusting of sulphate of potash. Such simple attentions are readily given when they are grown in the kitchen garden or allotment. Unlike *A. filipendulina* and *A.* 'Clypeolata' the foliage is neither ornamental nor aromatic.

Aconitum (Monk's-hood) *Ranunculaceae*

Aconitum × *cammarum* has a number of fine hybrids, of which

'Blue Sceptre' is the smallest at 24–27 in (60–67·5 cm). The deeply cut, delphinium-like foliage is attractive, as is the neat pyramid habit of the plant with its densely packed spikes of blue-white flowers. Similar in habit and colour, but much taller, is 'Bicolor', which may require a little support in windswept gardens. This grows to 4 ft (1·2 m), or a little more in good heavy loams. 'Bressingham Spire' is most distinctive. Its glossy foliage appears varnished in the sun, and it stands very erect, topped with spires of fine violet-blue flowers. At 3–3½ ft (90–105 cm) this is one of the most wind-resistant perennials yet raised. 'Spark's Variety' comes as a complete contrast with its more open, branched and bushier habit. It grows to 4½ ft (1·3 m) and its flowers are a deep Oxford blue. All these flower between July and September, with 'Spark's Variety' covering some three months and holding its flowers the longest. This is best given some simple group support when not planted in sheltered situations.

Both *A. septentrionale* 'Ivorine' and *A.* 'Arendsii' are valuable for their fine habit and flowering period. *A.* 'Ivorine', growing to 3 ft (90 cm), is very upright and neat with its ivory-white blooms touched with green in May and June. 'Arendsii' is a foot (30 cm) taller, wonderfully sturdy and erect, with fine blue flowers coming between late August and October. This is far too fine a plant to overlook, yet it remains curiously neglected by many gardeners.

All these forms of aconitum stem from fat crowns bearing a mass of gingerish fibrous roots. These, together with all other parts of the plant, are poisonous. Planting and cutting should therefore be followed by a thorough washing of the hands. This should not deter the gardener from raising these very fine and valuable perennials. They like moist loams, especially clay, and some shade, but all will grow in a remarkably wide variety of soils and aspects, and may be regarded as being among the most troublefree of plants. The cut flowers add a touch of sombre magnificence to a vase and dignity to the border, and the various shades of blue contrast splendidly with almost any other colour, toning down the more blatant to create a more acceptable harmony.

All make very fine border plants, 'Bressingham Spire' and 'Arendsii' in particular being bone-hardy, reliable, distinctive and long-lived. Flowering is prolonged where there is adequate summer moisture. Lighter soils should be generously enriched with compost, and a mulch given in early June.

As a contrast *A. orientale* grows bushily to about 5 ft (1·5 m). This is topped with lemon-tinged, ivory-white small flowers which are at their best in July and August. These mix very well with the cut blooms of the blue-flowered forms in a vase. As with these, partial shade is preferable to full sun.

Aconitum volubile is also a shade lover. This is a climber and a fine trellis plant, giving a wealth of violet-blue flowers between late August and October. Although little known and seldom grown, *A. volubile* is doubly valuable for its habit and flowering period.

Propagation is best undertaken in autumn and simply entails forking up and separating the crowns. These are planted with the heads of the crowns some 2 in (5 cm) below the soil surface. Within two years these will each bear a ring of further small crowns, usually about ten in number, but plants may be left undisturbed for several years without any deterioration in habit or flowers.

Agapanthus (African Lily) *Liliaceae*

Agapanthus is probably at its finest in the Headbourne Hybrids. These splendid, fully hardy perennials are the result of crossing several species of African lilies by the late Lewis Palmer. Raised from seed, a fine mixture of colour may be produced, ranging from violet-blue through azure to the most delicate china-blue. Flowering is at around the 2½–3 ft (75–90 cm) mark between July and September amid a wealth of rushy leaves. The roots are fleshy and brittle, making an initial purchase of pot-grown stock advisable. Plants are somewhat slow to establish and are best planted in a well drained but humus-rich soil in the sun. Some protection should be afforded over their first winter, and spring planting is to be preferred. Where aptly planted these will slowly expand so that four plants will duly occupy one square yard (1 sq m) of ground.

Agapanthus campanulatus 'Albus', with its heads of white flowers, graces July and August, while the related 'Isis' has more abundant

fine deep blue flowers a few weeks later. Slightly later still comes
A. patens, with its lighter blue flowers growing 6 in (15 cm) taller,
to 3 ft (90 cm).

All these, if protected over their first winter, may be regarded as
being fully hardy, perennial, very desirable, long-lived, and
troublefree plants to grace frontal positions in the border with
distinction. Both good winter soil drainage and summer moisture
in abundance are essential, and giving a pre-flowering mulch is a
good habit to acquire.

Agapanthus praecox (syn *A. umbellatus*) is also blue and beautiful,
but it is not fully hardy. It may be successfully grown in well
nurtured deep tubs kept moist in summer on a sunny terrace, and
suitably covered or moved to cover for the winter. Where there is
a small pool in the terrace it is entirely apt and delightful.

All agapanthus are best in a good, deep soil containing plenty of
leafmould. Plants resent any disturbance of their deeply probing
roots and are better left unmolested for many years. It may be two
or three seasons before any cutting for the house is worthwhile, but
such patience is generously rewarded. After flowering the green
seed vessels remain attractive for several weeks. Agapanthus remains among the choicer hardy perennials to grace any garden or
flower arrangement.

Alchemilla (Lady's Mantle)   *Rosaceae*

Alchemilla mollis is a most accommodating and good-natured
hardy perennial capable of growing well in both shade and sun, in
heavy and light soils, and in either moist or fairly dry conditions.
The roots are long-lived and expand at a steady pace, being readily
curbed when they exceed their allotted space. *A. mollis* may be
grown at the front of the border, in the kitchen garden, in the odd
shady corner, and very tellingly in raised beds or tubs in a gloomy
courtyard. Here it will softly illumine the greyness that may be
caused by shaded paving and confining walls.

The main beauty of *A. mollis* is in its leaves. These are very
attractive indeed and mound up in growth to some 10 in (25 cm),
a delight from spring until autumn. The leaves are refreshingly

green and prettily rounded and crinkled at the edges, becoming quite large, up to 6 in (15 cm) across, as the summer progresses. The surface is covered with very fine, soft hairs, and after a shower of rain these trap globules of moisture that glisten like beads of quicksilver that almost make one thirsty just looking at them. These beautiful leaves make a most handsome and valuable contribution to the flower vase—valuable because so few plants have rounded leaves, and few of these exceptions have leaves that excel those of the lady's mantle.

Between June and August the mounds of leaves are all but hidden by a profusion of wiry stems bearing loose sprays of mossy green-yellow flowers borne in soft clouds at about 1 ft (30 cm), so that one is greeted by a fine haze of golden-green. The flowers, too, provide delightful floral decoration for the house, blending beautifully with many other blooms, and providing a perfect contrast to their own leaves. A simple bowl of leaves and flowers on a dark mahogany table provides an apt reminder that green, in all its various shades, is without doubt the most important colour in the plant world, and certainly the most vital in any garden worthy of the name.

The dwarf, 6-in (15-cm) *A. alpina* is also distinctive but quite different in foliage. The leaves are long and silvered beneath, while the smaller sprays of flowers are the same lime-yellow. This, too, is extremely easy to cultivate and gives the flower arranger some useful material.

Allium *Amaryllidaceae*

Allium is a large genus overlooked by many gardeners and flower arrangers, and foolishly disdained by some as being a member of the onion family. The taint of onion is faintly noticeable only when handling the leaves or bulbs, and I find this far less objectionable than the smell of many pampered pelargoniums. One of the choicest and smallest is *A. cyaneum*, forming near-evergreen grassy-leaved clumps of bright green up to about 6 in (15 cm) high. Between July and September 7-in or 8-in (17·5-cm or 20-cm) stems bear loose umbels of beautiful turquoise-blue flowers. A group planted at the front of the border, in a rock garden or in a terrace tub always looks charming. This is a very useful allium, being fully hardy, long-lived, long-flowering, well foliaged, and of troublefree habit and easy cultivation in well drained soil. Most alliums relish sun but this will more than tolerate a little shade.

Allium beesianum is a little taller at 9 in (23 cm), with some purple in the blue flowers that appear in August and September. This, too, is a native of China, delightful of habit and graceful of flower.

Also about the 9-in (22·5-cm) mark, *A. narcissiflorum* is another charming plant, whose reddish purple pendulous umbels are a beautiful sight in July. This is not quite so robust and is best planted in a warm and well drained site open to the full sun.

Allium cernuum is another splendid plant for the sunny border. This grows to some 16 in (40 cm) and bears mauve, blue or purple flowers in fine nodding umbels between late June and mid-August amid a wealth of rushy leaves. Bone-hardy, fully perennial, re-assuringly reliable and good-natured, this is a fine plant. Its tang of onion is noticeable upon handling, but it is, nevertheless, one of the very best for the border.

Allium pulchellum is also full of merit and very graceful, with its loose umbels of nodding rosy flowers and protruding stamens, a delight throughout July and August. Its snow-white cultivar *A. p.* 'Album' also grows to about 15 in (37·5 cm) and flowers between July and September. Both these make splendid border subjects and are easy and troublefree to grow.

Taller at 18 in (45 cm) comes *A. caeruleum*, whose rounded golf-ball-sized, densely packed umbels of azure-blue cover several weeks between late June and August. Unlike any of the earlier noted alliums, this can become a little topheavy, especially after a shower of rain followed by a breeze, when the stems cannot always support the weight. Of the easiest cultivation in a sunny position and light soil, a site sheltered from the wind is desirable. Some pea-stick support is advisable if it is grown in the kitchen garden.

Of similar height but more sturdy of stem is *A. albopilosum*. The globose umbels of shiny deep violet flowers are three times the size of those found in *A. caeruleum*, and look very striking in sunny garden or vase.

All these bulbous perennials demand good soil drainage, but heavy loams give good results if lightened with grit and sharp sand. The bulbs are planted some 3 in (7·5 cm) deep in autumn. Sun is relished by all but those recommended for the border, *AA. cyaneum, beesianum, cernuum* and *pulchellum*, will all tolerate a little shade. Their pendulous umbels look charming both in the garden and in the house. The 'roundheads', *AA. caeruleum* and *albopilosum* look splendid in more formal floral arrangements. All make very fine cut flowers, however, as they have a long vase life.

Allium karataviense, with its lilac-white, round heads of flowers coming at the end of May, is also noteworthy for its very fine foliage. The leaves are very broad for an allium and have a metallic sheen of blue overlaying the speckled green.

There are hundreds of alliums, most of which are hardy and decorative, but I have confined my selection to those I have grown and found to be more than satisfactory. None of these spreads so freely as to become a nuisance. Propagation, after a few years, is by lifting and carefully dividing the offsets. Those planted in borders may be left down for a good number of years, where a light annual dusting of bonemeal and hoof and horn meal will keep them in good fettle.

Allium caeruleum, A. albopilosum, and other roundheads are very suitable for drying to give winter decoration.

For those who persist in dismissing all these as 'onions', the 2-ft (60-cm) *A. neapolitanum grandiflorum*, with its fragrant white umbels of May, has a less onion-like smell than the other alliums, and will add a touch of sweetness to their vases, if not their souls!

All these are available from nurserymen, especially those recommended for the border, and from bulb growers in the United Kingdom.

Alstroemeria (Peruvian Lily) *Amaryllidaceae*

Alstroemeria has ugly roots and brilliant flowers. The tuberous roots are a jumbled mass of fleshy fangs capable of probing deeply and, where suited, spreading quite widely in a manner not readily curbed. Mature plants deeply resent any attempts to transplant them, so correct siting at the outset is obviously important. Alstroemeria is therefore not a plant for the herbaceous border but better grown in the kitchen garden or, best of all, in a confined bed abutting a south wall of the house or greenhouse. The soil should be light, deeply worked and free-draining. Well made compost, peat, and grit or sharp sand are good additions to the soil. A warm and sunny site gives the best results.

Establishing plants more than two years old is very difficult, calling for deep planting. Fortunately, nurserymen sell pot-grown stock of a year's full growth and this presents no planting problems if the ball of soil and roots is carefully tapped out and planted direct without any interference into well-prepared ground. Alternatively, one may readily raise one's own stock from seed, using two or three seeds to a 3-in (7·5-cm) pot of a sandy, peaty mix. When these have sprouted they may be planted out as one, without any foolhardy attempt to separate or prick out. Establishment is slow and a season of hand weeding (only) will be called for, but once established the plants will steadily increase. Either of these means of establishment is better than trying to transplant older stock.

Alstroemeria aurantiaca, with its brilliant orange blooms, is well known to older gardeners but this, and its varieties, has now given way to the less rampant and very fine mixture known as the Ligtu Hybrids. These come in a splendid array of colours, sparkling pinks and flame-reds, together with softer rosy and apricot hues, orange and white, flowering at about 3 ft (90 cm) between July and September.

These Peruvian lilies, best cut when the buds colour up, give a wealth of very fine cut flowers. They drink well and last a long time in the vase. The plants are hardy and long-lived in deep, light soils. Planting is always best done in the spring to encourage uninterrupted growth. A light annual dusting of sulphate of potash is relished by roots which dread the fork and hoe.

Althaea (Hollyhock) *Malvaceae*

Althaea rosea has deeply probing fleshy roots which are adaptable to many soils that have been deeply worked. It is worth growing for its long spikes of single and double blooms, available in a wide range of colour, and appearing from July to October. These tall and homely perennials are fine plants for town gardens, where the exhaust fumes of traffic often act as an effective counter to the wretched rust disease that sometimes mars the leaves and stems of these good-natured giants, which reach 6–8 ft (1·8–2·4 m) in height. I admit to having a great liking for the single forms, some of which bear basal florets of great size. Plants are readily raised from seed to flower in their second year. The cutting of these heavy spikes is the same as for delphiniums, and they last well if the bases of the hollow stems are put into boiling water, which is then allowed to cool down with the stems remaining *in situ*. A deep drink before setting also adds to the hollyhock's vase life.

Anaphalis (Pearly Everlasting) *Compositae*

Anaphalis nubigena, *A. margaritacea*, and *A. cinnamomea* (syn *A. yedoensis*) form a trio of useful and valuable perennials. The fibrous roots of all three species are remarkably drought-resistant and adaptable to a wide range of soils. Plants will thrive in full sun and tolerate a remarkable degree of shade. Only in the heaviest loams and in wet soils are anaphalis likely to disappoint their unthinking guardians.

Anaphalis nubigena is probably the choicest of the trio. This forms a mound of fine spear-shaped leaves, soft to the touch and brightly silver-grey. In mid-August the loose sprays of small, paper-crisp pure white flowers borne at a height of 9–12 in (22·5–30 cm) are nicely proportioned. Flowering covers a very long period, often extending to the end of October. Cut flowers also last a very long time in the vase. They can also be dried and used as 'everlastings'. *A. nubigena* is fine at the very front of a shaded part of the border, where its contrast of flower and foliage with other plants is very valuable. Plants are well behaved, dying back in winter to leave the roots commendably compact. Fully hardy, long-lived and of easy cultivation, it may readily be grown in terrace tubs and other containers in shady courtyards where its tidy habit, fine leaves and multi-petalled flowers lighten the gloom.

Anaphalis margaritacea is similarly adaptable to many sites and uses. This is taller at 18 in (45 cm) and not so trimly neat, but the silver-grey leaves are attractive and the pearly white blooms dry better than those of *A. nubigena*. Flowering lasts many weeks between July and mid-September, but it is more suited to kitchen garden cultivation.

Anaphalis cinnamomea is taller still at just over 2 ft (60 cm), but it grows more erectly than *A. margaritacea* and the stems are quite sturdy. The leaves are again silvery but not so attractive as those of *A. nubigena*. Flowering begins in late August and extends into October. The flowers dry well and make good cut flowers.

Anaphalis cinnamomea is the most vigorous, expanding at a steady rate though readily curbed. The taller pair are not recommended for growing in the border, but all give a wealth of material for the flower arranger. Propagation is by simple division in spring, and a sharp knife is useful for the sake of neatness and speed.

Anemone   *Ranunculaceae*

Anemone hupehensis japonica is commonly known as the Japanese anemone in spite of its Chinese origins. This grows bushily to 30 in (75 cm) and bears a long succession of semi-double rose-carmine flowers between August and October. Its smaller cultivar *A. h. j.* 'Splendens' has finer and larger single pink blooms. This is one of the parents of *A.* × *hybrida*, which embraces a fine selection of cultivars.

Anemone × *hybrida* has very similar roots. These are partly fleshy and partly fibrous, slow to settle down but eventually probing to considerable depths. They relish some humus in a deeply worked, free-draining soil in sun or a little shade. Division of such roots is best not attempted, but new stock may be readily raised from root cuttings. Plants are tardy to show new growth in the spring, but all forms are fully hardy and very long-lived. Growth is slow but steady, and these anemones may be left undisturbed for years to give little or no trouble in almost any soil with adequate winter drainage. Once established the plants are remarkably tenacious of life.

Among the pink-flowered forms of *A.* × *hybrida* I find 'Queen Charlotte' at 30 in (75 cm) rather unregal. 'Lady Gilmour' may be 6 in (15 cm) shorter but her near-double pink blooms are much larger and purer in colour. Slightly smaller at just under 2 ft (60 cm), the old cultivar 'Profusion' is well named for its rose-pink blooms. The newer 'Bressingham Glow' is more rosy red and the blooms almost double. Both these are very good plants, as is the white-flowered 3-ft (90-cm) 'Louise Uhink'. 'White Queen' at 3½ ft (105 cm) has larger blooms and is more robust. These last two, with their golden stamens, have the most appeal for me because of their purity of bloom, but all are very good perennials. Bushily upright of habit and sufficiently sturdy to scorn staking, all are very valuable for their flowering period which covers many weeks between August and October. I have used the white-flowered cultivars in border work, but all these may be grown well in the kitchen garden.

Lesser known is the hybrid *A. lesseri*, which grows to just under 18 in (45 cm). This, too, is slow-growing, and the compact roots are happiest in a deep, light soil well laden with humus to retain ample summer moisture. Plants seem most content in a little shade and the flowers of May and June are a fine rosy red.

While all these herbaceous anemones are best in light soil, flowering is more profuse and the attractive leaves are enhanced by the presence of humus about the roots. Although the cut flowers are not particularly long-lasting, the blooms are appealing and come in good numbers during the early autumn. As garden plants these anemones are straightforward to cultivate. Even heavy and clay loams, suitably improved, can give very good results following a spring planting.

Among the so-called bulbous anemones one may find a few very good and colourful cut flower subjects. The tuberous-rooted *A. fulgens annulata grandiflora* and St Bavo are two kinds well worth growing in a well drained light soil and a sunny site. The former bears its yellow-centred brilliant scarlet blooms at a height of 1 ft (30 cm) in May, while the latter contains a fine mixture of colours, including lavender and rose. This anemone, raised by van Tubergen, is probably the more valuable plant as it flowers early in

March and April in the south, but both give very good cut flowers for the house.

The very popular 9-in (22·5-cm) stemmed anemones de Caen and St Brigid are best grown in a well-nurtured kitchen garden soil where successional plantings to extend the flowering season may be made. These tuberous anemones make extremely colourful subjects for the flower arranger. St Brigid and de Caen, in particular, respond best to generous cultivation after planting 2 in (5 cm) apart. Peat and leafmould and well made compost are good for these lime hating forms. Both forms of *A. fulgens* are the better for a planting in a warm site.

As a charming contrast *A. ranunculoides* bears its fresh buttercup-yellow blooms at a height of 8 in (20 cm) between April and June. While this, too, is a sun lover it must have its roots in a humus-laden summer-moist soil to give of its pleasing best.

Though none of these tuberous anemones can be called entirely troublefree, as the herbaceous forms are, they are ideal subjects for raising in the kitchen garden and give the brightest of blooms for the flower arranger, and *A. fulgens annulata grandiflora* and St Bavo last very well in vases. Their 10–12-in (25–30-cm) stems make them very suitable for small displays, and very cheerful they look at all times.

Anthemis   *Compositae*

Anthemis tinctoria revels in the sun away from all baneful influences. This incredibly floriferous plant has remarkably meagre fibrous roots, and is best planted in light, rather dry soils. Its habit is somewhat lax and planting in rich loam produces too lush a growth for the plant's own good.

Two of the best cultivars are *A. t.* 'Mrs E. C. Buxton' and 'Grallagh Gold'. Both these grow to about 30 in (75 cm). If given plenty of space and air the stems are reasonably straight and up-right above the deeply cut, bright green aromatic leaves, the basal clumps of which are virtually evergreen. The blooms of 'Mrs E. C. Buxton' are almost lemon-yellow, while those of 'Grallagh Gold' are more deeply golden. Flowering begins in late June and continues until early August. Cutting may be carried out weekly and benefits the plants. Indeed, it is good practice to cut the plants back in late August to stimulate the roots well before the onset of winter. These sun loving perennials left to their own devices may occasionally completely exhaust themselves and fail to survive a long, wet winter. This cutting back, together with sharp soil drainage, directly promotes longevity. These are fine plants for broad ridges in the kitchen garden. It is best to raise new stock from basal cuttings taken in early summer, rather than to propagate by division. Planting is always safest in the spring.

Anthericum (St Bernard's Lily) *Liliaceae*

Anthericum liliago's tuberous, fleshy white roots are very brittle and demand a well drained but humus-rich soil. These can be divided with a knife, but this means of propagation is best avoided as it is resented for a season thereafter. Plants grow fairly easily from seed, flowering in their second year. New growth is slow to appear in spring. The habit of *A. liliago* is very graceful, with dark green rushy leaves and slender 15-in (37·5-cm) stems bearing pure white star-like blooms with prominent stamens between late June and mid-August. Planted near the front of the border these St Bernard's lilies have an airy charm and a fragile beauty. These long-lived plants should receive summer moisture in plenty and be left down for many years. *A. liliago* is often confused with the related *Paradisea liliastrum major*, the St Bruno's lily, which grows a little taller and whose white petals are touched with green at the tips. Both are choice cut flower subjects.

Aquilegia (Columbine) *Ranunculaceae*

Aquilegia is a fleeting beauty. Many are far from perennial, and not all are very long-lasting either in the garden or as cut flowers. Even so these colourful columbines come readily from seed, and their wind-dancing blooms are delightful in early summer.

Aquilegia alpina, *A. glandulosa*, *A. flabellata* and the hybrid 'Hensol Harebell' are all useful garden plants but of little value for

Aquilegia

cut blooms. The longest-lasting cut flowers are to be found among those with long spurs to the bloom. The American McKana Hybrids are the largest-flowered strain, with blooms up to 4 in (10 cm) across and with spurs very nearly as long, Flowering at 2½–3 ft (75–90 cm) is profuse between June and early August. The range of colour is wonderfully wide.

Mrs Scott-Elliott's Long-spurred Hybrids also give a wealth of fine cut blooms for the house. These come in a range of beautiful shades borne at a height of about 2 ft (60 cm) between June and August. Red, pink, white, blue, yellow and purple, together with bicolour forms, afford the flower arranger a splendid choice of colour from these long-spurred columbines. These are raised from seed sown in the spring to flower the following year after an autumn planting.

Coming true from seed is *A*. 'Crimson Star', whose red and white blooms are borne at a height of 18 in (45 cm) in May and June. 'Snow Queen' likewise comes true from seed, as does 'Copper Queen', the soft yellow *longissima*, the blue 'Mrs Nicholls', and the delightful mixture of 'Dragonfly'. All these are long-spurred and last well in vases. *A. pyrenaica* is worth tracking down for, although the cut blooms are brief of life, the white-flowered form is lightly fragrant. For mixed colours Langdon's Rainbow Strain are long-spurred and superb.

Aquilegia will grow in a wide variety of soils so long as they are well drained, and plants seem equally at home in sun or partial shade. Although dry soils are tolerated some humus to retain adequate summer moisture gives the best results. Plants may be expected to flower well in their second and third years, but a few seedlings should be raised to replace those which have lost their vigour.

Cross-pollination among different kinds of aquilegia grown in kitchen garden neighbourliness is common, and seedlings may show a wide variation of colour and height. Blooms for the house should be cut as they begin to open.

Armeria (Thrift) *Plumbaginaceae*

Armeria is an attractive and accommodating perennial for well drained soils, sun loving but tolerant of some light shade. The fibrous roots will penetrate to a good depth and these make the plants drought-resistant. All the forms here, save one, make splendid front row occupants of the border, where their bright evergreen hummocks and wiry-stemmed flowers are attractive for months. These good-natured, long-lived plants are readily divided at almost any time of the year when not in flower, though care must be taken to plant the divisions deeply—well up to the basal leaves—and firmly. Plants may be left down for several years, the rate of growth being steady. Old plants tend to grow a little out of the ground, and although a mulch of gritty soil helps compactness this is better taken as a reminder to propagate new stock.

Armeria maritima has some very fine cultivars. 'Laucheana',

with its bright pink flowers held in the typical round heads, grows
to 8 in (20 cm) and flowers well between June and August. 'Blood-
stone' is of similar height and season but an intense blood-red.
About 2 in (5 cm) shorter come the white 'Alba' and the deep rosy
pink 'Vindictive', which often flowers from June to September
with memorable generosity.

Armeria latifolia 'Ruby Glow' and 'Bees' Ruby' are also fine.
The former grows to about 9 in (22·5 cm) while the latter is pinker
and 3 in (7·5 cm) taller. Both flower between June and August and
both are good perennials. *A. corsica* is shorter at about 7 in (3.5 cm)
with its bright brick-red flowers. The larger forms of armeria
offered as Giant Hybrids come in shades of pink and red. These
have stems of 18 in (45 cm) and give a profusion of cut blooms,
but the plants are not so perennial. They are better cultivated in
the kitchen garden where the plants may be frequently divided.

All the very slender wiry-stemmed flowers come in a fine succession, especially if they are judiciously cut and dead blooms
removed. The plants also make splendid subjects for raised beds in
sunny courtyards, and this makes cutting easier as one may more
easily avoid damaging those still in bud. Armeria is also useful for
patio tubs and window boxes. Cut blooms last well in water and
make ideal subjects for smaller vases and bowls.

Artemisia (Wormwood)   *Compositae*

Artemisia lactiflora, noble from root to topmost flower, is one of the
finest hardy perennials yet raised, 5 ft (1·5 m) tall. The fibrous
roots are remarkably compact for so tall a plant, well behaved, and
readily divided in spring or autumn. They are adaptable to many
soils so long as there is some summer moisture available. Clay
loams give magnificent results, and plants are equally at home in
sun or partial shade. The growth is a little bushy but very erect
and graceful with finely cut, delphinium-like leaves topped with
milky plumes redolent of meadow-sweet between July and late
September. Not only is *A. lactiflora* shapely and fine from top to
bottom, but the plant is wonderfully wind-resistant, and staking is
never necessary. This is a sterling subject for the border which is

still absent from far too many gardens, and fewer plants can screen off a kitchen garden with such distinction. Plants cut down in late October retain a basal clump of evergreen leaves, and one may sometimes glean a few small laterals of bloom in November. Bone-hardy, of easy cultivation, reliable and indispensable for good soils, this is the only flowering form whose blooms are worthy of com-mendation.

The remaining species of artemisia are grown solely for their decorative foliage. *A. absinthium* 'Lambrook Silver' is the late Margery Fish's silver-leaved form of wormwood growing to just under 3 ft (90 cm). The foliage is aromatic and bright, and the flowers grey. At half this height comes *A. maritima* 'Nutans', with deliciously dainty, aromatic silver filigree foliage. 'Silver Queen' is softly silver-white, with nondescript white flowers that are best removed, and growing robustly to 30 in (75 cm). Much smaller and choicer is *A. schmidtiana* 'Nana' at about 8 in (20 cm), a delightful dwarf with very finely cut silvery foliage.

All these silvery forms require full sun and a well drained soil. Most silver-leaved subjects definitely need a sandy or gritty soil, and very sharp drainage should be assured for the little *A. s.* 'Nana'. Only the smallest two are suitable for border work, while their more vigorous and taller relations are better confined to the kitchen garden, where any excess growth is more readily curbed. The leaves of all are valuable to flower arrangers, and plants are readily divided in the spring.

Asphodelus (Asphodel) *Liliaceae*

Asphodelus is the Greek name for the asphodel and Asphodeline refers to Jacob's rod which is one of the asphodels. The two names are often understandably confused, and growers use both names to prefix the two species generally available. *Asphodelus luteus* (or *Asphodeline lutea*) is the better known with its slender, ramrod, erect growth reaching up a good 3 ft (90 cm) from fibrous roots. The flower spikes of bright yellow, fragrant, star-like blooms are a sharp contrast to the almost glaucous grassy leaves. Flowering is through most of July and August, and cut blooms last well in water and scent the room sweetly. Plants grow well in most garden soils, including clay loams, and favour a sunny position. They make fine, distinctive border plants, valuable for their vertical accent and their compactness of root and habit.

Asphodeline liburnica (or *Asphodelus liburnicus*) is by no means a commonly seen plant and is now seldom offered by nurserymen. The roots are similarly fibrous and compact, and adaptable to a wide range of soils where the winter drainage is good and where there is some humus to retain summer moisture. Plants form a dense basal clump of very fine rushy leaves that are virtually ever-green, being very resistant to frost. The very slender stems rise to a little over 3 ft (90 cm) and between July and September flower most gracefully. This, too, is a splendid subject for the border, more graceful than *A. lutea*, and distinctively charming. Plants are fully hardy and reliable, with commendably steady growth, and may be left down for many years to remain troublefree and very desirable. Both these subjects may be divided, when mature, in autumn.

Asphodelus albus is still available via seedsmen. This is not such a good border plant, as the flowering season is short, but the fine white blooms come early in the season, in May and June. Plants grow to 30 in (75 cm). At nearly twice this height comes *A. cerasi-ferus* (or *ramosus*), but few nurseries stock this fine white-flowering asphodel which blooms in June and July. As with the others, it is best grown in a deeply worked, well drained soil, light soils being enriched with organic matter and heavy loams lightened with grit and sharp sand. Propagation is by division in spring or autumn, according to soil and climate. A number of seedsmen offer a choice of several species of asphodelus.

Aster (Michaelmas Daisy)   *Compositae*

Aster does not at first conjure up in my mind the vast army of named Michaelmas daisies but rather some of the lesser known forms. Among these *A. tongolensis* 'Berggarten', growing to 18 in (45 cm) and giving a wealth of fine cut blooms of a deep blue, and the closely related *A. yunnanensis* 'Napsbury', with its orange-

centred heliotrope-blue blooms and also flowering at 18 in (45 cm),
make superb subjects for cutting. Together with the 1-ft (30-cm)
A. subcoeruleus 'Wendy' of similar colour combination, these are
all valuable subjects for our purposes because they flower in June,
which few asters do.

Aster acris and cultivar 'Nanus' are unjustly neglected. These
grow to 30 in (75 cm) and 21 in (52·5 cm) respectively, and in
August and September the leaves are hidden by an almost incredible charming profusion of small lavender-blue flowers. Not
only are they very floriferous but plants are long-lived, reliable and
troublefree of root and habit in well drained soil and sun.

Paramount among asters, in my opinion, is the variety *A. thomsonii nanus*. From a spring planting, which is vital to success, comes
a lowly bush of soft leaves up to 15 in (37·5 cm) high. In July the
first beautiful lavender-blue flowers open. From then on these
come in increasing numbers with a wonderful abundance for a full
three months, often lasting into late October or November. The
fibrous roots are very compact and remain so for many years in
the lighter soils they prefer.

Aster amellus hybrids are similarly very fine plants for the border.
A. × *frikartii*, which has *A. thomsonii* as one parent, grows to
33 in (82·5 cm) and bears beautiful orange-centred blue flowers of
a good size from August until late October. Others of amellus
lineage that are full of merit are the deep blue, 2-ft (60-cm) 'King
George', the exquisitely pink 3-ft (90-cm) 'Jacqueline Genebrier',
and the magnificent 18-in (45-cm) German, glowing 'Violet
Queen'. All these flower profusely over many weeks between
August and the last days of October. All have fibrous and commendably compact roots, best suited to spring plantings in light but
humus-rich soils in the sun. It may be years before these are
divisible, but new stocks may be raised from basal cuttings taken in
spring. These are not plants for autumn lifting or planting, nor for
cold heavy loams. Plants should be left undisturbed for years.
None requires staking and all are troublefree perennials of the first
order, being prolific, beautiful and full of garden merit.

Aster ericoides also prefers lighter soils not bereft of humus. This,
too, is woefully neglected, yet the plants are healthy, well behaved

perennials giving very good cut flowers for the house in September and October. 'Brimstone' is very valuable at 30 in (75 cm) because the blooms are yellow—a rarity in asters. A few inches taller is 'Cinderella', with fine light blue flowers, and there is a pink form available from some growers. These are fine cut flower subjects for the kitchen garden.

Cut flowers of *A. novae-angliae* obstinately refuse to drink, but the old cultivar 'Harrington's Pink' is the exception. It drinks and lasts well in a large vase if the bases of the stems are split. Fibrous of root, woody of stem, very floriferous, it grows well in clay loams and will reach 5 ft (1·5 m). The sturdy bushes require a midriff band of stout cord but seldom need any staking. Flowering extends from mid-August until October, the blooms being graced by many feeding butterflies.

Lastly, *A. novi-belgii*, or the Michaelmas daisies. Many of these are not good garden plants, being untidy, unreliable, prone to mildew and far from troublefree. To grow them well the soil must contain humus in plenty, and plants must have space and air and sun. These requirements are therefore best attended to in the kitchen garden, as is their need for fairly frequent division to retain flowering vigour. The following selection is deliberately brief but gives a choice of colour and height.

'Fellowship' at 3½ ft (105 cm) remains one of the best soft pinks, and 'Freda Ballard', of similar height, is a very good semi-double red. The name 'Ballard' is synonymous with Michaelmas daisies, and it therefore seems right to include 'Marie Ballard', whose double light blue flowers borne on leafy bushes to 3 ft (90 cm) remain unsurpassed. 'Eventide' is an old 3-ft (90-cm) favourite with excellent, large, violet-blue blooms, while 'Royal Velvet' at 2 ft (60 cm) gives a wealth of gleaming violet flowers. At the same height 'Little Boy Blue' should not be overlooked. In the 3-ft (90-cm) range again, 'Crimson Brocade' is also good, while the precise white ruffs of 'Choristers' have a delightful purity. There are dozens more I have not grown and some I have no wish to grow, but this wealth of bloom coming in autumn acts as a wonderful tonic to ward off the impending winter gloom.

To leave the colourful realm of Michaelmas daisies thus would be both foolish and ungracious. The dwarf forms come as a boon to those whose soil space is precious. Some of these smaller asters are very fine border plants requiring but a minimum of attention. They can also be grown in well tended terrace tubs and deep window boxes.

'Little Pink Beauty' reaches 21 in (22·5 cm) and is a fine and prolific plant, as is the 10-in (25-cm) 'Rose Bonnet' whose blooms are a beautiful misty pink. 'Little Red Boy' at 15 in (40 cm) is similarly good and the nearest to red there is. 'Blue Bouquet' is the same height, and although the colour is good the plant is not so compact as the 10-in (25-cm) 'Lady in Blue'. The best white still remains the 1-ft (30-cm) 'Snowsprite'. All these are valuable plants which give many fine cut flowers for the house in September and October. None requires any support, and they are seldom, if ever, much troubled with mildew if the cultivation is sensible and there is free circulation of air among the plants.

Michaelmas daisies flowering in late October are often spoiled and wasted with prolonged rain by day and frosts by night. Often a host of unopened flowers will be thus ruined. The more dwarf forms may be protected with cloches, and the taller cultivars are well worth shielding with polythene sheeting stretched high over the plants. By such kitchen garden tricks one may have a good supply of Michaelmas daisies for cutting well into November.

Mildews are the main curse of Michaelmas daisies, and while some cultivars are very prone to this disfigurement, some of the blame must fall on the gardener who crowds his plants and gives them too rich a diet. Humus the plants must have, and watering during the summer months should never be neglected, but the use of farmyard manure galore is better checked in favour of an annual dose of sulphate of potash for the roots and, therefore, the betterment of the bloom. Sensible planting and good cultivation early in the season produce strong, healthy plants better able to resist the damp trials of autumn. Too many only remember their asters in September—fortunately for them there is now a very effective spray to apply, yet even this is best applied once or twice early in the season, and in any event long before flowering begins.

Astilbe

Saxifragaceae

Astilbe is among the most beautiful of hardy perennials. It is a plant for borders where the soil is deep, humus-laden and in some shade to prolong flowering. Clay loams give splendid support to the tough, woody and fibrous roots, and light soils should be deeply enriched with organic matter to hold an abundance of summer moisture. This ideal is worth attaining for it brings an added luxuriance to these splendid perennials. A few species and cultivars will flower remarkably well in ordinary garden soil, and the genus is noted for its longevity and tenacity of life. Astilbe is also noted for its perfect contrast of graceful plumes and very fine foliage. The flowers cover a colour range from white to deep red, passing through many beautiful shades of rose and pink, while the leaves vary in their intricacy. The colour of the leaves changes as the season progresses, and some are decidedly dark and glossy for good measure. Height also covers a wide range from just under 1 ft (30 cm) through to a statuesque 6 ft (1·8 m), and while the main flush of flowering is in July and August by selection the season may extend from June until the end of September. The emerging vernal leaves of many are richly tinged with pink and rosy hues, and these have a fine disposition and a soft beauty.

There are many fine cultivars and hybrids available, and while all are very good garden plants not all are suitable for cut flower requirements. One of the very finest for the flower arranger is *A.* 'Gertrude Brix'. This is a beautiful plant with attractive deeply cut foliage from spring until autumn. The slender but sturdy stems bear their fine crimson plumes between July and September up to a height of about 3 ft (90 cm). The cut flowers last longer than most in a vase where they make an immediately distinctive contribution. The 30-in (75-cm) 'Bressingham Beauty' is a magnificent pink, while the white plumes and dark leaves of the 2-ft (60-cm) 'Irrlicht' are very fine. The red 2-ft (60-cm) 'Federsee' is less demanding of moisture than many, as is 'Granat', which is a little taller and another excellent red. Indeed, it is difficult to pick out an astilbe that is not full of merit.

Mature plants may be lifted and divided in autumn with the aid of a hefty, sharp knife. This may also be undertaken in the spring if the divisions are kept well watered.

Astrantia (Masterwort)   *Umbelliferae*

Astrantia is a charming plant for the summer-moist border, where it will flourish in sun or shade. This fibrous-rooted perennial will grow in a wide range of soils so long as they are not dry in summer or waterlogged in winter. Plants are more telling in a little shade, where their glossy, deeply lobed, fresh green leaves, and intricately wrought flowers on their slender wiry stems, make excellent neighbours to such as astilbe and phlox

Astrantia carniolica gives a fine clump of lobed basal leaves, and the flowering stems grow to some 30 in (75 cm). The flowers are typically intricate with their grey-white petals flushed at the centre and decorated with a mass of stamens. These come in good numbers over many weeks between June and September. 'Rosea' is similarly long-flowering with the grey flowers more deeply flushed with rose at their centres. 'Rubra' is more decidedly red and more dwarf at 15 in (37·5 cm), flowering more briefly in June and July. In *A.* 'Major' the blooms are also rosy-centred and further graced with pale green without. These unusual and beautiful flowers come for some eight weeks or more between June and August, the plants growing up to 30 in (75 cm). *A.* 'Maxima' also flowers at the same time at about 2 ft (60 cm), the blooms being finely flushed with a rosy pink.

Astrantia carniolica and its relations are easy to grow, making a steady increase that is never troublesome. *A. c.* 'Rubra' is the slowest-growing form, remaining very compact of root. The type is readily raised from seed, plants flowering in their second year.

All these astrantias give the flower arranger a subtle choice of bloom that is both distinctive and charming. Pride of place for a long vase life must go to *A. involucrata*, which gives excellent cut flowers of green-grey-white over several months. This is also a fine plant for cool, light shade, growing to just over 2 ft (60 cm) and flowering from early June to late September. Sprays with long stems look fine in large vases, and blooms with shortened stems make dainty posies. Curiously, these distinctive, easily cultivated masterworts are still neglected by many gardeners, yet they are full of merit, being fully hardy, reliable and troublefree. Several forms will gently seed themselves but propagation by division is simple and may be undertaken in autumn or spring. All are prolific plants with well behaved shallow roots.

Astrantia

Bellis (Daisy)   *Compositae*

Bellis perennis deserves more than a fleeting mention. This daisy is a delightful plant for moister soils, either in a little shade or in the full eye of the sun. The plants expand steadily, and curbing of their fibrous roots is an annual or biennial child's play. Where there is a little moisture flowering will extend over a very long period, often from March until November. In the damper days of early autumn the spoon-shaped leaves take on an added luxuriance of deep glossy green, and the golden-eyed white flowers have a simple appeal that is a delight among paving crevices and damp rocks, in raised beds and tubs in courtyards, and in window boxes, while the cut flowers can make a charmingly simply contribution to a small bowl or vase for several days. This daisy has two or three delightful cultivars, the white-flowered 'The Pearl', the deliciously pink 'Dresden China', and the larger-flowered double red 'Rob Roy'. All these have stems of about 3 in (7·5 cm). Bellis, from the Latin *bellus*, means pretty—and this is true of these small, easy-going, hardy perennials.

Bergenia *Saxifragaceae*

Bergenia is a very valuable genus both to the gardener and to the flower arranger. Plants will grow in a wide range of soils in either shade or sun. All have large, near-evergreen leaves and both fleshy and fibrous, very long-lived roots. While plants may be left down for many years, older plants are not so free-flowering. Indeed, the gardening trick with these is to keep them young and floriferous by a surgical division every three or four years.

The first to flower, and one of the most dwarf, is the hybrid *B. schmidtii*. This gives a mound of large spoon-shaped leaves, very finely serrated at the edges, and 1-ft (30-cm) stems clustered with a beautiful profusion of pure pink flowers between the very end of January and the middle of March. After flowering the plants remain a mound of flat, leathery leaves. Obviously such an early-flowering plant gives the discerning flower arranger most valuable cut blooms in the cold months.

Bergenia cordifolia grows to about the same height but with more rose in its pendant sprays of flowers, which appear in April and May. The leaves are heart-shaped. Its cultivar 'Purpurea' is very similar, but the pink sprays are flushed with light purple. The blooms have a light fragrance when warmed by the sun.

Bergenia delavayi is the smallest species generally available,

c

growing to some 9 or 10 in (22·5 or 25 cm). The rosy purple blooms come in March and April after the winter has flushed the leaves to red.

Other forms of bergenia that flower in April and May include some very fine hybrids. 'Ballawley' (once known as 'Delbees') has large glossy leaves that colour well in winter, while the deep rose-red flowers of spring are borne on stems growing up to 18 in (45 cm). 'Margery Fish' is a fine pink cultivar growing to about the same height. Flowering at just under 1 ft (30 cm) is the newer 'Bressing-ham Bountiful', which is very generous with its fuchsia-pink blooms in April. With larger flowers and growing some 6 in (15 cm) taller is the seldom offered 'Pugsley's Pink'.

Among the recent German introductions we have two very fine bergenias. 'Abendgut' ('Evenglow') and 'Silberlicht' ('Silver Light') both grow to about 1 ft (30 cm). The former has glowing blooms of a rich rosy red while the latter has only a very light blush to its white flowers.

All these are of easy cultivation and best suited to partial shade where there is some moisture, and all give valuable cut blooms when there is a natural scarcity of pink flowers.

Brunnera   *Boraginaceae*

Brunnera macrophylla (once, more tellingly named *Anchusa myoso-tidiflora*) grows very well in the conditions favoured by bergenias. It has both fleshy and fibrous roots, which are long-lived and expand at a steady pace. Plants mound up to 18 in (45 cm) to give a wealth of large heart-shaped leaves covered, between May and July, with fine wiry sprays of innumerable tiny but brilliant blue flowers that are strongly reminiscent of the forget-me-not. Seen en masse, these intensely blue flowers are both striking and charming. The variegated form *B. m.* 'Variegata' is very similar in root, habit and flower, but the leaves are mottled with creamy variations. Plants are not so vigorous as the type, making this more suitable for growing in the border. *B. macrophylla* becomes rather large and coarse if left to its own devices for many years, and plants are better for fairly frequent division with a knife in spring or autumn.

Cut blooms may last only a few days but because of their daintiness and intense colour they make a valuable contribution to any vase or bowl, and the leaves are very decorative, giving a cool contrast to the flowers.

Calamintha (Calamint) *Labiatae*

Calamintha nepetoides remains curiously neglected by growers, gardeners and, therefore, flower arrangers. This fibrous-rooted perennial remains so compact that division is mostly impossible. Fortunately firm cuttings give a ready means of propagation. Plants grow best in lighter soils bearing humus, in partial shade or sun. *C. nepetoides* grows bushily erect, in soils not over-rich, to a little over 1 ft (30 cm). The slender woody stems are well clothed with small leaves strongly aromatic of peppermint. Much of the stem forms a spike of tiny, lipped flowers of white and lavender-blue, so numerous that the gardener is greeted by a delightful haze of light blue. Not only is flowering profuse, but the established plant's flowering period of July to October is exceeded by a full month in young plants. In my garden these begin flowering in the earliest days of June and continue without diminishing until the end of October, making a fine sight at the front of the herbaceous border. Plants remain troublefree for years and give the flower arranger a wealth of spikes to tone down the more blatant blooms of summer.

Caltha (Kingcup, Marsh Marigold) *Ranunculaceae*

Caltha palustris will grow in many soils so long as these are moist in summer. If this basic requirement is met the cheerful kingcup will grow equally well in full sun or partial shade. Clay loams well worked with sedge peat give very fine results, and the lightening effect of the peat makes division after flowering a simpler and less tearing task. *C. palustris* gives a mass of hollow, branched stems growing to about 1 ft (30 cm). To these cling the very rounded, heart-shaped, fresh green leaves. These stemless leaves are very attractive and form a refreshing contrast to the buds and to the bright golden-yellow blooms with their wide open petals and

golden stamens. Flowering extends through most of April and May.
The best time to cut flowers for the house is when the topmost bud
is open. Short stems often bear a loose cluster of five or six buds,
and these open in a vase. Although the blooms bear a likeness to
those of the buttercup, the petals are of a better substance and do
not drop. As I write these words the calthas on the table have been
in their vase for eight days and not shed a single petal. The clean
brightness and generosity of this spring-flowering, bone-hardy
perennial makes it a valuable subject. Plants are of the easiest
cultivation if the soil is kept moist in summer. The equally bright,
double *C. p.* 'Plena' is not so good as a cut flower subject, but it is
well worth growing.

Camassia (Quamash)   *Liliaceae*

Camassia quamash (or *C. esculenta*), are rare bulbs in that they are
both edible and quite at home in heavy, even ill drained clay loams.
Strangely enough, the bulbs do not rot away under such wet conditions, and copious summer moisture is vital to these neglected
hardy perennials of easy growth. Bulbs are best planted 3 or 4 in
(7·5 or 10 cm) deep in autumn, and will sprout very narrow light
green leaves by early April. Plants then grow away well and by June
there will be a clump of rushy basal leaves and very upright stems
growing to some 30 in (75 cm) and bearing fine spikes of richly
blue, star-like flowers. The colour of these charming blooms may
vary from pale china to deep blue, according to the soil in the
locality. Clay loams give both a nice proportion of foliage and
beautiful blue blooms. Good results may also be obtained in
terrace tubs kept moist, whether in full sun or a little shade. The
cut blooms last well and look fine in a vase. A white-flowering
form of *C. quamash* is sometimes obtainable.

The bulbs of *C. cusickii* are very much larger, being the size of
a good onion. Planted in a deep, humus-rich loam the flowering
stems of light blue blooms may attain almost 3 ft (90 cm).

Camassia leichtlinii also has large bulbs, and the sturdy stems
can reach 3 ft (90 cm). The blooms may come in a range of blue
and purple, cream and white, and there is even a double-flowered

milky white form in *C. l.* 'Plena', and an even rarer violet-purple cultivar in *C. l.* 'Atroviolacea'.

Other forms of camassia include the light purple *C. howellii*, and the pale blue *C. scillioides*, but these are seldom offered, whereas *C. quamash* and *C. leichtlinii* are more freely available and make very good border plants when given the dignity of a group planting in the heavier, moisture bearing loams.

The bulbs of these camassias are fully hardy and may be left down for many years. In a suitable position they will slowly increase and expand, making propagation by division of the offsets a simple matter. This may be undertaken in early autumn, after the foliage has been allowed to die right back. Alternatively, *C. quamash* and *C. leichtlinii* (together with its white flowered form 'Album') are offered by some seedsmen, so one can raise one's own stock, which gives one a wider range of colour variations to choose from. *C. quamash* remains the strongest grower and makes a good introduction to these little grown plants.

Campanula (Bell-flower, Harebell)   *Campanulaceae*

Campanula is a genus giving many fine and diverse hardy perennials. Treating a selection alphabetically, the first is *C. alliariifolia*. This flowers well in sun or a little shade, a choice given by many campanulas, and grows to just under 2 ft (60 cm), with its pendant creamy white blooms dancing on arching stems between June and August. Plants come readily from seed, whereas division is required for the more refined and garden-worthy cultivar 'Ivory Bells'.

Campanula burghaltii, with its wafer-thin blooms of pale violet-blue coming between late June and the end of August, grows to 18 in (45 cm) and is a gracefully lax plant.

The well known *C. carpatica*, growing to 9 in (22·5 cm) and flowering very profusely over many weeks between June and September, gives charming, slender-stemmed blue and white bell-flowers for the flower arranger. 'Blue Moonlight', 'Bressingham White' and 'Wheatley Violet' are all very fine hardy perennials of the easiest cultivation in well drained soils with a little humus for the fibrous roots.

Campanula glomerata, 15 in (37·5 cm) high, has a valuable trio of cultivars in 'Joan Elliott', producing violet-blue harebells in May and June; the white 'Nana Alba', flowering later, between June and August, and the violet 'Superba', which grows a little taller, to 2 ft (60 cm), and blooms at the same time. All these give good cut flowers of fragile bells which need careful handling.

Campanula lactiflora, unlike the preceding campanulas, is more fleshy than fibrous of root, and is propagated by basal cuttings in spring rather than by division. This species is more sturdy of growth and bushier of habit than the foregoing. *C. l.* 'Alba' grows to a good 4 ft (1·2 m) to give a profusion of white bells between June and August. 'Loddon Anna' can reach 5 ft (1·5 m) and is similarly floriferous with very light pink flowers. Both these tall cultivars may require some support. 'Prichard's Variety', at 3 ft (90 cm), with its deep blue flowers delightfully covering most of its leafy profusion between late June and late August, seldom needs any support, however. This is a very commendable cultivar. Lastly here, comes the little *C. l.* 'Pouffe', a delightful 9-in (22·5-cm) mound of light green leaves and a wealth of charming and nicely proportioned lavender-blue flowers lasting from late June until September. This is a superb plant at the front of the border, and the cut blooms are ideal subjects for small table bowls.

Campanula latifolia also grows robustly and gives a wealth of fine cut blooms for the house. While these grow well in sunny borders, a shady site and soil with some humus give a longer flowering season. The roots, which are more fibrous than fleshy, are more readily divisible than those of *C. lactiflora*, and plants grow very erectly, and far less bushily, to 3½ ft (105 cm) or a little more. In sheltered borders no staking is required, but kitchen garden plants are better given some elementary support. Two very good cultivars are 'Brantwood' and 'Gloaming'. Both grow to 4 ft (1·2 m) and bear fine spikes of long bell-flowers throughout July and August. 'Gloaming' is the palest silvery mauve imaginable, and the name gives the clue to the gardener that they should be viewed at dusk for their beauty to be fully appreciated. The blooms of 'Brantwood' are larger, and a splendid deep purple. While both plants are similar in root, height and flowering period, the leaves differ very noticeably, those of 'Gloaming' being narrow, whereas those of 'Brantwood', especially the basal leaves, are larger and much broader. These heart-shaped leaves are often beautifully variegated with hues of buff and old gold. Both forms come readily from seed, but with the usual variations of colour, whereas division retains the parent's characteristics. While *C. latifolia* is fully hardy, reliable and floriferous in soils with adequate summer moisture, the blooms share the fragility of the genus; they are poor travellers but splendid for home use.

Campanula latiloba raised from seed produces 2-ft (60-cm) stems of pale violet-blue blooms each up to 2 in (5 cm) across. An improvement is to be found in the Bressingham-raised hybrid 'Percy Piper', which grows to 3 ft (90 cm) and gives a good number of larger blooms of a deep blue. Flowering covers several weeks in June and July, giving the flower arranger many fine cut blooms for the house.

Campanula persicifolia has several fine cultivars, one of the oldest and best being 'Telham Beauty'. This grows to nearly 3 ft (90 cm) and flowers profusely between late June and early September. The rich blue blooms look charming in both garden and vase. 'Fleur de Neige' is a very good double white cultivar, and the single 'Snowdrift', the double deep blue 'Pride of Exmouth', and the more violet, double 'Wirral Belle' give the gardener and flower arranger a charming choice. Plants are kept most healthy and floriferous if divided every three years or so. These, together with *CC. burghaltii, carpatica, lactiflora* and *latifolia*, are fully worthy of a border planting.

The fine, fibrous roots of *C. portenschlagiana* (an ugly-sounding substitute for *C. muralis*) are wonderfully adaptable to a wide range of soils, and accept full sun or a remarkable degree of shade. The dense mounds of fresh green leaves are all but evergreen, and the profusion of flowers which nestles on these lasts months on end. These 4-in (10-cm) high, steadily expanding mounds may be smothered with fine, deep blue bell-flowers from June until late October, and these look equally delightful at the front of the border, in a shady corner, among rocks, in raised beds, tubs, and window boxes, or as cut blooms in a small table bowl. This is a sterling hardy perennial full of merit based on hardiness, longevity, and troublefree cultivation.

Campanula poscharskyana also has a very long flowering season lasting four months in an average year. The light blue flowers are more open and star-like than those of *C. portenschlagiana*, and are borne on slender stems up to 9 in (22·5 cm) high. Growth is very vigorous and far too rampant to admit planting in a border, but this bone-hardy, sheet forming campanula looks fine on a sunny bank and gives a host of cut blooms for the smaller vase, while the white-flowering form of 'Alba' provides a useful admixture.

The harebell, *C. rotundifolia*, with its delicate pale blue blooms on very slender 10-in (25-cm) stems, is undeniably charming. This is readily raised from seed, the fibrous roots being best suited to lighter soils with some humus and in some shade. The cultivar *C. r.* 'Olympica', with its deeper blue harebells, grows to nearly 1 ft (30 cm). From a mound of small, light green, rounded leaves rises a host of stems so slender that the flowers dance in the lightest summer breeze. These graceful plants flower very well between July and September, and are more than fit to grace the front of any border. Plants in my garden have always been reliable, troublefree and prolific, even flowering well in quite heavy shade when not deprived of summer moisture. They are far too seldom seen.

The taller campanulas are best cut when the spikes are half in bloom and half in bud.

Catananche (Cupid's Dart, Blue Cupidone)   *Compositae*

Catananche caerulea has very fleshy roots. It should be planted in the spring, and where the soil is heavy this advice is best taken as a direct order. Autumn plantings may be followed by an unacceptable winter toll of stock. Nurserymen usually offer pot-grown stock, as the roots deeply resent disturbance. Plants do not have time to establish their roots in autumn, and are not to be hurried even when planted in spring. Established plants are tardy to show much new growth until the latter part of spring. Light, free-draining soils and a sunny site promote longevity. Heavier soils will give good results if thoroughly lightened with plenty of grit and sharp sand.

Catananche caerulea is of easy cultivation and a valuable perennial for those with dry, stony gardens. Plants form a dense clump of grey-green, narrow, evergreen basal leaves. The slender wiry stems arise in profusion to about 18 in (45 cm). In early June these are topped with buds nestling in beautiful silvery calcyes. Towards the end of the month these silver cups will open to reveal fine blue flowers with thin, crisp-looking petals. Flowering is incredibly profuse and lasts for a full three months. Indeed, plants are so free-flowering that some may exhaust themselves, and the old practice of cutting back all the stems in mid-September is a wise one to emulate.

The cultivar *C. c.* 'Major' also demands sharp soil drainage and plenty of sun. This is a distinct improvement on the type, both for the gardener and for the flower arranger. The stems are remarkably wiry and straight considering their slender height of 30 in (75 cm), while the flowers are a very fine deep lavender-blue held in crisp, silvered saucers.

Catananches make splendid border plants and must be considered one of the most valuable blue-flowered subjects for the summer garden. Cutting over three months gives the flower arranger a wealth of very long-lasting subjects for the house. Those long-stemmed blooms cut towards the end of the summer, if dried slowly, provide very valuable and primly attractive winter decoration.

Plants are best left undisturbed but new stock of the type may be grown from seed, whereas the cultivar *C. c.* 'Major' must be propagated from root cuttings taken in mid-spring.

Cedronella   *Labiatae*

Cedronella foeniculum has been so neglected in recent times as to become almost impossible to obtain except from a few determined nurserymen. Seedsmen, too, have sensed this decline and most sadly omit this hardy perennial from their catalogues. The recent spate of comparatively wet and mild winters has gravely reduced the stocks of the nurserymen, for this plant, with its rather meagre fibrous roots, is a subject for well drained, preferably light soil and sun. Plants grow bushily and upright to $2\frac{1}{2}$–3 ft (75–90 cm), and are well clothed with fine, narrow bright green leaves and spikes of soft deep blue flowers lasting from July until September. Where *Salvia superba* flourishes, this distant relative will grow well and give cut blooms to tone down the harsher hues of other flowers in large vases. *C. foeniculum* is suitable for sunny borders and for growing on broad ridges in the kitchen garden. Judicious cutting encourages root vigour and longevity. A little annual potash is always preferable to any manure.

Centaurea (Perennial Cornflower)   *Compositae*

Centaurea is another genus of perennials most suitable for well drained, well worked soils that have not been enriched with manure. Rich clay loams will require 'diluting' with grit and sharp sand because they are generally full of plant nutriments that noticeably tend to induce too much leaf and a subsequent decrease in the flowering. *C. dealbata* is a good example of this, and plantings in well fed kitchen gardens produce a wealth of very fine, deeply cut leaves and only a few blooms of pink cornflowers between June and August. The cultivar 'Steenbergii' also has deeply cut silvery leaves, but the flowers are finer, being a deep purply pink. Plants grow to about 30 in (75 cm) and bloom later in the season. The best cultivar available is 'John Coutts'. This flowers well for several weeks between June and August with large clear pink blooms.

The 2-ft (60-cm) *C. montana* has pink, purple and blue forms flowering in May and June. The more openly wrought flowers make splendid subjects for the house. *C. pulchra* 'Major' flowers more erectly at 2 ft (60 cm) in July and August above sharply cut silver-grey leaves, but for silver foliage one must turn to *C. simplicicaulis*. This, too, has pink blooms (in June), but it is half the height at 1 ft (30 cm).

All these are fully hardy subjects propagated by division in spring or autumn.

Centranthus, see Kentranthus

Cephalaria (Giant Scabious) *Dipsaceae*

Cephalaria gigantea (also known as *C. tatarica*) is well named by
the botanists. This is another plant far too seldom seen in gardens.
Although this giant scabious will grow in many soils, those that
have been deeply worked and bear a good supply of humus give
the most impressive results, as long as the site is sunny. Planted in
such a soil the roots probe deeply to provide a firm anchor for the
sheer weight of the bushy growth, which can attain 5–6 ft (1·5–
1·8 m). This is a handsome giant with deeply cut edges to its leaves,
which partly clothe the massive stems topped with large heads of
yellow pincushion flowers. In good soils flowering covers many
weeks between July and September. The branching stems of
flowers make fine long-lasting subjects for large floral displays, even
if some buds are thereby unavoidably wasted. *C. gigantea* is a
splendid subject for the sunny kitchen garden, although a little
shade is well tolerated. Plants should be allowed ample room and
are best stationed at least 2 ft (60 cm) apart. Staking in gardens is
generally unnecessary, except in exposed positions when substantial support is required before the plants have reached their
full stature. The labour of division is best undertaken in spring but
plants may be raised from seed.

Cheiranthus (Wallflower) *Cruciferae*

Cheiranthus, the wallflower, is an extremely popular plant, and
where thoughtfully planted will flourish longer than many suppose.
On top of a 30-ft (9-m) wall of the London Transport bus garage in
Tottenham there are five cheiranthus bushes planted by beak
wiping birds. These have flourished in this apparently inhospitable
place for the last eight years, to my certain knowledge. That they
should survive in this admittedly well drained but soilless and
exposed site makes a mockery of those short-lived plants coddled
and cajoled each year by the gardener. The lesson is that cheiran-

thus demands sharp soil drainage and an open situation, coupled with a selection from those whose perennial qualities have been proved.

The well tried old hybrid *C.* 'Harpur Crewe', growing bushily to about 1 ft (30 in), is still to be valued for its reliability and abundance of fragrant, double golden-yellow blooms between April and June. It can be raised from spring-sown seed, but quicker results come from cuttings taken immediately after flowering. The hybrid coppery orange 'Rufus' is another old favourite of similar stature, and a good lilac-mauve is to be found in the 1-ft (30-cm) *C. linifolius* (*Erysimum linifolium*). The newer *C.* 'Constant Cheer' is an aptly named hybrid capable of flowering for months on end with amber tints to its rich mauve blooms. All relish a little lime in the soil.

Chrysanthemum (Shasta Daisy, Tansy, Feverfew)

Compositae

Chrysanthemum maximum, also known as the Shasta daisy, has been greatly improved by plant breeders over the years to give a number of fine cultivars suitable for the kitchen garden. These fibrous-rooted perennials are fully hardy and of easy cultivation in ordinary well drained garden soil with some humus. Among the doubles the 3-ft (90-cm) white 'Wirral Supreme' grows sturdily and flowers well in July and August, and the 30-in (75-cm) 'Cobham Gold' is fine if left undisturbed for a few years to develop a flush to live up to its name. 'Jennifer Read' has mostly ousted the older and unforgettable 'Esther Read', with its slightly larger blooms on sturdy 3-ft (90-cm) stems. Of the semi-double or anemone-centred forms 'Wirral Pride' bears blooms up to 5 in (12·5 cm) across on stems a little over 3 ft (90 cm). The semi-double 'T. Killin' is a very fine and sturdy grower bearing blooms of great substance up to 4 in (10 cm) across. This is a very commendable cultivar also growing to 3 ft (90 cm). The smaller, by 6 in (15 cm), 'Horace Read' with 4½-in (11-cm) blooms of ivory-white is also a good plant. 'John Murray' is another double with good-sized, substantial, pure white blooms that come for many weeks between late July and September on very sturdy stems. Among the simpler, single-flowered varieties 'Everest' remains supreme for cutting, the strong 3-ft (90-cm) stems being topped with large white blooms that have both substance and style. All these provide the flower arranger with a wealth of cut blooms between July and September. All may be divided with benefit every three years or so, but 'Cobham Gold' is worth another year's wait. Division should be undertaken in the spring, or immediately after flowering where the garden soil is not heavy. Where the soil is heavy then a generous quantity of grit and sharp sand must be worked in, but plants do respond to humus and some potash. By careful selection among the cultivars and by cunning use of cloches the cut flower season may cover over three months. Blooms are best cut when half-open.

Other forms of summer-flowering chrysanthemums are well worth cultivating. The tansy, once *Tanacetum vulgare*, now *Chrysanthemum vulgare*, grows very erectly to 30 in (75 cm) to give a pretty bush of delicately cut aromatic foliage topped with plates of little yellow flowers between July and early September. Similarly attractive and also with fine, aromatic leaves is *C. parthenium*, or feverfew, with an incredible number of dainty, golden-centred, small white flowers. The double form known as 'White Bonnet' is equally floriferous between June and early September, and both will grow in a very wide variety of soils, in sun or shade. While neither is very perennial unless cut back severely in early September, plants are readily raised from seed, and the cut blooms make charming floral decorations. A spartan diet suits them best.

Two autumn-flowering forms of fully hardy and perennial chrysanthemums are to be found in *CC. rubellum* and *uliginosum*. The latter is remarkably unfussy as to soil, although some humus is always noticeably appreciated. This grows strongly and erectly to an unsupported 5 ft (1·5 m) and bears appealingly simple single, golden-eyed white daisies in September and October. *C. rubellum* grows to only half the height and is best represented in the cultivar 'Clara Curtis'. This bears a fine array of pure pink blooms between late August and October. *C. uliginosum* is bone-hardy and long-lived, whereas to be on the safe side *C. rubellum* should be raised anew fairly frequently from basal cuttings taken in mid-spring.

Among the spray chrysanthemums the Koreans are the most valuable to us here. These are sufficiently hardy to be left down for a number of years, but plants are best kept young and floriferous by fairly frequent division or by taking basal cuttings. The chief value of the Korean chrysanthemums lies in their late flowering. They require a little support for the taller forms, but no disbudding. The kitchen garden soil should be deeply worked and well fed for these gross feeders. This especially applies to those cultivars growing to 4 ft (1·2 m) such as the September-flowering rosy pink 'Autumn Day', the October-blooming old gold 'Charles Nye', or the deep crimson 'St George's Day'.

At about the 2-ft (60-cm) mark the orange 'Carlene', 'Coral Mist', and the peachy pink 'Polly Peachum' all flower in August. The old 2-ft (60-cm) 'Margaret Simpson' also begins flowering in August and continues until the harsher frosts of autumn scythe down her rusty blooms.

Among the last to flower, at about the 3-ft (90-cm) mark, comes the October-blooming pure white 'Wedding Day', the fine single 'Lilac Time', and the flushed lime 'Yellow Maize'. These are old and well tried cultivars known for their abundant flowering.

Recently the more dwarf Otley Koreans have superseded many of the spray forms. These are valuable and very floriferous hardy plants suitable for growing in large borders, raised beds, terrace tubs, and even window boxes. Most, being under 2 ft (60 cm), require no form of support whatever, nor is any stopping or disbudding necessary. The blooms of these Otley Koreans cover a good range of colour and are remarkably resistant to, even disdainful of, October frosts. These autumn-flowering dwarfs are greatly prized for their cheerful blooms to brighten house and garden. Among the tallest, at 2 ft (60 cm), are the double silvery pink 'Gloria', the primrose-yellow, semi-double 'Shining Light', and the crimson 'Firestone'. In the 1½-ft (45-cm) range the semi-double 'Amber Glory', the double 'Copper Nob', the vivid red semi-double 'Pirate' and the pink 'Rapture' are all good. Smallest of all, at just 1 ft (30 cm), a fine choice is offered by the glowing orange double 'Cheerfulness', the semi-double rich red 'Dandy', the double pure yellow 'Gold Dust', and the green-centred, semi-double white 'Powder River'.

Cimicifuga (Bugbane)   *Ranunculaceae*

Cimicifuga is among the most beautiful and stately garden plants. Its toughly fibrous roots are similar to those of the astilbe and are likewise best planted in a deeply worked soil laden with humus. Improved clay loams give very fine results, especially if the plantings are in the shade. Where ample summer moisture is available cimicifugas are of simple cultivation, being fully hardy and very long-lived. Plants are finely proportioned with beautiful, deeply cut leaves and slender stems topped with very graceful spikes or spires of tightly packed creamy white flowers that are also attractive when in bud. Although plants may attain 5 ft (1·5 m) or more, no form of staking is required to detract from their statuesque beauty. As border plants cimicifugas are magnificent and make a distinctive contribution when carefully sited so that neighbours do not mask their overall virtues.

Of the several forms available *C. cordifolia* (often catalogued as *C. americana*) is perhaps the most graceful. The specific name *cordifolia* is a little misleading, for the leaves are heart-shaped only by stretching the description. They are very similar to those of *Tiarella wherryi*, that is, a beautiful golden-green and maple-like. Indeed, there is a form where this is acknowledged in the name, *C. japonica acerina*, but I have not seen or grown this. The leaves of *C. cordifolia* are a delight from spring until autumn, being very nicely disposed about the base of the remarkably slender, almost black stems. These are well under $\frac{1}{4}$ in (0·6 cm) in diameter and rise to a full $5\frac{1}{4}$ ft (1·6 m), yet they are wonderfully resistant to summer winds. In July the stems are gracefully crowned with slender spires of buds. In early August these open into little star-like white blooms, and flowering continues until the end of September. I find this plant so beautiful that it is now safe from any scissors of mine.

Cimicifuga foetida intermedia 'White Pearl' begins flowering in early September and continues through October. This hybrid is different in many respects from *C. cordifolia*. The leaves are deeply divided and astilbe-like, and the branched flowering stems barely reach 4 ft (1·2 m). The flower spikes are a little broader and not so upright. While *C. cordifolia* is by far the more imposing garden plant, *C.* 'White Pearl' is the better plant for cutting because its blooms have a delicious scent when they first open, and last well in water. This, incidentally, makes the common name of bugbane a downright lie.

Cimicifuga racemosa also grows to just 4 ft (1·2 m), but there is more cream in the spikes of white blooms that grace August and September. The tallest species is *C. ramosa*, which grows remarkably erect to nearly 7 ft (2·1 m) and bears large spikes of creamy white blooms between mid-August and the end of September. This, too, is very resistant to winds.

All these are very fine and distinctive hardy perennials giving the flower arranger some choice and graceful blooms that are doubly valuable because of their season. Like astilbe, these cimicifugas may be divided with the aid of a hefty sharp knife.

Convallaria (Lily-of-the-valley)   *Liliaceae*

Convallaria majalis is well known as the lily-of-the-valley. This is a lover of dappled shade and soil rich in humus, and while it is sufficiently common to be found naturalized, it remains a perennial of considerable charm with its fine pale green leaves and delicate pendant bells of pure white. This sweetly fragrant flower of May and June deserves a bed to itself, where the soil has been deeply worked and generously enriched with compost, peat and well rotted manure. The crowns are best firmly planted very shallowly and just 1 ft (30 cm) apart. Heavy loams must be lightened. Once plants are established it is an old and sound practice to give an annual mulch of organic matter, and a pre-flowering liquid manure feed works wonders on the quality and longevity of the blooms. Any form of potash is likewise good.

Plants expand steadily, and after three or four years tend to become overcrowded with a resultant decrease in flowering. This is a signal to lift, divide and replant in re-enriched soil. Strangely, lily-of-the-valley is a splendid plant for draughty sites, such as is often found between houses, and it is a very valuable subject for well tended tubs in a shady town courtyard.

For the garden the 9-in (22·5-cm) *C. majalis* is unsurpassed, but the 1-ft (30-cm) *C. m.* 'Fortin's Giant', with its fragrant, larger flowers, is a splendid subject for indoor decoration. *C. majalis*, of course, is charming for small table bowls. For those seeking a choice of colour the softly pink blooms of *C. m.* 'Rosea' on 9-in (22·5-cm) stems are similarly useful to the flower arranger.

Plantings in rich soil give longer stems, to the heights indicated, and this makes cutting quicker. The quality of the leaves is also greatly enhanced.

Coreopsis   *Compositae*

Coreopsis provides some striking contrasts in its species. The most garden-worthy, and fit to grace any select herbaceous border, is the ferny-leaved *C. verticillata*, which forms a delicate wind-proof bush smothered in yellow starry blooms throughout the summer, but this sterling perennial is of little use as a cut flower subject. The most suitable species for our purpose here is *C. grandiflora*. This gives very good long-stemmed flowers that drink well and have a long vase life.

Coreopsis grandiflora is not a plant for heavy or richly fed loams. Such plantings lead to a lush growth and a short life. Planted in light soils bearing some peat or compost, but no manure, and in the full eye of the sun. *C. grandiflora* is both hardy and perennial. Plants are very readily raised from seed, and grow bushily up to 3 ft (90 cm). It is admirably suited for kitchen garden cultivation, where the plants may receive early support and regular cutting. Three or four cultivars are available. One of the oldest is *C. g.* 'Mayfield Giant', so named for its larger, yellow blooms. *C. g.* 'Sunburst' also grows to about 30 in (75 cm), but the yellow blooms are more densely petalled. Both come reasonably true from seed. Another old form is *C. g.* 'Perry's Variety', growing to about 2 ft (60 cm), but although the deep yellow blooms are semi-double the stems are far from sturdy. While all these are very useful cut flower subjects their longevity is rather suspect, but the frequent raising of new stock is both simple and interesting.

The best variety of *C. grandiflora* is the newer 3-ft (90-cm) 'Badengold'. Planted in light, even poor soils in a sunny position, this is reliably perennial. Plants grow bushily erect and the 3-in (7·5-cm) golden-yellow blooms are borne on sturdier and straighter stems. This is a very good cut flower subject, flowering between June and the end of August, as do the other cultivars, but not so profusely. Longevity is enhanced by cutting back plants in early September, and new stock is raised by division of the more fibrous roots, a feat not always possible with other cultivars.

Similar to *C. grandiflora* is *C. lanceolata*, with its narrower leaves making a bush capped with a profusion of yellow blooms between late June and the end of August. Plants grow to a little over 2 ft (60 cm) and, while not choice, they are perennial and give useful and long-lasting cut blooms for the house.

Corydalis   *Fumariaceae*

Corydalis lutea is a beautiful small perennial of fragile appearance, but the fleshy roots are both hardy and long-lived. Plants mound up to about 9 in (22·5 cm) with a mass of delicately cut leaves. These are delightful from March until November. In early April the first sprays of tiny, tubular lime-yellow flowers appear nestling on, and amid, the foliage. Flowering continues for months, until the more severe frosts of autumn at last put an end to this charming bounty. Corydalis is of the easiest cultivation, tolerating full sun, relishing dappled shade, and capable of flowering in fairly heavy shade, as long as the soil is not dry. Plants remain compact and well behaved in clay loams, but in fertile, moist, light soils self-sown seedlings can be a serious nuisance. *C. lutea* is a delightful and troublefree plant if grown in tubs in courtyards, and in town window boxes, and I have seen less floriferous plants growing in the vertical crevices of brick walls bonded with the old mortar mix. Both the foliage and the sprays of flowers look delightful in small bowls and vases. *C. ochroleuca* is similar except that its flowers are creamy in colour.

Crambe (Flowering seakale) *Cruciferae*

Crambe cordifolia, by comparison, is a giant, yet this, too, is a fleshy-rooted hardy perennial adaptable to sun or partial shade. Crambe develops massive and deeply penetrating roots, and propagation by root cuttings is laborious but worthwhile. Although seeds germinate well it takes three years to produce a good flowering plant. The huge crowns of mature plants can be split apart, and these, if replanted immediately (leaving 2 in (5 cm) proud of the soil) will establish themselves in well prepared and moistened soil. The fat red buds about the proud crown open to give a wealth of very large deep green leaves, up to 2 ft (60 cm) long by nearly as much across. Amid these the lightest of green flowering stems rapidly ascend in May. These are much branched and divided to hold clustered buds in great profusion. In June these open, and one may then marvel at the basal leaves, mounding up to 3 ft (90 cm), topped by the 6-ft (1·8-m) stems bearing a vast airy cloud of tiny white flowers that are redolent of a heavy honey. This giant gypsophila-like, honeyed cloud lasts for four or five weeks. Thereafter one is left with a green tracery hung with little globular seed cases for the rest of the summer. Allowed 5 ft (1·5 m) square, crambe will remain troublefree in well drained soil and give innumerable sprays of bloom that last well in a vase.

Crinitaria (Goldilocks) *Compositae*

Crinitaria linosyris was for many years known as *Aster linosyris*. Conforming to the botanist's change gives one a welcome opportunity to rescue this from being submerged in that flowering army. The common name for this often overlooked perennial is Goldilocks, which is both affectionate and apt. This fibrous-rooted, good-natured plant grows to nearly 2 ft (60 cm). No support is required for the slender, upright stems, closely clothed with narrow leaves and topped with a profusion of golden-yellow sprays of clustered flowers in August and September. Revelling in full sun and well drained soils, *C. linosyris* is propagated by division of the roots. The tough stems are best cut with secateurs and slit at the base. This is a very good garden plant and cut flower subject, the cut blooms being both bright and long-lasting.

Crinum   *Amaryllidaceae*

Crinum is a bulbous genus giving a few distinctive and valuable subjects for both gardener and flower arranger. Only the hardy forms can be considered here. Crinum bulbs have very long necks and extremely large bases closely resembling the gymnast's Indian Clubs. Deeply worked, free-draining and preferably light soils are essential, as is a generally warm and sunny site. Crinum obviously requires deep planting because bulbs 1 ft (30 cm) long are not uncommon, and the tips of the vernal emerging leaves can be singed by frosts if the planting is a little too shallow. These make fine border plants, the two species most commonly available and suitable for border cultivation being *C. bulbispermum* and the hybrid *C. × powellii*. Both produce a wealth of fine, long, rushy leaves, wavy-edged in the former, and the loose, nodding umbels of lily-like flowers on graceful stems have a certain fragile richness. The blooms of *C. bulbispermum* are shell-pink and borne on 2-ft (60-cm) stems. These are lightly fragrant and make very valuable cut flowers for the house.

Crinum × powellii has *C. bulbispermum* as one parent and is the hardier of the two plants. Established plants are very impressive, with bright green leaves up to 4 ft (1·2 m) long and gracefully arched, and flowering stems a full 3 ft (90 cm) long bearing drooping clusters of large rose-pink trumpets in July and August. Bulbs increase steadily but may be left undisturbed for forty years, where space permits, to form magnificent clumps. Dividing the offsets calls for profound work, but the sight of a bulb up to 6 in (15 cm) in diameter makes the task enjoyable.

Crocosmia, Curtonus (Montbretia)   *Iridaceae*

Crocosmia and curtonus have some fundamental points in common and may be conveniently considered together. Both plants stem from corms best suited to well drained soils bearing some nutriment, and while a little shade is well tolerated, full sun is to be preferred.

Curtonus has only one species, and this was for long classed among the *Antholyza,* and confused among the mass of plants loosely labelled montbretia. *Curtonus paniculata,* like crocosmia, has very fine and decorative pleated leaves. The branched stems bearing rich orange-red flowers grow to a full 3 ft (90 cm) and sometimes top 4 ft (1·2 m).

These give splendid cut blooms for the house in August and September. Plants are both long-lived and fully hardy when the corms are planted about 4 in (10 cm) deep in well drained border soil.

Crocosmia now gives the gardener a wide choice of plants as the montbretia of old are now included in the genus. Before turning to these old favourites there are two species to note. *C. pottsii,* growing to 4 ft (1·2 m) and bearing spikes of fine yellow blooms, often flushed with orange, in August, is hardy in southern gardens. This is one of the parent plants of the old montbretias and is still available from some growers.

Crocosmia masonorum is the best of the genus. The narrow sword-like leaves are finely pleated and form a splendid foil to the gracefully arching 30-in (75-cm) stems with their vivid orange flowers, stamened in gold and facing the gardener's downward gaze. Flowering covers many weeks between July and September, giving the flower arranger some startlingly beautiful subjects. Cutting of leaves should be severely restricted, as these are best left to die back and wither off in winter. Corms planted 4 in (10 cm) deep require a season or two to settle down, and are better left undisturbed for several years. Propagation calls for a careful lifting of the linked corms. Some will be found to have little bulbils attached, and these should not be severed but replanted with the parent corm as a pair. *C. masonorum* planted as a group makes a fine contribution to the herbaceous border, and this hybrid plant is fully hardy and perennial—far more so than either *C. pottsii* or the general run of montbretias.

Botanists have been among the montbretias of late (they often

Crocosmia

keep far worse company!) sorting out a complex of crocosmia, curtonus, and tritonia, hitherto jumbled together under the great-coat of montbretia. We are thus left with the solitary species *M. laxiflora*, but this is not hardy and cannot be considered here.

What were once known as montbretia have been reclassified rather preciously, as *Crocosmia × crocosmiiflora*. This is a fact I hardly stomach, but I have dutifully assimilated the hybridizing between *Crocosmia aurea* and *C. pottsii*, and remain delighted to know that this was first made by the versatile French nurseryman Victor Lemoine of Nancy.

Some of the old forms of montbretia, with their flame-orange flowers in July and August, proved to be remarkably long-lived. In the Kent garden of my childhood, corms were left undisturbed for a decade, receiving an occasional dusting of bonemeal or sulphate of potash and an annual autumnal mulch.

These old varieties, so popular for cut blooms between the Wars, are now seldom seen, growers having forsaken them in favour of the Earlham Hybrids. These are an improvement on the older montbretias in that the growth is stronger, the stems taller and the blooms larger, often 3 or 4 in (7·5 or 10 cm) across. They are hardy enough if given a mulch after being planted in March 3 in (7·5 cm) deep and an annual autumn blanket of leaves. One of the finest cultivars is 'Marjorie', elegantly tall to 3½ ft (105 cm) with a deep central flush to her orange blooms. 'Kathleen' is another desirable lady at 3 ft (90 cm) with her flowers a fine orange overlaid with apricot and primrose at the centre. 'His Majesty' is suitably impos-ing at just over 3½ ft (105 cm) with his velvet-scarlet and golden flowers of regal size, while his companion 'Fire King' is a brilliant golden-centred flame-scarlet, but not so robust a grower. The lemon-yellow 'Citronella' begins flowering a few weeks earlier, thus making possible, by selection, a season extending from late June until September. A number of growers offer a selection of such cultivars, but most offer corms as a mixture, and these re-present very good value for their modest cost.

All these are fine subjects for sunny sites with well drained, lighter soils, giving a profusion of elegant cut flowers for the house. Early March remains the best time for planting the corms, and autumnal plantings should receive adequate protection to last the winter.

Delphinium   *Ranunculaceae*

Delphiniums require good cultivation to attain their true magnificence. Basically, this entails good soil drainage, a deeply worked soil laden with humus and sufficient nutrients to keep the fibrous roots healthy and vigorous. A little lime in the soil is always desirable as delphiniums dislike acid loams. A generally sunny site should be selected, and one sheltered from the worst summer winds. In a good garden soil and suitable position these stately plants present no difficulty in growing. Staking for varieties in the 5–6-ft (1·5–1·8-m) range need only consist of a triangle of canes, tied twice at 18-in (45-cm) intervals to form a 3-ft (90-cm) cradle in which the plants may gently rock in the breeze without breaking. Extra height alone does not necessarily mean raising the level of this cradle support. The 6½-ft (1·9-m) 'Great Scott', for example, is remarkably sturdy, more so than many in the 5-ft (1·5-m) range. Thus selection with delphiniums plays a very important part in their successful cultivation. Of paramount importance, however, to all these lofty perennials is an assurance of abundant summer moisture about their roots. This is particularly vital in early summer, both when the plants are coming into bud and when they are in flower. Indeed, spires cut from delphiniums selected for their suitability as cut flower subjects will too readily drop if the plants are not kept moist right up to the time of cutting.

Many of these noble spire plants are of little value as cut flower subjects, as the blooms too often drop in prodigious profusion. Some of the older cultivars, raised several decades ago are still among the best for cutting purposes. Outstanding in this regard is the early-flowering, near-double mauve 'Alice Artindale', which grows to 5 ft (1·5 m). The azure-blue, later-flowering 'Artist' and the flushed and glowing blue 'Evenglow' complete an old trio still unsurpassed for the lasting properties of their cut blooms. The newer 'White Nylon' may not last quite so long, but its blooms have a delicious light scent of vanilla—a rarity among delphiniums.

The pure sky-blue 'Betty Hay'; the very early brilliant blue 'Cristella'; the late, fully double and magnificent 'Purple Ruffles'; the well prized 'Silver Moon'; the famous 'Blue Nile'; and the newer 'Strawberry Fair' and 'Sungleam' are all superb plants and sturdy growers, giving a rich choice. There are scores of others.

Cutting of these noble flowers is best done in the cool of the evening, the time to cut being as soon as the lowest florets begin to open. They should then be given an immediate and very deep drink of fresh water. Stems should be cut diagonally at the base and filled with water, keeping a finger over the base when inverting the stem into its container. These valuable cut flowers may also be made to last longer if the stems are reduced by an inch or two every other day, and re-set in a vase of fresh water. Those who understandably find it hard to rob the garden of the large spikes may console the flower arranger by cutting the laterals instead, and these add a very graceful touch to any vase.

Plants raised from firm basal cuttings taken in spring will often flower in September, and it is sound practice to cut these for the house, as this promotes root vigour before the onset of winter. With a little ingenuity it is possible to have cut blooms of delphiniums from June until September. Plants of the popular Pacific Hybrids strain are readily raised from seed, and many give magnificent spikes.

The Belladonna Hybrids are the most commendable, however, for both the gardener and the flower arranger. These will grow very well in ordinary border soil so long as it is not lacking in humus. Most grow to between 3 and 4 ft (90 and 120 cm). The Belladonnas form graceful, finely leaved, upright bushes. Their habit is altogether attractive, and in reasonably sheltered gardens no form of staking is required. The spikes of flowers are finely proportioned and give the best cut blooms of all delphiniums. Plants come readily from seed but with the usual variations of colour which will call for some rogueing in the second season. The tallest cultivar is 'Wendy', whose single-flowered, dark blue spikes, which come in mid-season, grow to nearly 4 ft (1·2 m). A few stout pea-sticks inserted early in the season will soon be hidden beneath the graceful foliage. 'Blue Bees' grows unaided to about the 3-ft

(90-cm) mark, and the fine rich blue spikes appear some two weeks earlier than those of 'Wendy'. 'Moerheimii' also grows to a little over 3 ft (90 cm), but here the single blooms are a pure white and come in July. Raised over half a century ago, 'Lamartine' is a fine violet-blue growing to 3½ ft (105 cm).

In addition to the Belladonnas there are half a dozen splendid border delphiniums under the 4-ft (1·2-m) mark raised by Blackmore and Langdon. 'Betty Baseley' at 3½ ft (105 cm) has black eyes to her gentian-blue florets. 'Blue Tit', at the same height, is another deep blue, but 'Cinderella' is a fine heliotrope-mauve. Smaller still at 3 ft (90 cm) is the white-eyed, sky-blue 'Cupid', and the white-eyed 'Pageboy' is a brilliant blue. None of these require staking in sheltered gardens, and all are very fine plants requiring the same conditions as their loftier brothers and sisters.

Delphinium nudicaule is a neglected perennial that comes as something of a surprise to those who first think of those opulent blue spires. This small delphinium is readily raised from seed. It is not a plant for cold, winter-wet areas or ill drained loams. *D. nudicaule* has tuberous roots, which need a light, gritty soil to permit rapid drainage in winter. This is a plant for the front of a sunny border or a raised bed, where its 12–18-in (30–45-cm) stems of vivid orange-red blooms are borne in loosely packed spikes in June and July. Even a skilled surgical division of the tuberous roots is fraught with risks, and plants raised from seed occasionally show the expected variations of colour, some having more orange than red, and vice versa.

Even more valuable as a cut flower subject is the related hybrid *D. ruysii* 'Pink Sensation', whose strawberry-pink blooms cover a longer season, between late June and September. This grows to about 3½ ft (105 cm) and also demands sun and a well drained soil for its fibrous roots. *D. r.* 'Pink Sensation' is easy-growing, good-natured, and fully hardy and perennial. Its habit is graceful like the Belladonnas, the blooms being freely borne in loose racemes. The cut flowers last well in water, even a little longer than the Belladonnas.

The more ephemeral *D. grandiflorum (chinense)* 'Blue Butterfly', with its airy blooms of brilliant blue borne at 3 ft (90 cm), is not long-lived, but it is well worth growing from seed and cultivating in the lighter garden soils for its summer blooms, as they look quite charming in a vase.

Even more neglected than *D. nudicaule* is *D. zalil*. This, too, is tuberous-rooted and therefore best raised from seed and planted in a warm, well drained site laden with grit. It is worth giving *D. zalil* some winter protection from wetness and the destructive action of frost. This Belladonna-like delphinium's yellow blooms always come as a pleasant surprise, and the cut flowers last for several days.

Dianthus (Pink, Border Carnation) *Caryophyllaceae*

Dianthus includes the border and cottage carnations of July and August. These, being hardy and perennial, are the only form of carnation to be included here. Although they demand good soil drainage, very good results can be obtained from plantings in well drained heavy loams. Over-rich conditions are to be avoided, as these bring a crop of troubles in the form of ungainly behaviour, and too lush a growth, and its attendant ills of disease and brevity of life. A little potash or bonemeal does nothing but good, but nitrogenous fertilizers should only be used where the need is proved, and then with a miserly hand. Planting is best undertaken in autumn in light to medium loams, but in spring where the soil is heavy or the district one of high rainfall. Winter wetness is more trying to the roots than any frost. Very firm planting at 18 in (45 cm) apart in moistened stations will allow for several seasons' expansion. Plants are more floriferous in their second year and will need some timely support from short twigs. Disbudding is only necessary if blooms are to be exhibited, but the undecided may indulge in partial disbudding. Shallow and firm planting is more important.

One of the best ways to increase stock is by layering in July, but plants may be raised from seed and from cuttings or 'pipings'. In addition to good soil drainage border carnations require an alkaline soil (lime), full sun and plenty of air. Plants should never be hemmed in or overhung by grosser neighbours, and garden cleanliness is vital to their well-being.

Some of the older cultivars with martial names, such as 'The Rifleman' and 'The Grenadier', are still available, but their rather dull red blooms have been surpassed and superseded by a host of new cultivars covering a very wide range of colour. Some of the older cultivars, however, were compact and short enough to grow unaided, whereas many of the newer introductions are longer in the stem and need some garden support. These are, paradoxically, not fit plants for the border but are better suited to kitchen garden cultivation, border occupants being chosen from the more dwarf kinds and the garden pinks.

All make basal clumps of narrow, silvery grey foliage that is pleasing throughout the year. Single-coloured, or 'selfs', include many forms of red, pink and white, and border carnation cultivars now cover a range of orange, yellow, apricot and purple. 'Beauty of Cambridge' is aptly named for its soft yellow blooms, and 'Fiery Cross' is a magnificent searing scarlet. 'Madonna' is a white of great purity and substance, whereas 'Robin Thain' is white but edged and striped with crimson, and strongly redolent of cloves. Other richly fragrant cultivars include the carmine 'Imperial Clove', 'Salmon Clove', and 'Scarlet Fragrance'. These are but a few of the proven cultivars growing to just about 1 ft (30 cm), but dozens of others are available from specialist growers. Cut blooms should have their stems slit at the base and set in deep water.

The more dwarf border pinks require no support, and all the following are both garden-worthy and sufficiently prolific to give an abundance of cut flowers for the house, with stems growing to just under 1 ft (30 cm). One of the oldest is the very fragrant, double white 'Mrs Sinkins', but sometimes she splits her calcyes, which the similar 'White Ladies' do not! The rosy pink double 'Excelsior' and the curious chocolate-marked, double white old 'Dad's Favourite' are also very familiar.

Dianthus allwoodii give the gardener a wide range of sterling subjects for house and garden. These are of easy cultivation, being fully hardy and perennial, forming fine groups of narrow silver-grey leaves and dainty blooms on wiry stems, many in the 6–9-(15–22·5-cm) range. These sweetly scented flowers, which appear between June and September, make delightful groups planted at the front of a sunny border. Among the *D. allwoodii* cultivars is 'Doris', a very good perpetual pink, and her daughter (a sport) 'Diane', a fine red. 'Helen' is salmon-pink, 'Ian' a rich crimson, and 'Robin' a bright scarlet-orange double. 'Lilian' is pearly white, fragrant and very floriferous, while 'London Poppet' has a flush to its white blooms, which are prettily zoned and laced with deep red. This, too, is very fragrant and semi-double. Many of those offered by nurserymen in mixed lots include a number with such delicate refinements of marking and colour variations.

Alpine forms of dianthus contain some of the most delightful flowers of the summer, and the cut blooms make ideal subjects for tiny vases and bowls. *D. deltoides* is known as the maiden pink, and several cultivars of this are available. 'Hansen's Red' is rosy; 'Albus' is white with a red eye; 'Brilliant' is crimson and brilliant, and 'Erectus' is vivid red with upright stem and dark green foliage. All these flower at a height of about 6 in (15 cm).

Dianthus gratianopolitanus is the Cheddar pink, renowned for the richly fragrant blooms that come in June. At 6 in (15 cm) high we have 'Baker's Variety' and 'Flore Pleno'. The former has larger and more deeply pink flowers than the type, while the latter's are almost double.

Dianthus plumarius is the common garden pink, flowering between late May and July, and bearing sweetly scented, delicately fringed blooms of pink, rose and white in single colours, or in variations, and growing to nearly 1 ft (30 cm). This is one of the parents of the allwoodii strains usually offered by growers in a mixture. These, too, give the flower arranger an additional choice.

Some distinctive and diminutive hybrids are also available from growers of alpines. There is a fine old trio in the double and deeply red 'Mrs (Nellie) Clarke', the dark-eyed pink 'Little Jock', and Mr Alan Bloom's 'Oakington Hybrid', a floriferous double pink raised in 1932. All three grow to about 6 in (15 cm) and are very fragrant. These are splendid subjects for a raised bed or at the very front of a sunny border where the soil is light and drainage assured. All are fully hardy and very reliable.

The alpine forms of dianthus must have sharp soil drainage and a sunny site, and those forming more tufted growth make ideal subjects for dry stone walls and raised beds. Characteristic growth is maintained by a rather spartan diet, and while an occasional fillip of bonemeal is good no rich manures should be given. The alpine forms, in general, also dislike acid soils and relish chalk or lime in the soil. These are then of the easiest cultivation, seeming mere child's play to those who have grown carnations. Plants are remarkably hardy and perennial, making splendid occupants of well prepared and sunny window boxes, where they may be a feast for both eye and nose. These little dianthus are mostly raised from cuttings taken about every three years. By this means plants are kept neat, vigorous and free-flowering.

The so-called border carnations are best grown in a slightly raised bed to themselves in the kitchen garden, and it is well to stress that plantings must be shallow and very firm. Slugs seem to be irresistibly attracted to all forms of dianthus, so a sharp eye must be kept on these night spoilers; both soot and lime have uses here.

Dicentra (Bleeding Heart, Dutchman's Breeches)

Fumariaceae

Dicentra comes as a complete contrast to dianthus. These sterling perennials demand a cool, deeply worked, good border soil laden with humus and sheltered from the full stare of the sun and the harrying winds which mar the fragile blooms. The best known species is *D. spectabilis*, a plant with hideous roots that give rise to beautiful blooms and foliage. The roots form a jumbled mass of fleshy fangs bearing little fibrous attachment. In a mature plant these probe to considerable depths and, being somewhat brittle, division in autumn calls for the skilful use of a sharp knife. Plants may be raised from seed sown as soon as ripe under glass, but it takes some three years to produce a good flowering plant. Curiously, this dicentra may be treated as a pot plant for greenhouse cultivation, and although the roots become so congested as to fill a large pot, earlier flowering can thereby be induced. As border subjects dicentras are splendid. *D. spectabilis* forms a delicate bush up to about 2 ft (60 cm) high, by as much across, of deeply and delicately

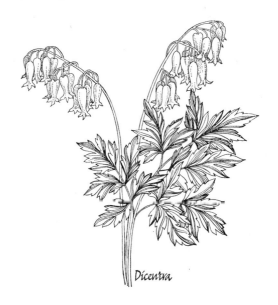

Dicentra

lobed leaves, reminiscent of corydalis, and gracefully arched sprays on which hang little red and white locket-like blooms commonly known as bleeding hearts. In well grown plants, flowering is profuse for several weeks between late April and June. There is a fragile, elfin charm about this plant, but this is based on fully hardy and long-lived roots.

Dicentra eximea 'Adrian Bloom' reveals not quite such ugly roots, and this, too, has beautiful leaves and flowers. The leaves are so finely cut as to appear decidedly ferny, and the pendant deep crimson flowers, held in terminal clusters, often first appear in early April on upright stems at just about 1 ft (30 cm). There is also a white-flowering form in *D. e.* 'Alba', and both these will divide more readily than *D. spectabilis*.

Dicentra formosa 'Bountiful' is a fine American hybrid, also ferny of foliage but growing a little taller at 18 in (45 cm), and bearing a mass of larger, deep pink blooms over many weeks from May until the end of August.

All these give the flower arranger some very choice and charming subjects, though great care is needed in the handling of their fragile blooms. If forced to restrict the choice, *D. spectabilis* would come first, both for garden and house, followed by *D. e.* 'Adrian Bloom'. The former bears its pendant lockets in horizontal sprays, and these look particularly graceful in floral arrangements.

Dictamnus (Burning Bush)   *Rutaceae*

Dictamnus also has fleshy roots, but they are more finely divided and fibrous than those of dicentra, and like light, well drained soils in the full sun. Division of the brittle roots is similarly difficult and not without some risk. Dictamnus deeply resents disturbance, and autumn surgical divisions will seldom produce flowering plants the first year. The hard-coated seeds should be scratched and planted as soon as ripe, and the boxes or pots kept moist until germination has taken place. Raising plants from seed requires patience, as flowering plants are seldom produced in less than three years. Dictamnus are a little slow to establish, but they are fully hardy and very long-lived perennials of troublefree cultivation in a sunny, well drained border or kitchen garden. Plants are tardy to emerge in spring, sending up slender pale shoots only when the worst frosts are over.

Dictamnus fraxinella forms an upright bush, and its name gives the clue to the plant's foliage, as it has deep green leaves like those of the ash tree. The 30-in (75-cm) flowering stems of mature plants bear fine racemes of white or lilac-pink, open, five-petalled flowers in June and July. Botanists have changed the name to *D. albus*; there is also a purple-flowering form. Colour apart, the two plants are the same. While these give some cut blooms for the house, plants should not be robbed of all their flowers in July, for in September the seed pods give a source of valuable decoration. The cut stems should be hung upside down with their pods in paper bags. The little black seeds literally explode from their pods, leaving the silvery-lined seed cases wide open on their hinges. It is these which provide autumn and winter decoration for the flower arranger.

Dictamnus is redolent of oranges because of volatile oil that is exuded by both stems and leaves in the warmth of the sun. On calm warm evenings this may be lighted to give a brief flame—hence the true common name of the burning bush, which should not be confused with an annual sold under the name. The decorative seed pods of autumn retain that delightful aroma of oranges throughout the winter, adding a touch of richness to any dried flower arrangement.

Plants may be left down for a decade even in quite poor soils, the rate of expansion being slow, but the roots do respond well to a little compost, and this is duly reflected in both the quality and the duration of the flowers.

Dierama (Wand Flower, Angel's Fishing-rod)   *Iridaceae*

Dierama has but one species in garden cultivation. This is *D. pulcherrima*. Its swollen rootstock is almost a corm, from which slender, fibrous roots emanate. These are totally unsuited to cold, heavy, limy loams on the one hand, and dry, light soils on the other. Plants are hardy enough in southern gardens in well drained soil containing humus, and while sun is relished a little shade is readily tolerated. Plants demand sharp drainage in winter, but copious summer moisture is always to their benefit. A liberal admixture of grit and peat, in equal parts, thoroughly incorporated to a good depth in the border has suited the plants in my garden. Slightly acid or neutral soil should be aimed for. Such a brittle and meagre root system will not readily respond to division, and plants are usually raised from seed. Most nurserymen offer pot-grown stock, and a spring planting of this gives the safest means of establishment in the garden. Even then one must wait a few years to have freely flowering, full-sized plants.

Dierama pulcherrima is worth such patient attention, for it is one of the most graceful and distinctive hardy perennials. Growth in spring is tardy, as if plants were nervous of late frosts, but by July they have a fine growth of tall, ribbed, grassy leaves gracefully arched at the tips. The slender stems up to 5 ft (1·5 m) long are similarly arched and hung with beautiful narrow bell-like blooms

D

in various shades of light purple and, occasionally, white. Mature plants will flower over many weeks between mid-July and September. The blooms, which dance in the lightest of summer breezes, are commonly known as wand flowers, and the plants as angels' fishing-rods. By raising stock from seed one may have blooms more pink than purple, and some with hues of violet and rose. Until one has grown and seen these plants their full beauty and graceful habit cannot be appreciated. Plantings in borders should never be masked or accompanied by unsuitable neighbours. I like to plant them at the end of an island bed so that I can see them face to face as I pass by.

There is also a charming dwarf version, which grows to 30 in (75 cm) and is hung with pinker bells in July and August. In rich light soils laden with peat, so as to provide humus, this is a splendid subject for the front of the border.

Cut blooms make very choice subjects for large floral displays—if one can bear to cut at all.

Digitalis (Foxglove)   *Scrophulariaceae*

Digitalis is widely known as the foxglove, and those growing in humus-rich hedgerows and in the dappled shade of glades are often imposing plants with a sinister and speckled beauty. These, alas, are biennials, as are the magnificently floriferous and colourful Sutton's Excelsior Hybrids, whose long flowers are held at near right-angles to the stem to reveal the dainty speckling within. While these biennials do provide a wealth of colour and give distinctive cut flowers, they must be lightly passed by in favour of the perennial species in keeping with our brief.

The perennial forms of digitalis are very much neglected, and most growers now offer only two or three species. *D. ambigua* (now *D. grandiflora* to some) planted in a group is fully worthy of border cultivation as long as it is placed in cool shade, and the fibrous roots in a soil laden with peat and leafmould to retain summer moisture and to counteract any lime present. Digitalis dislikes lime and thrives best in slightly acid and leafy soils. *D. ambigua* grows leafily erect to nearly 3 ft (90 cm) and is hung with nicely proportioned soft yellow blooms between June and the end of August. If it is raised from seed one may obtain some very subtle variations bearing light brown markings and a flush of orange. These blooms above the fresh green foliage give their shady corner a quiet charm. Plants grown in shade seem to give longer-lasting cut flowers than those grown in the sun. *D. ambigua* has proved to be both fully hardy and reliably perennial.

Digitalis ferruginea is another reliably perennial species. This grows a little taller but the unusual bronzed flowers come at the same time, and these give the flower arranger curiously attractive blooms.

The hybrid *D. mertonensis* occurred as a chance seedling at the John Innes Institute. In ordinary soils this grows to nearly 3 ft (90 cm), but I have grown plants reaching twice this height and bearing very large blooms up to 4 in (10 cm) long. The colour is rightly described as a crushed strawberry shade. The leaves are dark and glossy, and noticeably broad. The flowers are much larger than in the two previous species, but these look better, to me, in a vase than in the garden, *D. ambigua* being the more graceful border plant. Cut blooms of this species are delightful in their simplicity, whereas those of *D. mertonensis* are more showy. The cut blooms are fragile and call for careful handling, but they make very telling vase subjects.

Doronicum (Leopard's Bane) *Compositae*

Doronicum plantagineum is a very old favourite cut flower perennial. This is a valuable subject for kitchen garden cultivation, but not suitable for the select border. Doronicum will generally grow in a wide variety of soils not lacking in some nutriment, and gives excellent results in improved clay loams. *D. plantagineum* 'Harpur Crewe' (or 'Excelsum') was introduced nearly a century ago and is still very much in demand for its cut flowers of mid-spring. Its popularity is mainly based on its large, bright yellow blooms borne on 3-ft (90-cm) stems, which give a wealth of first-class cut flowers between late April and June. As a hardy perennial, however, it has a tendency to die out occasionally in patches after flowering. For-

tunately this can be remedied by lifting the newer (outer) growth
and replanting this in any gaps at the end of the summer. The
newer 'Miss Mason' is 1 ft (30 cm) shorter but begins flowering
some two weeks earlier while still a small plant. Slightly shorter
still is the German 'Spring Beauty', a fine plant with double flowers
a good 2 in (5 cm) across which come in a rich profusion between
the end of March and May. The type, *D. caucasicum*, is also a
floriferous, easy, good-natured plant, which flowers well in quite
heavy shade as long as there is sufficient moisture. The finely rayed
blooms are reminiscent of the later-flowering *Inula oculis-christi*,
but the leaves are heart-shaped, freshly green and glossy, strongly
suggestive of moisture.

Doronicums are propagated by division of the crowns. This may
be done immediately after flowering if the position is moist, or in
the autumn. Those of *D. plantagineum* may require the use of a
knife, but those of *D. caucasicum* almost fall apart upon lifting
with a fork. Plants seem to grow equally well in chalky soils and
lightly acid loams, in sun or partial shade, so long as there is
moisture for the roots. Plants are best kept fairly young and more
vigorous by division every two or three years.

All these doronicums are best planted in early autumn to ensure
some flowers for cutting the following spring. While none may be
regarded as very choice, plants have the merit of being reliable,
free-flowering and early. Cutting is best when the topmost blooms
open and the laterals are still in bud. These latter will often open
in the vase. *D. p.* 'Harpur Crewe' remains the longest-lasting in a
vase, but *D. c.* 'Spring Beauty' is superior for the garden.

Echinacea (Cone Flower)   *Compositae*

Echinacea purpurea, for long known as *Rudbeckia purpurea*, is a
striking perennial suitable for inclusion in the border where the
soil is deeply worked, well nurtured and open to the sun. Raised
from seed, plants grow leafily and stems rise to 3 ft (90 cm) and
bear blooms of rose through to a plum-purple. The open, rayed
flowers with their curiously reflexed petals have, at first, a large

flattened central boss of stamens. These shortly develop into their prominent cones, making the common name of cone flowers very apt. *E. p.* 'The King' has for many years been a favourite for its more crimson rayed flowers measuring up to 5 in (12·5 cm) across borne on sturdy stems up to 4 ft (1·2 m) high between late July and September. Some old German cultivars are no longer available. This is to be regretted, for while the blooms were smaller, I recall one of a deep red that when cut lasted much longer in a vase than the very popular 'The King'. The newer 'Robert Bloom' grows erectly to a full 3 ft (90 cm) and carries fine, deep red cone flowers in profusion for many weeks in late summer, and a most welcome 'White Lustre' provides a valuable contrast. Spring divisions are a little risky but a careful surgical approach gives a means of raising plants true to the parent plant. The cut flowers with the longest vase life are those cut late in the day and late in the season. Those cut in the sun or wind flag rapidly. Curiously, plants raised from seed often give better-lasting cut blooms.

Echinops (Globe Thistle)   *Compositae*

Echinops will grow in heavy or light soil, sun or partial shade. It has fleshy tap-roots, and forms a stout bush of jagged leaves and sturdy branched stems which bear their distinctive globe thistles of steely grey or bright blue for much of July and August. These spiky globes later consist of innumerable tiny flowers which open to become small blue crosses much worked by bees. When these are open to present a blue globe it is time to cut a few stems for the house, and these will last a full two weeks. *E. ritro* flowers well between July and September at about $3\frac{1}{2}$ ft (105 cm), but *E. humilis* 'Taplow Blue' will grow to a massive 7 ft (2·1 m) in rich clay loams, with a wealth of large and sharply cut grey leaves. Both forms expand steadily, making these indestructible plants more suitable for the kitchen garden than the border. Any piece of root left in the ground will sprout afresh, making correct siting at the outset important. Stems bearing a completed globe dried for two weeks at 50° F (10° C) give lasting floral decoration for winter.

Eremurus (Foxtail Lily, Desert Candle)   *Liliaceae*

Eremurus is known as the foxtail lily, but the alternative desert candle is more evocative of this noble spire plant. Those who have grown *Thalictrum dipterocarpum* 'Hewitt's Double' and delphiniums with success will find eremurus a very rewarding plant. It enjoyed a certain vogue in Victorian days but has been unduly neglected in more recent times, yet the cut blooms provide the flower arranger with some distinctive and magnificent material, both fresh and dried, and with a long vase life.

The fleshy roots of eremurus radiate from a central crown that is best planted on a little saddle within the wide planting hole so that it is 6 in (15 cm) deep. The brittle thongs of root are then spread out radially and slightly downwards. Heavy soils must be lightened with grit and sharp sand to ensure sharp drainage. Plants are hardy in southern gardens, but a quilt of leaves or straw is useful to ward off the frosts following the preferred spring planting. Although they are difficult to propagate from surgical separations and very slow from seed, eremurus is less expensive to buy today than twenty years ago.

Established plants give a wealth of rushy basal leaves and tall stems of long spires which call for a site sheltered from the wind. Several species and hybrids are available. *E. stenophyllus* (syn. *E. bungei*) is one of the most garden-worthy, being comparatively short at 4½ ft (1·3 m) and bearing elegant golden-orange spires in July and August. Of similar vintage and stature is *E. olgae*, whose white spires are flushed with rose.

In addition to the taller *E. himalaicus* and the huge *E. robustus*, nurserymen occasionally offer hybrid strains growing from 5 to 6 ft (1·5–1·8 m) high. The Highdown Hybrids with their pink, yellow, apricot, amber and coppery spires are a magnificent living tribute to the memory of their raiser, Sir Frederick Stern. Growing to between 4½ and 6 ft (1·3 and 1·8 m) these are more suitable for small gardens than the 9-ft (2·7-m) spires of *E. robustus*.

Good soil drainage is vital to prevent the crowns rotting in winter, but plants rejoice in ample summer moisture and rich fare.

The heavier the soil the nearer to the surface the crowns should be planted. Eremurus is best left undisturbed for several years, when a lifting might reveal a new root system capable of being divided with a sharp knife. Crowns may be bared of soil in autumn and capped with grit and a blanket of straw, and they must be guarded against slugs.

Erigeron (Fleabane) *Compositae*

Erigeron is a good-natured and floriferous subject, and more suited to planting in spring than autumn. The compact fibrous roots will grow in almost any garden soil, but the best plants are grown in lighter soils bearing a little humus. Rich loams tend to produce too lush and lax a bush. Erigeron is a sun lover but tolerant of a little light shade. Some of the oldest cultivars have been discarded in favour of the brighter, newer introductions, yet the pale pink-lavender 'Quakeress' grows erectly to 2 ft (60 cm) in fairly poor soils and flowers very generously from mid-June until September year after year. Not only has this flowering period remained unsurpassed but the cut flowers are among the longest-lasting of all erigerons. 'Foerster's Liebling', produced by the late Karl Foerster, at 18 in (45 cm) remains one of the best semi-double, deep pink, golden-eyed erigerons, flowering between late June and August. A little taller at just 2 ft (60 cm), 'Darkest of All' bears its single blooms of deep violet-blue at the same time. The old mauve-flowering 30-in (75-cm) 'Merstham Glory' has been surpassed in the lilac-mauve 'Wupperthal', but 'Rose Triumph', growing to 2 ft (60 cm), is a fine light pink with near double blooms. The dwarf white *E. simplex* at just 1 ft (30 cm) is very valuable for its early flowers, which come in May and June.

The greatest contribution to the genus was made in the 1950s by Alan Bloom of Bressingham who launched his now famous 'ity' range of erigerons. We now have a range of height and colour to cover most of the summer. The smallest of these is 'Dimity', at just 1 ft (30 cm), bearing surprisingly large pink flowers. Giving some of the best cut blooms are the 18-in (45-cm) violet-blue 'Dignity' and the slightly taller deep pink 'Gaiety', while 'Pros-

perity' is a fine semi-double light blue. Larger with its single
mauve-blue blooms is the very long-flowering 'Sincerity', but
perhaps the best cut flowers are given by the June to September-
flowering 'Serenity', whose very large blooms are a deep mauve.
There are several more 'itys', but the above is a fair selection.

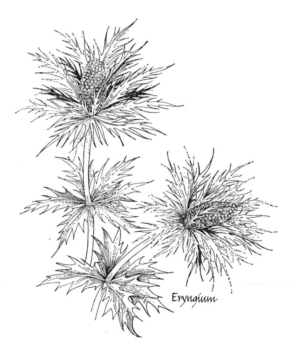

Eryngium

All these easy-going hardy perennials are readily divided in
spring. Fully open blooms give the best material for the flower
arranger, as partially open flowers will seldom completely unfurl
their rays in a vase. Plants may be used as border subjects or
grown in a kitchen garden where the soil is well drained and not
too rich. As long as there is a little humus some bonemeal or
potash is preferable to any manure.

Eryngium (Sea Holly) *Umbelliferae*

Eryngium and echinops are in some ways similar. Both have deeply probing fleshy roots, an air of prickliness, and blue flowering heads. Eryngium, however, is far more insistent on sharp soil drainage and a sunny aspect. This striking plant is best suited to deeply worked soils and a rather spartan diet. When thus planted no support is necessary for any of those below.

Eryngium alpinum and its 'Improved' variety grow to a little over 2 ft (60 cm). The basal leaves are large and the stems bear almost too large heads of thistly-looking, but soft, bright blue coned flowers in July and August.

Eryngium bourgatii is more dwarf at 18 in (45 cm) with deeply cut, marbled foliage and stems bearing heads of more spiky flowers between late June and August. The whole plant is then silvery blue.

Eryngium planum grows to 3 ft (90 cm) with fine blue heads of flowers in July and August. *E. tripartitum* is of similar height, but its stems are much branched to bear a wide array of small blue cone flowers above the silvery-veined, jagged leaves.

Eryngium variifolium gives a dense basal clump of deep green, glossy, heart-shaped leaves marbled in cream. These are evergreen and attractive throughout the year. The very slender, erect, silvery stems rise to 2 ft (60 cm) and terminate in very distinctive spiny, open heads also silvery in colour.

One of the most graceful and border-worthy is *E.* 'Violetta', a well proportioned plant growing to some 30 in (75 cm) and capped with small blue cones. The whole plant takes on a soft violet-blue appearance as the summer progresses.

All these may be propagated from root cuttings taken in spring, and plants are fully hardy and long-lived in light soils. Division is a laborious alternative with mature plants; eryngium is better correctly sited and left undisturbed for several years. The time to cut is when stems, leaves and flowers have coloured up. These make a striking and long-lasting contribution to floral decorations. The dried stems of eryngium give an additional source of material to the flower arranger, and those of *E. variifolium* in particular may

be gilded to provide some dramatic winter decoration for the
house. Eryngium is not so prickly to handle as it appears, though
echinops most certainly is.

Eupatorium (Hemp Agrimony)   *Compositae*

Eupatorium purpureum is worth growing in heavier loams which
retain moisture in summer but are adequately drained in winter.
The fibrous roots are hardy and long-lived, giving rise to strong
bushy but upright growth to 5 ft (1·5 m). In clay loams it will
grow to an imposing 6 ft (1·8 m) A plant of *E. purpureum* in the
kitchen garden is valuable for its wide plates or heads of plum-
purple flowers in August and September. Long stems of cut
flowers look and last well in large floral arrangements. *E. ageratoides*
is not so tall. Plants grow to 4 ft (1·2 m) in good kitchen garden
soil, and these too are worth growing for their long-lasting fluffy
white heads of flowers in late summer. This, too, is of easy cultivation in either sun or partial shade, and is readily raised from
seed or by division.

Euphorbia (Spurge)   *Euphorbiaceae*

Euphorbia has two or three species of interest to the flower
arranger. *E. polychroma* is among the most garden-worthy, being
fully hardy, long-lived and troublefree. The fibrous roots emanat-
ing from a tough rootstock remain compact, and are adaptable to
most garden soils in sun or partial shade. In April the vernal shoots
unfurl to reveal green leaves and lime-yellow bracts. Plants mound
up steadily to become a beautiful mass of lime-yellow lasting well
into May. By then the rounded, dense bush is about 18 in (45 cm)
high by as much across. Then, imperceptibly, the whole bush
slowly dissolves into green and remains thus for the rest of the
summer. Vernal stems of bright yellow give the flower arranger
some valuable material with which to enliven any room. Division
after flowering is something of a butchering job, the rootstock
being very tough and woody, but basal cuttings give an alternative
means of increase. This is worthy of border cultivation.

Euphorbia veneta (syn *E. wulfenii*) grows strongly to nearly 4 ft (1·2 m) high. The growth is shrubby, the stems being densely whorled with narrow, grey-green leaves and topped with broad spikes of greenly yellow flowers and bracts between April and June. These provide the flower arranger with unusual and colourful subjects for the larger display. Plants are readily raised from seed and flower in their second year. Mature plants will measure 5 ft (1·5 m) across, making this a subject for the shrubbery or kitchen garden, while plantings on low dry stone walls accentuate its striking habit. *E. characias* is similarly decorative but more insistent on a warm site and sharp drainage. This, too, requires ample room for its shrubby growth, up to 3½ ft (105 cm) high

Foeniculum (Fennel) *Umbelliferae*

Foeniculum vulgare is the herb fennel, redolent of aniseed, its thick fleshy roots, leaves and seeds being edible. In a deeply worked light soil in the sun it is fully hardy and perennial. Fennel grows into a delicate light green bush up to 5 ft (1·5 m) high when mature, with leaves so finely divided as to be ferny and reminiscent of asparagus. Young plants are best supported by a few pea-sticks early in the season, but well grown mature stock requires no support. Between July and September these fine bushes are topped with umbels of small mustard-yellow flowers which make charming subjects for vases. The tender green youngest leaves should not be cut, the older leaves giving longer-lasting decorative material for the vase. A bush or two of fennel is worthy of inclusion in a border, where it will act as a fine foil or background to such as border phlox, and any red or round-leaved plants. The red or bronze form of fennel is similarly useful, forming a backcloth to lower-growing subjects with light green leaves. Both forms are valuable plants for dry, sandy or stony soils, and while some humus is relished no feeding is required. Any self-sown seedlings are readily lifted in a moist spring and either eaten or used for new stock.

Fritillaria (Snake's-head Fritillary) *Liliaceae*

Fritillaria is a large genus of charming bulbous plants. The 6–10-in (15–25-cm) stemmed snake's-head fritillary is one of the most garden-worthy as long as the soil is always damp. The pendant chequered bells come in a wide range of charmingly subtle shades, while the white forms are outstandingly chaste and delightful in April. But for cut flowers we must turn to *F. persica*, a comparative

Fritillaria

giant which grows to nearly 3 ft (90 cm) and demands a warm and sunny site with sharply drained soil, a general requirement among fritillaries with almost the sole exception of *F. meleagris*.

Fritillaria persica has slender stems topped with spikes of pendant, deep purple bell-flowers in late April and May. These distinctive spires make very good cut flower subjects for large vases. The bulbs are three or four times larger than those of *F.*

meleagris, and, being somewhat fragile, call for careful handling. Bulbs should not be allowed to dry out, and planting in early autumn should be 6 in (15 cm) deep in light soils. Bulbs are neither cheap nor common, and it is worth encouraging their early growth by providing a little protection in early spring.

Gaillardia (Blanket Flower) *Compositae*

Gaillardia aristata, or *G. grandiflora*, is lost as a species in an abundance of cultivars. These hardy perennials are noted for their profusion of blooms from June until October. Gaillardias grown indifferently are an abomination of tangled crooked stems. To grow these colourful fat daisies well, the needs of good soil drainage, full sun and adequate spacing must be fully met. While dry, light soils are always preferable to heavy loams, plants do like to have their fibrous roots in a little humus for the necessary summer moisture, but they abhor winter wetness above all else. The reason for this is obvious when one sees the remarkably compact roots and compares these to the sheer volume of flowers produced. By the end of the summer the roots must be heavily taxed, and if they are then left to a winter's rest in cold wet soil some losses of stock can hardly cause surprise. None of this implies that gaillardias are difficult to grow; on the contrary, if the needs just indicated are met, then regular cutting of blooms throughout the summer encourages both straight stems and longevity of the roots. Cutting back plants in September likewise encourages root vigour before the onset of winter, and a modest dressing of bonemeal then pays dividends the following summer. Old well rotted manure may be used for forming humus as opposed to unwise rich feedings that do nothing but court trouble.

Gaillardias are readily raised from seed but with very variable results. Cultivars are propagated by taking firm basal cuttings, with fibre attached, in April. The popular and flamboyant orange-yellow 'Dazzler' is an exception in coming true from seed. 'Wirral Pride', of similar 30-in (75-cm) stature, bears its deep fiery-red blooms up to 5 in (12·5 cm) across between June and September—a period of flowering common to many. Gayborder Nurseries'

'Golden Giant' is a splendid strong grower to 3 ft (90 cm), while 'Mandarin' is a firmly established flame-orange. 'Wirral Flame' has some mahogany in its red, while 'Ipswich Beauty' is yellow and crimson. 'Mrs Harold Longster' is a very old cultivar with large red-centred yellow blooms. There are more, but these are as good as any, and all give first-class long-lasting cut flowers over many months. The old advice of seeking local confirmation of selected cultivars still holds good. Stock is best kept vigorous and floriferous by propagation every third year, and spring planting is to be preferred.

Galega (Goat's Rue)   *Leguminosae*

Galega officinalis gives a wealth of pretty mauve and white pea-like blooms over several weeks in early summer. The compact, fibrous roots are adaptable to light and medium soils in sun or partial shade, and give rise to a remarkable bushy growth of short-stalked, narrow, glaucous leaves. Plants grow up to 4 ft (1·2 m) and measure as much across, yet they have a certain leguminous daintiness when smothered in sprays of bicoloured spikes some-what reminiscent of buddleia or wisteria in miniature. The type readily seeds itself in light and fertile soils. Of the cultivars 'Lady Wilson' is lilac-blue, which is a little lighter in 'Her Majesty', while the white 'Alba' gives a simple contrast. The more upright sprays are not so attractive as the more drooping spikes of the type, which give a very graceful display in a vase if some of the feathery foliage is also used. Flowering finishes in July, making these galega more suited to the kitchen garden or allotment than the border. *G. orientalis* is offered by some growers, and this bears more up-right spikes of good, bright blue flowers. All are good plants for rather dry and poor soils, these being preferable to rich loams which engender rather lax, untidy growth.

Galtonia (Summer Hyacinth)   *Liliaceae*

Galtonia candicans stems from bulbs the size of a medium onion. Its main requirements are a well drained soil, light rather than heavy, and a planting in autumn at a depth of some 6 in (30 cm) and 1 ft (30 cm) apart. While good winter drainage is vital to longevity, the brittle roots must have some summer moisture, and some humus for these should be assured before planting. Slugs are a serious foe in heavier loams, and precautions against these dispoilers should also be taken before planting by thoroughly cleansing the soil and setting the bulbs on a sandy saddle within the planting station.

Bulbs of galtonia are slow to send up vernal shoots, but as soon as they appear in May growth is rapid. The leaves are basal, very long, narrow and almost rushy. From the centre of these rise sturdy stems up to 5 ft (1·5 m) hung with large white bells, tinged with green, in a loose spike between July and October. The stems of these giant summer hyacinths are solid and very heavy, calling for a substantial or weighted vase. The large, bright green seed pods are also very decorative. Bulbs may be left down for years before dividing the offsets in autumn.

Gentiana (Gentian) *Gentianaceae*

Gentiana septemfida is free-flowering and easy-growing, a sterling alpine that is a delight at the very front of the border or in a raised bed, or even in a well tended terrace tub in sun or a little shade. Unlike many gentians it is remarkably unfussy about lime in the soil, and so long as the soil is well drained it will grow in light or medium loams. Light, dry soils should be enriched with humus,

Gentiana

but no rich feeding is required or desirable as this would induce uncharacteristic growth. The small fleshy crowns bear fibrous roots that penetrate to almost 1 ft (30 cm), and these are understandably resentful of disturbance. Late spring sees the emergence of stems well set with small, deep green leaves, mounding up to give in July 6–8-in (15–20-cm) arching stems of beautiful, deep blue trumpet flowers. Flowering is continuous and extends into September. Well grown, mature plants are floriferous, and a few stems for cut flowers are not missed. These make charming subjects for small table bowls.

Geranium   *Geraniaceae*

Geranium is a large genus containing a number of very fine hardy perennials, some of which give the flower arranger some dainty and choice subjects. The three chosen here are fully hardy, long-lived and worthy of border cultivation. All grow well in ordinary garden soil with some humus, and while they flourish in full sun some light shade hardly detracts from their obvious virtues.

The most robust of this trio is *G. armenum* (now, alas, *G. psilostemon*). In ordinary soils this grows bushily to 30 in (75 cm) and bears a mass of black-eyed, vivid magenta, open blooms between June and August.

The hybrid *G.* 'Johnson's Blue' has attractive, deeply cut, rounded leaves and gives a wonderful profusion of bright blue open saucer flowers between May and August at just under 18 in (45 cm).

Lastly, *G. wallichianum* 'Buxton's Blue', with its white centres, is a sterling prostrate plant flowering from late July until November. Unlike the others it dies back to a central crown that is insufficient to divide, but seed promptly sown under glass germinates well. Plants have a wide spread and mound up to 9 in (22·5 cm). These are very valuable for their late and reliable flowering, and cut sprays of 'Buxton's Blue' last very well.

All these geraniums are best cut when the blooms are not quite fully open. Individual blooms are charming in small bowls.

Geum

Rosaceae

Geum is prone to flag quickly after cutting. It is best to cut small bunches in cool and calm conditions and give them an immediate deep drink before setting in a vase. The finest garden form is the hybrid *G. borisii*. This is the first to flower, plants in my garden coming into bloom with the *Orchis mascula* in mid-April. The fibrous roots are compact, adaptable to a wide range of soils, fully hardy and long-lived, in sun or a remarkable degree of shade as long as the soil is not too dry. The low mounds of rounded, crinkled leaves, which are attractive throughout the summer, and the host of 10-in (25-cm) stems bearing fragile blooms of vivid orange, delicately centred with a shower of golden stamens, together make this a plant fully worthy of the border. Flowering covers many weeks and often extends into August. Division of the roots is elementary after flowering.

The well known trio of ladies raised from seed are free-flowering but not so border-worthy. 'Mrs Bradshaw' is a fine semi-double crimson, flowering at 2 ft (60 cm) between June and the end of August. Of similar height 'Lady Stratheden' is a semi-double bright yellow, while 'Dolly North' is a fine single orange-flame. These are so floriferous that cutting does nothing but good. All three demand good soil drainage for their meagre roots and are far less tolerant of shade than *G. borisii*. Some humus is always relished, but a spartan diet is best.

Gypsophila

Caryophyllaceae

Gypsophila revels in sun and deeply worked, free-draining soils bearing some chalk or lime. The fleshy root resembles a well grown parsnip and penetrates far into the soil to become drought-resistant. *G. paniculata* is the old favourite single form, giving a mounded cloud of tiny white flowers borne on a haze of finely branched stems between July and September. This form is very hardy and reliable, and in well drained soils plants may be left down for years to become capable of occupying a full square yard

(1 sq. m) of ground abutting a path. Here it may tumble over tellingly and conveniently for the cutter. 'Bristol Fairy' bears masses of double white blooms in clouds up to 4 ft (1·2 m), 'Flamingo' grows to the same height to give showers of double pink blooms between July and September, and 'Rosy Veil' is a more lowly cloud at 18 in (45 cm) bearing little fully double blooms of soft pink. Lime around the plants also helps to keep slugs away from the vernal shoots.

All these provide valuable foils to blooms with too military a bearing in the vase. Sprays may also be dried in the dark for winter decoration.

Helenium (Sneezeweed)   *Compositae*

Helenium grows from fibrous roots remarkable for their ability to grow well in heavy loams. While all are sun lovers and very free-flowering plants giving a wealth of cut flowers between June and October, cultivars worthy of border cultivation need to be carefully selected. Among these some of the older cultivars remain unsurpassed, the 3½-ft (105-cm) 'Moerheim Beauty', with its large crimson, mahogany-centred blooms coming between July and September, being a splendid example. The taller 'Baudirektor Linne' bears fine orange-red blooms in August and September. Older still, but very reliable and sturdy at 4 ft (1·2 m) is 'Chipperfield Orange'. Among the newer introductions at 3 ft (90 cm) the tawny-orange 'Gold Fox', the copper-orange 'Coppelia' and the long-leaved 'Bressingham Gold' are all fine plants to cheer July and August. In the 2–2½-ft (60–75-cm) range, the orange-gold 'Wyndley' and the neat 'Mahogany' are both worthy of border cultivation.

More suitable for kitchen garden cultivation, *H.* 'Pumilum Magnificum' makes a lax 30-in (75-cm) bush, but the sheer wealth of fine clear yellow blooms, which begin in June and extend well into August, make this a valuable cut flower subject. Another fine yellow is found in 'Golden Youth', flowering between June and August at a more upright 30 in (75 cm). The pure yellow 'Butterpat' is a few inches taller but flowers from late August to October, as does the $3\frac{1}{2}$-ft (105-cm) crimson-mahogany 'Bruno'. Should one be forced to restrict the choice severely then 'Moerheim Beauty' and 'Wyndley' would have to be included, as these give some of the longest-lasting cut flowers. Were a yellow essential then 'Pumilum Magnificum' would be my choice for the vase.

Growing heleniums has taught me some humiliating lessons. At one stage my stocks were decimated by a wet winter to such an extent that I nearly gave up these cheerful plants. Reason prevailed, however, and I improved the soil drainage with grit. Clearly the fault lay with the gardener, for now losses are minimal. Another lesson learned is that heleniums give the best cut flowers if kept young by division every two or three years, and not crowded together or given short measures of moisture and nutriment.

The woodier stems of such as 'Chipperfield Orange' should be split at the base, but 'Pumilum Magnificum' drinks well through its much softer stems. If the vase water is changed frequently cut flowers last very well.

Helianthus (Perennial Sunflower) *Compositae*

Helianthus decapetalus has two very fine 5-ft (1·5-m) representatives in the single 'Maximus' and the double 'Loddon Gold'. The former is the better garden plant in that the stems are sturdier and the spent flowers less unsightly than those of the double form. Flowering, on upright leafy bushes, extends from July to September, and while the branched stems cannot be cut without sacrificing some buds short-stemmed individual flowers have a cheerful if short life in a vase. Both plants grow well in clay loams and readily divide in spring or autumn. Staking is seldom necessary, and plants are good enough to grow in borders or to be used as kitchen garden screens in a mainly sunny aspect.

Helianthus atrorubens is not such a worthy plant but its cultivars give better cut flowers. It is an easy plant for kitchen garden cultivation, where its wandering tuberous roots may be kept under control, and where ample spacing and frequent division will produce the best plants for giving cut blooms. The tallest is aptly named the 'Monarch'. This grows vigorously up to 6 ft (1·8 m), and some timely staking will be of great benefit later in the season. The 'Monarch' may be somewhat ungainly and sparse of foliage, but it is to be valued for its fine large golden-yellow flowers in September and October. These may measure up to 6 in (15 cm) across following a little disbudding, and it will also give stems up to 18 in (45 cm) long for the flower arranger. These large and cheerful late blooms are among the best cut flowers of all helianthus. 'Soleil d'Or' grows to 4½ ft (1·3 m) and gives a wealth of large, quilled, golden-yellow blooms which make this old cultivar a favourite. 'Capenoch Supreme' justifies its name only by comparison with the smaller blooms of 'Capenoch Star', but both are clear yellow singles, while the blooms of 'Triomphe de Gand' are attractively anemone-centred. All these respond well to some annual attention to their curiously erratic roots and an early preflowering mulch. While plants tolerate remarkably dry conditions these make the undistinguished leaves unsightly.

Helianthus rigidus is also fully hardy and perennial, and remarkably unfussy as to soil. The hard dark stems bear finely proportioned golden flowers giving the arranger some useful late blooms. 'Miss Mellish' once held the stage but is now seldom available. She is confined to a dry corner in my garden and remains admired. Helianthus require timely cutting and an immediate deep drink before setting in a vase.

Heliopsis (Orange Sunflower)   *Compositae*

Heliopsis is a sun loving hardy perennial admirably suited to cultivation in heavy loams. The smaller forms are suitable for inclusion in the larger herbaceous borders, and the more robust make fine kitchen garden plants. Most heliopsis have very compact, tough fibrous roots that are both fully hardy and perennial. Unlike helianthus, plants may be left down for years in good soils without undue expansion or deterioration. Plants may be divided or raised from basal cuttings taken in spring. Heliopsis grows strongly, erectly and bushily when not overfed, to give sturdy stems clothed with fine dark green leaves. The branched stems bear clusters of golden blooms, 3 or 4 in (7·5 or 10 cm) across, between June and September.

The German-raised *H.* 'Golden Plume' remains unexcelled for its compact, troublefree roots, sturdy growth to just 4 ft (1·2 m) and flowering period covering some eleven weeks between July and September. The double blooms are so deeply gold as to be almost orange-yellow in the evening sun. Very similar in all respects is *H.* 'Goldgreenheart'. The small greenish centres to the blooms are the only noticeable difference. The name of the much older *H.* 'Incomparabilis' is hardly an exaggeration, for this is often the neater plant at just over 3 ft (90 cm) and from July to September bears a rich profusion of large, double, zinnia-like blooms of a fine orange-yellow. This probably makes the most valuable contribution to the border. Another commendable old kind is *H. patula*, growing to 4 ft (1·2 m) and bearing a wealth of frilled, bright yellow flowers.

Cut flowers of heliopsis flag rapidly unless cutting is done in the cool and calm of the evening, and the stems are immediately immersed in fresh water. Cut blooms that have wilted will seldom revive. It is equally important to cut stems not when the central bloom is open, but when several laterals are in flower, for buds are very reluctant to open in a vase. The choice of cutting for one bloom or several on a stem is left to the cutter, however. Individual blooms on short stems may be gleaned late in the season as one removes the very unsightly spent flowers during one's rounds of the garden and these, together with a few of the attractively saw-edged leaves, have a cheerful small vase or bowl life of about a week.

Deprived of mid-summer moisture the leaves of heliopsis droop and the quality of flowering is diminished, making humus in the soil a basic requirement.

Helleborus (Hellebore, Christmas Rose, Lenten Rose)
Ranunculaceae

Helleborus niger is the optimist's Christmas rose, and while many are familiar with it few are conscious of the dozen or so other species and hybrids commonly available from growers of hardy perennials, to say nothing of the several hybrid forms of *H. niger*.

Hellebores are members of the buttercup family, and this gives a vital clue to their cultivation—a moist soil. Moisture is important during the summer for these shade loving plants, and a site sheltered from winds which can damage their dog-roses. Hellebores revel in a well drained soil laden with a mixture of grit, peat and leafmould. Plants do not like the heat of the sun on their roots and crowns in summer, and partial shade suits them to perfection. Planted in such conditions *H. niger* may be encouraged to become a Christmas rose by the timely use of a cloche to ward off the rains that so rob the blooms of their purity. Thus the flowers that come between December and March are not wasted. One can seldom cut stems longer than 6 in (15 cm) in the garden, and these must be put in water immediately or they will wilt. If the stems are very short the blooms may be floated in a table bowl. A few of the attractive leaves may be used, but great restraint is needed here as these later form a natural protection for the crowns.

Helleborus orientalis is the Lenten rose, whose blooms of greenwhite, deep rose or light purple are borne at a height of 12–18 in (30–45 cm) between January and March. Also with evergreen leaves is *H. lividus corsicus*. The leaves are large and glaucous, and the lime-green flowers of February and March are borne on stems up to 2 ft (60 cm). These give the flower arranger some valuable and unusual material. As with all hellebores there must not be the slightest delay between cutting and immersion of the stems. A small container should be taken to the plants, and not vice versa, but any cut flowers that have flagged may have their stems removed and the blooms floated in a bowl.

Helleborus antiquorum is a valuable species for growing in quite heavy shade. Again, the leaves are evergreen and the stems, up to 1 ft (30 cm) long, bear clusters of pink flowers measuring some 2 in (5 cm) across between March and May.

Raising plants from seed is a slow business calling for great patience, and division immediately after flowering or in the autumn needs considerable care, even with mature plants grown in good deep soil.

Hemerocallis (Day Lily) *Liliaceae*

Hemerocallis has rhizomatous roots that are remarkably adaptable to a wide range of soils in sun or some shade. It is a fine plant for the heavier loams or other soils that retain summer moisture in abundance, and the finest plants are those whose roots are in a good soil laden with organic matter. Here the foliage is improved and the flowering prolonged, and the presence of sun or partial shade is then immaterial. These are invaluable plants for the discerning gardener. The wealth of bright green rushy leaves adds vital contrast to borders with rather too many bushy subjects. The flower arranger also has a fine choice among the clusters of day lilies borne on stems from 2 – 5 ft (60–150 cm) in a good range of colours from May until mid-September.

One of the oldest forms is *H. fulva*, grown in England for some three centuries. In summer-moist soils this is still a splendid plant giving an imposing clump of bright green rushy leaves that is not surpassed by any of the newer introductions. Stems grow up to 4 ft (1·2 m) and are forked near the top to bear clusters of copper-orange blooms between July and September. Just as old and fine is the 3-ft (90-cm) *H. flava* with finely arched foliage and valuable lemon-yellow clusters of fragrant flowers in June and July. The modern 3-ft (90-cm) 'Imperator' is also highly commendable for its good-sized amber-bronze blooms. The 3½-ft (105-cm) 'Hyperion', introduced fifty years ago, remains one of the best yellows, while *H. dumortieri* is less robust at 2 ft (60 cm) and valuable for its soft yellow blooms beginning in late May. The taller 'Fandango' has fine ruffled orange blooms in July and August, while 'Stafford', at 30 in (75 cm), is a glowing red. At the same height 'Whichford' has green-throated lemon-yellow blooms of good substance. Also valuable to the flower arranger is the 3-ft (90-cm) 'Black Falcon', the name of which is only a slight exaggeration. 'Pink Prelude' and the flushed apricot creamy blooms of 'Halo Light' conclude a brief selection from the scores of cultivars available, to which others are somewhat unnecessarily added each year.

While hemerocallis grows robustly in good soils, it is never a troublesome plant. If after several years it has filled more than its allotted space then the surplus may be spaded out. The leaves should be left to wither over the winter, and a rich pre-flowering mulch is always worthwhile. If spent flowers are removed daily, cut blooms will last a week in a vase.

Hesperis (Sweet Rocket, Dame's Violet, Damask Violet)
Cruciferae

Hesperis matronalis has a trio of common names, sweet rocket, dame's violet, and damask violet. The generic name translates, via the Greek *hesperos*, to give evening. All are apt, for the loose spikes of purple, lilac or white blooms are delightfully fragrant, especially in the warm evenings of early summer. The rather meagre-rooted plants are hardy enough, and though they may not be long-lived any losses are readily made good from self-sown seedlings. *H. matronalis* grows easily to 2 ft (60 cm) in any adequately drained soil not lacking in moisture, and as it will also tolerate either sun or a little shade it has a wide range of uses. Plants are very free from seed to produce a variety of colours. One used to see double-flowering forms of white and purple. These seem to be no longer available. They were raised from cuttings, no seed being set. They must now be classed as rare, but the single forms give the flower arranger a small range of very good cut flowers for the house between May and July.

Heuchera (Alum Root)
Saxifragaceae

Heuchera × *brizoides* and *H. sanguinea* between them have given both the gardener and the flower arranger a first-class range of hardy perennials. The former hybrid form is the smaller and more graceful plant bearing tiny pink or red blooms in spikes topping 1-ft (30-in) stems, while *H. sanguinea* is taller at 18–20 in (45–50 cm) and bears its coral spikes of little bells over a very long period in summer. Both plants have rounded, pretty, near-evergreen basal leaves, while the roots become more woody than fibrous with age and tend to grow out of the ground. Mulching or a deeper replanting helps, but plants are better lifted every four years, after flowering. Pieces of the root bearing eyes or buds with fibrous roots attached can then be broken off and replanted. Heuchera is a drought-resistant plant for well drained, deeply worked soils in sun or partial shade.

H. × brizoides 'The Huntsman' is a border favourite of mine for his 1-ft (30-cm) graceful spikes of long-lasting tiny red bells, and the taller H. *sanguinea* is more than useful for its flowering period from June till September. The flower arranger and gardener must, however, also turn to the charming Bressingham Hybrids. Many of these have beautiful variations of leaf, and the choice of season, height and colour makes these indispensable plants. The 20-in (50-cm) stemmed 'Red Spangles' and the slightly taller vivid pink 'Scintillation' are two of the best, while 'Coral Cloud' and the sulphur-green spikes of the tall 'Greenfinch' are a flower arranger's delight. Of the white cultivars the small 'Pearl Drops' is preferable to the taller 'Snowflakes', but the latter is a vigorous, reliable and early-flowering plant tolerant of a remarkable degree of shade.

Heucherella 'Bridget Bloom' is a dainty hybrid ideally suited for dappled shade in a border. Where the soil is deep and light with some humus, this will grow a shower of graceful stems to nearly 18 in (45 cm) topped with fine spikes of pink blooms lightly touched with white. The fact that it is bicoloured is only noticeable upon close study, the total effect being a light airy cloud of pink lasting, where aptly planted, from late May until late August. The leaves are cut like those of the maple, similar to those of one of its parents, tiarella, and these remain attractive for most of the year. As with a number of other good perennials, flowering is often longest with young plants. This has been known to flower from May until September in many gardens.

Both heuchera and heucherella make excellent border plants for frontal positions where their attractive basal mounds of leaves are not masked by neighbours. The range of colours and colour combinations, the graceful disposition of the spikes with their minute bell-flowers available for up to four months of the year, and the long slender yet wiry stems make these most attractive hardy perennial cut flower subjects, either on their own, in variety, or mixed with other cut blooms in a vase.

Hosta (Plantain Lily)   *Liliaceae*

Hosta, which has both fleshy and fibrous roots, is an excellent plant for deep summer-moist soils and some shade. It is a fully hardy and long-lived plant with a steady rate of expansion. Many forms of hosta will give a good account of themselves in ordinary garden soil, and some are adaptable to both sun and shade. While

Hosta

even comparatively dry soils will support the plants, they take on an added luxuriance where there is moisture and a little shade. In such a sheltered site hosta, often grown for its beauty of foliage alone, will not have its leaves torn by winds and the flowering will be prolonged. Mature plants may be lifted and divided, or pieces simply dug out with a sharp spade.

Hosta fortunei 'Albo-picta' has the most beautiful leaves in spring. These are lightly golden and edged with bright green, becoming suffused with pale green all over as the summer progresses. The stems, rising to 21 in (52·5 cm), bear spikes of lilac blooms in July and August. *H. f. aureomarginata* is an inversion of this, having golden-edged green leaves, while *H. f.* 'Aurea' has completely golden leaves until midsummer.

Hosta sieboldiana has much larger and rounder heart-shaped leaves that are more blue than green. In *H. s.* 'Elegans' they grow very large, up to 2 ft (60 cm) or more long by nearly as much across. From the centre of this sumptuous basal clump of blue-grey stems rise to 3 ft (90 cm) bearing pale lilac blooms between July and September. *H. ventricosa* gives large tufts of broad glossy leaves and 3-ft (90-cm) stems of fine bold purple flowers in July and August. In *H. plantaginea* 'Grandiflora' the broad green leaves are topped with 18-in (45-cm) stems bearing spikes of fragrant pure white blooms in August and September.

The green-leaved *H.* 'Honeybells', flowering in July and August, is a most desirable hybrid bearing stems up to 3 ft (90 cm) of fragrant mauve flowers. Two fine dwarf forms are to be found in *H. minor* 'Alba' and *H. tardiflora*, both valuable for their late flowering at 10 in (25 cm) between August and late September. *H. tardiflora* is like a small version of *H. lancifolia*, but *H. m.* 'Alba' has white blooms with a sweet scent.

All these, and others, give fine cut flowers and choice foliage for the flower arranger. The cut leaf stems must first be submitted to the ordeal of boiling water, and the leaves may also be treated with olive oil to prevent their transpiring moisture. Dried leaves curl and these, too, may be used for winter floral arrangements.

Incarvillea   *Bignoniaceae*

Incarvillea delavayi has both thickly fleshy and fibrous roots. These call for a planting in a generally sunny site where the soil has been deeply worked and good drainage is assured. Well made compost should be incorporated deep into the soil, and while no rich feeding is required fertility should be maintained to a reasonable level if plants are to be left down for many years. Plants are very tardy to show new growth in spring, and it may be the very end of April or early May before new shoots appear. By late May these suddenly erupt to give quite large rose-pink Chinese trumpet flowers above the bare earth. Thereafter growth is rapid, and stems rise to nearly 2 ft (60 cm) by late June, and the flowers are then borne above glossy green, narrow leaves neatly paired and arranged like those of the Rowan tree.

In *I. grandiflora* the leaves are broader and the trumpet flowers a little larger than those of *I. delavayi* and the insides of the trumpets are marked with orange. Plants are much more dwarf at around the 1-ft (30-cm) mark, but the roots are identical. Incarvillea is an ideal subject for light but not starved soils, and both species may be planted near the front of the herbaceous border. Flowering is continuous over several weeks between late May and early July, the gloxinia-like blooms never failing to startle pleasantly both gardener and flower arranger.

Such fleshy roots deeply resent any disturbance, and plants are better left alone. Where the drainage is good incarvilleas are long-lived, fully hardy and troublefree. While a skilled surgical division is possible, this is fraught with too many risks to both parent plant and offspring, and new stock is better raised from seed, sown under glass in April, even though this calls for care and two years of patience. Plants respond best to spring planting.

Inula   *Compositae*

Inula is a sadly neglected genus with three species that are of interest here. The best cut flowers come from *I. orientalis* (and the less common *I. oculis-christi*). This makes quite a handsome garden plant with stems growing to 2 ft (60 cm) bearing a profusion of finely rayed, golden-yellow blooms of a good size between June and August. *I. ensifolia* is 6 in (15 cm) shorter, bushier of habit and narrower of leaf. The smaller, sparsely rayed, blunt-ended, bright yellow flowers have a simple appeal. These are borne profusely on branched stems between late June and September. Shortness of stem makes these more suitable for small flower displays. Both plants are of the easiest cultivation in the sun, and both cope with clay loams remarkably well.

Iris *Iridaceae*

Bearded irises far outnumber *I. sibirica* in cultivars. The bearded flags relish a little lime in the soil and sun on their rhizomes, but *I. sibirica* dislikes lime and is best grown in neutral or slightly acid loams laden with peat to retain copious summer moisture. In such a soil our native *I. pseudacorus* will grow well, but in mud this is a magnificent plant of handsome proportions. Three more moisture loving irises which give cut blooms of considerable beauty are *I. chrysographes, ochroleuca* and *delavayi.* These six species and their cultivars will be given preference here over the well known bulbous trio of Dutch, English and Spanish irises, though these give excellent cut flowers, and the Spanish irises are particularly graceful and sweetly fragrant subjects. Blooming in June and early July these bulbous irises are best planted in lighter soils at a depth of 3 in (7·5 cm) in early autumn. All three are of easy cultivation and may be divided when overcrowded after the foliage has died right back. Neither should the 15-in (37·5-cm) *I. stylosa* (now *I. unguicularis*) be overlooked. Planted in sharply drained, gritty or stony soil in the full sun, it gives lavender-blue blooms in the chill days between January and March. A poor, limy soil suits it, as does a summer's baking of its rhizomes. The golden-speckled blooms should be gathered for the house as the buds colour up, and these give valuable winter decoration.

The bearded hybrid irises should be planted in a bed to themselves where the ground has been thoroughly prepared well in advance, having been dressed with chalk or lime and dusted with bonemeal. The rhizomes should be set very shallowly on saddles and the roots very firmly planted. The top half of the rhizome is left bare to receive a baking from the sun. After flowering the seed pods are removed and the sword-like leaves may be reduced a little. Division calls for a knife to produce 2-in (5-cm) pieces of rhizome with roots attached. This may be carried out every three years to keep plants healthy and floriferous. Cultivars are legion and the following selection is necessarily brief. The $3\frac{1}{2}$-ft (105-cm) 'Blue Valley' is very desirable for its fragrant blooms, while 'Gold Flake' and 'Golden Fare' are two fine tall cultivars at 4 ft (1·2 m). 'Cliffs of Dover' and 'Gudrun' are a pair of strong-growing whites, and 'Senlac' is a rich mulberry-red. 'Helen McGregor' is justly popular for her beautiful silvery blue and 'Ola Kala' is a splendid rich orange-yellow. 'Paradise Pink' and the deep violet-purple 'Sable' conclude this brief selection to give a fine choice of colour. All these are best divided and planted after flowering, early autumn being the next best time.

Iris sibirica forms fine clumps of more rushy leaves to give a graceful habit to the plants. In summer-moist soils these are imposing hardy perennials fully worthy of growing in borders. 'Perry's Blue', together with the deep violet-purple 'Caesar' and the veteran golden-touched white 'Snow Queen' were raised decades ago, yet they remain very desirable cultivars. All three grow to a little over 3 ft (90 cm) in good soil, and give longer-lasting cut blooms than the bearded irises.

In moisture retaining clays and bogs *I. pseudacorus* is a majestic and graceful iris growing to $4\frac{1}{2}$ ft (103 m). The broad arched leaves are among the most handsome to be found among the green-leaved irises, and the large golden-yellow blooms cover a longer period than most, coming between May and July. The seed pods are also very decorative, being shiny, green and elongated.

In moist border soils *I. chrysographes* with its rushy leaves grows to 30 in (75 cm). The glowing light purple blooms appearing in June are undeniably beautiful, while *I. c.* 'Black Knight' is strikingly dark and worthy of his name. *I. delavayi* bears its deep violet blooms above rushy foliage, but the golden-suffused white flowers of *I. ochroleuca* top a wealth of tall and slender sword-like leaves. Both grow to a little over 4 ft (1·2 m) when planted in good summer-moist soils, and while partial shade is tolerated a sunny aspect produces freer flowering.

One must not leave this large genus without mentioning *I. foeti-dissima*. This is a slanderous botanical name for our native Gladwyn iris. While iris lovers are apt to look askance at the lilac-blue blooms, none save the foolish despise this plant, for its vivid scarlet seeds make such colourful winter decoration. Combine these with the knowledge that this easy-growing iris will tolerate a remarkable degree of shade, even where the soil is dry, and we have a most valuable plant. The variety *I. f.* 'Lutea' bears burnt-yellow blooms, and the bright orange seeds of autumn and winter are very useful. In *I. f.* 'Variegata' we have one of the finest variegated irises available, with cream and green striped leaves, and this makes a splendid, if shy, flowering subject for a shaded site.

The stems of irises should be put into hot water before setting in cold. Irises should be cut when the blooms are half-open and put into deep water.

Ixiolirion   *Amaryllidaceae*

Ixiolirion ledebourii (or *I. montanum*) is one of a small genus of bulbous plants suitable for cultivation in well drained soils in a warm sunny site. The flowers open into six-petalled stars of a violet-blue centred with golden stamens. The blooms, measuring about 2 in (5 cm) across, are borne on 12–15-in (30–37·5-cm) stems above basal grassy leaves in late May and June. The colour is variable but van Tubergen's form is a beautiful glowing violet, with blooms up to 2½ in (6 cm) across. Ixiolirion makes fine cut flowers of graceful habit, and is an ideal subject for well prepared tubs on a sunny terrace. It should be protected in cold districts during winter.

Kentranthus or Centranthus (Valerian)   *Valerianaceae*

Kentranthus is the valerian that grows so well in dry soils and upon

walls. The red valerian is *K. ruber* but there is also a finer and
deeper red in *K. r.* 'Atrococcineus' and a seldom seen white-
flowering form in 'Albus'. All grow bushily erect from 2–2½ ft
(60–75 cm). These plants will grow almost anywhere and are
valuable for poor, stony soils baked by the sun, and for waste
corners in partial shade. Although well grown plants flower profusely between June and September and are of pleasing habit, they
should be banned from the border because their self-sown seedlings are such a nuisance. Confined to the kitchen garden the
flowering stems may be cut before any seed has set. Besides giving
cut blooms for the house kentranthus is a valuable plant for tubs
in courtyards where its long season will bring a welcome splash of
pink, red and white. Kentranthus bears its blooms in fine branching heads over shiny deep green leaves. The only fault with this
most adaptable and generous perennial lies in those self-sown and
quite deep-rooting seedlings. This apart, one would have to
search far to find a better plant for poor, dry soils.

Kniphofia (Red–hot Poker)   *Liliaceae*

Kniphofia demands good soil drainage as a prime requirement for
its deeply penetrating and somewhat fleshy roots, and sun is
always preferable to the light shade many of these misnamed red-
hot pokers will tolerate. Allied to faultless drainage, these drought-
resistant plants do respond very well to ample summer moisture.
Although it is resented, kniphofia can be carefully divided in
spring, but it should be replanted without delay to obviate any
rapid drying out of the brittle roots. Such rude interruptions often
entail the loss of flowering for that season, and plants are best left
undisturbed for years. The persistent leaves must be omitted from
the autumnal shearing, and tied together to form a winter tent to
protect the crowns from excess wetness followed by the destructive
frosts. Most kniphofias are then both fully hardy and perennial,
and good soil drainage makes them long-lived. Many are valuable
border plants providing a distinctive contrast of foliage and flower.
Spring planting is advisable unless one is prepared to ensure some
winter protection following an autumn planting.

By selection a flowering period extending from late June to October may be obtained in a range of yellow, orange, red and white with many subtle overtones, and height can vary from 2 ft (60 cm) to a full 5 ft (1·5 m). The soft orange *K. galpinii* is grassily graceful at 2 ft (60 cm), while the 5-ft (1·5-m) scarlet 'Samuel's Sensation' has a rigid magnificence. Both are doubly valuable for their September and October flowering. The named hybrid forms of *K. galpinii* are really too good to cut, but these give some of the most decorative and graceful vase subjects among this fine genus. Less wastefully, a few plants of Stark's Hybrids give good returns of variable pokers in many shades of orange and yellow. Cut before the lowest blooms fade, the spikes of tubular flowers continue to open up the stem in a vase.

Lamium (Dead Nettle)   *Labiatae*

Lamium maculatum grows vigorously to give dense mounds of white-splashed leaves beset with many pink-lipped flowers borne up to 10 in (25 cm) and beginning as early as March or April. The fibrous roots are remarkably adaptable to almost any soil in sun or shade, even where dry. While flowering often covers six months and the leaves are ornamental, the vigorous spread in good soil makes it unsuitable for the border. It is, nevertheless, a valuable plant for dry and shady places, and in courtyard tubs where its exuberance may be confined. The sprays of bright pink flowers, deeper in *L. m.* 'Roseum', make colourful subjects for small informal displays. One may often fill a small bowl with cut flowers as late as November. The galloping *L. galeobdolon* 'Variegatum' similarly thrives in shade, giving bright yellow sprays in May and June, while the leaves remain attractively splashed with silver for the rest of the season. Division is elementary at almost any time of the year.

Lathyrus (Everlasting Pea, Spring Vetch)   *Leguminosae*

Lathyrus latifolius is the everlasting pea. This climbing hardy perennial will cover a 6-ft (1·8-m) trellis in the kitchen garden. The

E

fleshy roots demand a deeply worked soil in a generally sunny aspect. Rather than disturb these roots by division, plants are better raised from seed sown in pots in late spring. These may be transplanted to the garden in autumn. While the flowers are smaller than those of the annual sweetpeas, the pink blooms are attractive between July and September. In the cultivars 'Pink Beauty', 'Pink Pearl' and 'Rose Queen' the blooms are much the same colour but of better substance than those of the type, while 'White Pearl' gives a good and useful alternative. Cut sprays of flowers and foliage provide the flower arranger with attractive and informal decoration. Easily raised from seed, the everlasting pea is tolerant of a little shade.

Lathyrus vernus is the attractive spring vetch, an herbaceous plant growing to a densely leaved bush about 1 ft (30 cm) high and bearing charming clusters of violet-blue pea flowers for a few weeks in May and June. Raised from seed these may give blooms of near-white, pink, lilac and purple, and an occasional blue of some substance. These too are best suited to informal arrangements. Plants are more rewarding in good, deeply worked, well drained soils in the sun, though they will tolerate a little shade. Both species are fully hardy and reliably perennial. Those who have grown sweetpeas with success will find these perennial forms of easy cultivation.

Lavandula (Lavender)   *Labiatae*

Lavandula spica (syn *L. officinalis*), is the old English lavender of Elizabethan gardens which forms aromatic bushes of narrow, silver-grey leaves and short spikes of flowers for much of the summer. Although this will grow well in many well drained loams, the finest and most floriferous plants are those in deep light soils bearing some chalk, and in the full eye of the sun. A number of good forms exist, the strongest and tallest being 'Grappenhall', which grows to a full 3 ft (90 cm). 'Hidcote', sometimes offered as 'Nana Atropurpurea', is less vigorous at barely 2 ft (60 cm), but it is a splendid, compact form, deep violet and very floriferous. 'Munstead Blue' is also very commendable and compact, bearing its bluer spikes at just under 18 in (45 cm). 'Backhouse Variety' is also dwarf at just over 1 ft (30 cm), and a fine deep violet-purple. 'Folgate Blue' is also good at 15 in (37·5 cm). 'Nana Alba' is sufficiently pale to merit its name, while 'Nana Pink' adds to the choice available to the flower arranger. Some of the more compact forms may be used in borders, while others make good edging to a sunny path. Any deterioration in the plants may be taken as a sign to take cuttings and these, crowded into pots and kept in humid conditions, soon form replacements for old or tired stocks.

Lavatera (Tree Mallow)   *Malvaceae*

Lavatera olbia rosea is another shrubby perennial which thrives in the same conditions as those enjoyed by lavender, but its height and bushy nature makes it more suitable for a dry, even stony soil in a sunny corner. Once planted this tall mallow is best left undisturbed for good. *L. o.* 'Rosea' will grow to a full 6 ft (1·8 m) and bear a profusion of beautiful pink salvers, up to 3½ in (8·5 cm) across, from late June until October. Their size and simplicity make the pink flowers very appealing, and if their vase life is somewhat brief then one is never short of replacements throughout the summer. The sturdy, woody stems of soft grey-green leaves should never be cut back in autumn. Plants are best established (and cut back) in the spring, allowing a good square yard (1 sq. m) of ground for each plant. Good soil drainage is vital to longevity and if, after several seasons, some deterioration is apparent one can take some heeled cuttings in spring as a precaution against loss. These root readily enough under favourable conditions. In poor, light soils plants may be expected to thrive for some five years, but in heavier loams three years might prove the limit of reliability. As with many mallows, *L. olbia* comes easily from seed.

Liatris (Blazing Star, Button Snake–root)   *Compositae*

Liatris grows from curiously fleshy and hairily fibrous roots akin to corms, and while these must have a well drained soil in a sunny site they do not do so well if they dry out. A little humus for the roots greatly benefits these striking perennials. The flower spikes of liatris are remarkable in that flowering begins at the top and continues downwards. This has a startling effect which makes them more worthy of being called red-hot pokers than most kniphofias. The leaves are dark green and very narrow, ascending the stems. Plants may be left down for several years and the roots may then be divided by hand in spring.

Liatris callilepis grows stiffly to 3 ft (90 cm) to give magenta-purple fluffy pokers. In 'Kobold' the stems are shorter by 1 ft (30 cm) but the spikes are intensely lilac and very erect. Both these make striking border groups when closely planted, and neither needs any support, whereas the 3¾-ft (1·1-m) *L. pycnostachya* often needs some help. This ugly-named species, together with *L. callilepis*, gives the best cut flowers if they are taken before the topmost blooms have faded. Cutting is good for the plants and by this means flowering sometimes extends from late June until September.

Ligularia   *Compositae*

Ligularia comes as a complete contrast. It has more fibrous than fleshy roots that are best suited to a deeply worked soil laden with humus to retain copious summer moisture. Light shade is always to be preferred for this distinctive perennial. In the sun the leaves droop pitifully. They are far too handsome to be so tried by heat. In *L. clivorum* the leaves are large and round, plum-purple or freshly green according to variety, and while I have used some flowering stems of these I found this wasteful, and confine my cutting to a few spires of *L. przewalskii*. Its leaves are deeply dissected and very handsome beneath the slender, near-black, 5-ft (1·5-m) stems topped with long yellow spires of blooms in July and August. In *L. p.* 'The Rocket' the leaves are large and heart-shaped, jagged at the edges, and altogether attractive throughout the entire season. The black stems are very erect to 5¼ ft (1·6 m) and topped with more slender golden-yellow spires. These magnificent plants require no support whatever. They look fine in the border and, if cut in good time, in a vase. The flowers are lightly fragrant. Plants are fully hardy and long-lived, thriving where such as astilbe flourish and adding a welcome luxuriance to the summer garden.

Lilium (Lily) *Liliaceae*

Lilium is a large genus of bulbous subjects which can only be dealt with briefly here, where the emphasis will be laid on lilies that are reliable and fairly easy to cultivate and give good cut flowers, with a preference given to the most fragrant. As with other bulbous subjects, good soil drainage is a prime need to be fully met. Clays and sandy soils will yield poor results in comparison with good medium loams, unless they are suitably improved. Farmyard manure is safest left alone in favour of well made compost to supply a deep layer of humus. Leafmould is best of all if this is available. Lilies like their heads in the sun and their nether parts in shade. These are simple but fundamental requirements for growing good plants. Selection must also take into account that some are lime haters while others are lime lovers. Depth of planting is also very important as species rooting from the base of the bulbs obviously require a more shallow planting than those rooting from stems above the bulbs. The bulbs of lilies are best left undisturbed until overcrowding occurs. Division should only be undertaken after the foliage has been allowed to die back, and bulbs must not be allowed to dry out before replanting.

Lilium candidum is the very popular madonna lily, with pure white fragrant blooms on 4-ft (1·2-m) stems in July. This is an exceptional lily whose bulbs are planted in mid-summer so shallow that 1in (2·5 cm) of soil above her crown is sufficient, while her basal roots are best in rather poor gritty soils bearing some lime or chalk. The madonna lily is also exceptional in that she relishes sun on all her parts. She is healthiest when given ample space about her foliage.

Lilium regale is remarkably unfussy as to soil, and of easy and reliable cultivation following a planting at 8 in (20 cm) deep to allow for stem rooting. This, too, has fragrant white flowers, and is readily raised from seed to flower in the second or third year. Plants attain a full 5 ft (1·5 m).

Lilium henryi

Lilium henryi is another stem-rooting lily for an 8-in (20-cm) planting, and one famed for its orange blooms of turk's-caps borne up to 6 ft (1·8 m) in August. Lime in the soil is relished.

Lilium speciosum also grows to 6 ft (1·8 m) to give a wealth of turk's-caps in August and September. The fragrant flushed blooms of great substance make this a florist's favourite, and gardeners have found this a fine lily for partial shade. All these will need some simple support to counter the wind.

Limonium (Sea Lavender) *Plumbaginaceae*

Limonium latifolium has long been prized by both gardeners and flower arrangers as statice. The deeply penetrating roots demand a well drained, preferably light soil in the sun. Plants form a rosette of large, broad, deep green leaves, later hidden by a haze of finely branched stems smothered with clouds of tiny lavender-blue flowers between July and September. In mature plants this will occupy a square yard (1 sq. m) of ground and mound up to a good 30 in (75 cm). It is a fully hardy perennial best left undisturbed for a decade. Division is something of a butcher's job but plants may be raised from seed. A few cultivars are available, of which 'Violetta' is fully worthy of its name, as is the much lighter 'Blue Cloud'. Both these mound up to nearly 30 in (75 cm) in time, and make a charming contribution in a well spaced border planting. They can only be propagated from root cuttings taken from mature plants. While some short branches may be cut for small bowls, mature plants are sufficiently prolific to allow a cutting from the base when the flowers are open. A similar cutting made a little earlier should also be taken for hanging upside down in any airy outhouse where it may be left to dry slowly. The colour will then hold very well and provide the flower arranger with some valuable and delightful winter decoration.

Linaria (Toadflax) *Scrophulariaceae*

Linaria purpurea has fine, fibrous roots giving rise to a splendid basal clump of narrow glaucous leaves and graceful stems rising up to 3 or 4 ft (90 or 120 cm). These hold very slender spires of lavender-blue flowers between June and September, aided by the well balanced secondary spikes to the sides. No staking is necessary for these remarkably adaptable and hardy perennials, and plants can be faulted only on one score. *L. purpurea* will bestrew too many seedlings unless plants are cut back immediately after flowering.

The equally graceful *L. p.* 'Canon J. Went' differs only in the colour of its slender spires. Its blooms are a beautiful soft light pink, and flowering covers the best part of three months. This, too, may be raised true from seed with a little culling of young plants. Both the type and the Canon are worth growing for their cut flowers and their ease of cultivation in sun or shade, light or heavy soils, regardless of dryness. Only sites that are waterlogged in winter are unfavourable to the compact roots. The attractive basal leaves are evergreen while those around the stems are borne in fine whorls. Canon Went is even better than his parents!

Lobelia   *Campanulaceae*

Lobelia gives a fine trio of perennials that are hardy in most southern gardens. These give most valuable cut flowers of blue, red and violet-purple in late summer and early autumn. The fine fibrous roots of all three should be planted in adequately drained, summer-moist soils in sun or partial shade.

The best known member of this trio is the brilliant scarlet-bloomed *L. cardinalis*, which grows sturdily erect to 2 or 3 ft (60 or 90 cm) according to site and moisture. The leafy stems are topped with spikes of the most vivid red between August and October. Hybrids of this and the somewhat tender and softer-stemmed *L. fulgens* have proved to be fully hardy in my Essex garden, given a quilt of peat, well drawn up over the crowns, for the winter. *L.* 'Queen Victoria' is beetroot-red of foliage and scarlet of flower, whereas *L.* 'Jack McMasters' is hung with deep purple blooms. *L. f.* 'Bees Flame' also has deep red leaves and stems, bearing fine spikes of glistening vivid red blooms. Height, according to moisture, is between 2 and 3 ft (60 and 90 cm). *L. cardinalis* is often grown as a marginal plant by ponds, where it remains fully hardy and long-lived so long as the crowns are protected against frosts by a few inches of water or by the foliage of neighbours. The finer and more tress-like roots of the hybrids must be assured of good winter drainage.

A fine contrasting neighbour to *L.* 'Bees Flame' is the hybrid *L.* × *vedrariensis* of identical roots. This is freshly green of leaf. Plants in rich soils can attain a full 4 ft (1·2 m), but in ordinary border soil a more restrained and troublefree 3 ft (90 cm) is usual. The spikes are packed with glowing violet-purple flowers. These are typical of lobelia in having a trio of lower petals and two above, each bloom being touched twice by a speck of white within. Flowering covers many weeks between early August and mid-October. Plants are more vigorous than those of *L.* 'Bees Flame' and may be readily divided, but I prefer to raise stock from seed to obtain some beautiful hues of maroon and deep violet. *L.* × *vedrariensis* is fully hardy in the south and revels in a peaty-gritty soil in the shade.

Lastly, a few words for *L. syphilitica*. This is quite hardy in sheltered sites and valuable for its bright blue spikes of blooms borne on 2-ft (60-cm) stems in late summer. It is best on light soils with some humus. All these lobelias require spring planting, and give the arranger fine and colourful subjects for the early autumn vase.

Lunaria   *Cruciferae*

Lunaria rediviva is a perennial relation of the splendid biennial honesty. This, too, is content in well drained soils and a little shade, where it grows leafily erect to about 3 ft (90 cm). The deep mauve-purple flowers are as attractive as the biennial beauty's, and lightly fragrant for good measure. Flowering is profuse in May and June above a wealth of deep green, heart-shaped, saw-edged leaves. The crisp, thin, silvery seed pods are equally decorative and make splendid substitutes for everlasting flowers. *L. rediviva* comes readily from seed or mature plants divided in autumn.

Lupinus (Lupin)   *Leguminosae*

Lupinus polyphyllus was transformed by the late George Russell from a 30-in (75-cm) plant with rather dull blue spikes into a taller plant bearing magnificent spikes covering a wide range of colours and colour combinations. To grow these well a poor soil is preferable to a rich loam, and a light, well drained, deep soil lacking in lime promotes longevity. Plants thrive in sun and tolerate a little shade quite well. The deep, fleshy roots of lupins should not be fed with farmyard manures, but they do relish a little humus by way of well made compost to give the flower spikes some substance not attainable in very dry soils. Thus lupins are ideal subjects for kitchen garden cultivation where the soil is suitably light and free of lime or cold clay.

Since Mr Russell introduced his improved lupins in the mid 1930s, other plant breeders have continued this work to such an extent that one is now faced with legions of cultivars. One is left wondering if such intensive propagation has proved tiresome to the plants, for many cannot be regarded as being long-lived perennials. With some a marked deterioration sets in about the third year. While fine mixtures of Russell lupins may be raised from seed, cultivars are propagated from firm basal cuttings taken in early spring rather than from tearing divisions. The following five remain among the most rewarding and reliable. The 4-ft (1·2-m) 'Josephine' is still unsurpassed for her deep blue and golden standards, while the 3-ft (90-cm) 'Thundercloud' is profuse with its shorter spikes of flushed purple. The soft rose and coral 'Lady Fayre' and the longer-spiked 'Lilac Time' are both good, while the much newer 4-ft (1·2-m) 'Bressingham Sunshine' is a fine yellow. Spikes are best cut when the lowest blooms are open. Some people split the stem bases and add a pinch of household starch to the vase water.

Lychnis   *Caryophyllaceae*

Lychnis has two species giving striking cut flowers, yet the plants' needs are quite different. In an adequately drained, good loam laden with sufficient humus *L. chalcedonica* can hardly have too much summer moisture. Its fibrous roots are fully hardy and long-lived, easy-natured yet remaining compact. In good soils the leafy stems rise erectly to a full 4 ft (1·2 m) to bear fine domed heads of closely packed scarlet flowers, recalling Maltese crosses, throughout July and August. The colour is probably the truest scarlet in the garden, but cutting poses a nice problem in that the flowers do not always open together to give a complete dome of bloom. This is mere carping, however. The sturdy stems drink well, and a little experience in cutting is readily gained from these prolific and reliable sun loving perennials. Plants grow well enough in ordinary border soils, but where it is too dry in summer the leaves hang sadly from the stems, and some of the basal ones may wither. This is hardly a fault but rather a condemnation of the lazy gardener. *L. chalcedonica*, aptly planted, may remain down for several years, a colourful and troublefree subject. The roots readily divide in spring or autumn, and this good-natured plant comes easily from seed. Some purists find *L. chalcedonica* a little too long in the leg, but the stems are readily concealed by intelligent siting in the border.

Lychnis viscaria would not long survive the conditions favoured by *L. chalcedonica*, for although the two have similar fibrous roots that is all they have in common. *L. chalcedonica* will tolerate partial shade as long as there is moisture, but *L. viscaria* will only flourish in the full sun and prove fully hardy and truly perennial in sharply drained, light soils. *L. chalcedonica* will thrive in improved clay loams that would soon prove fatal to this somewhat spartan relation. Plants give a low mound of dark green leaves topped by 1-ft (30-cm) stems of flowers. In *L. v.* 'Splendens Plena' the double vivid rose-pink flowers are quite large and colourful for a few weeks in June and July, but much smaller in the white *L. v.* 'Albiflora' which is seldom seen today. While flowering is not nearly so prolonged as in *L. chalcedonica*, both cultivars give good cut flowers for smaller displays. Lychnis as a genus is noted for the vivid colouring of its blooms, and some other species might prove of value to the flower arranger.

Lysimachia (Loosestrife, Creeping Jenny) *Primulaceae*

Lysimachia has two contrasting species giving distinctive cut flowers. *L. clethroides* is the easier plant to grow, its fibrous roots being content in most well fed border soils with a generally sunny aspect. It grows bushily up to a full 3 ft (90 cm). The very leafy stems terminate in a profusion of long tapered spikes, tightly packed with small white flowers between July and September.

These spikes are curious in that they are arched to nod more in the horizontal than vertical plane. This curious disposition of the flowers is not unattractive in the garden when plants are sited among suitable neighbours, and the cut flowers give the arranger some distinctive and valuable material. *L. clethroides* is propagated by division, and plants are fully hardy and long-lived, expanding steadily but not excessively in soils with adequate humus to retain summer moisture.

Lysimachia ephemerum needs more attention to its requirements. The roots are partly fleshy and partly fibrous, and these must be planted in a well drained soil, preferably light, yet not subject to drying out in season. A thorough incorporation of well made compost and peat will provide the probing roots with vital humus. Once they have this, *L. ephemerum* will develop into one of the most imposing hardy perennials. The basal leaves are virtually ever-green, narrow and almost glaucous. From among these the slender stems rise erectly to $4\frac{1}{2}$ ft ($1 \cdot 3$ m) to bear very fine spires of densely packed, tiny globular white buds. These open to reveal a mass of small stars, very lightly touched with a suggestion of purple. These exquisitely formed spires recall those of *Veronica virginica* and some of the cimicifugas. *L. ephemerum* flowers with a quiet beauty from late July until October. A group of well grown *L. ephemerum* in the border, in sun or light shade, is an impressive sight. Plants lend a valuable note of vertical distinction, effectively counter-pointing the lowlier and bushier subjects. Their successful culti-vation depends primarily on the gardener striking a nice balance between winter soil drainage and summer moisture, for both bad drainage and drought can inflict losses. My experience tends to show that plants dislike lime. *L. clethroides* is far less fussy but *L. ephemerum* is the more imposing garden plant. The cut flowers of both last very well in a vase.

L. nummularia, our creeping jenny, is a useful little plant for damp and shady courtyards, and the severed stems bedded in a bowl of moist moss make charming indoor decoration.

Lythrum (Purple Loosestrife) *Lythraceae*

Lythrum is among the most reliable and hardy of all perennials. Its very tough fibrous roots are adaptable to all soils except those that are both light and summer-dry. The purple loosestrife of our river banks, itself a noble spired plant, is the sire of many fine garden forms. *L. salicaria* and *L. virgatum* have willow-like leaves and tough fibrous roots that are almost identical. Both species make splendid border or pool-side subjects for the garden where the merits of good behaviour, long life and gracefulness are so valuable.

Lythrum salicaria grows bushily erect. The smallest cultivar is the Bressingham-raised 'Robert', which grows to 30 in (75 cm). As with all lythrums, flowering is most profuse and prolonged where there is ample summer moisture, and *L. s.* 'Robert' is then a delight of clear pink spikes between late June and September. *L. s.* 'Brightness' grows between 4 and 5 ft (1·2 and 1·5 m) to give a wealth of rosy pink spikes, as do 'Lady Sackville' and 'The Beacon'. The newer German 'Firecandle' is an intense rosy red growing to nearly 4 ft (1·2 m). None of these requires any support, even in wind-swept sites.

Lythrum virgatum is more slenderly erect, making this a most graceful and rewarding plant to cultivate. 'The Rocket' grows bolt upright to 3 ft (90 cm) with narrow rosy spires. 'Rose Queen' is aptly named for its graceful colour and habit, growing to 30 in (75 cm). Both these valuable border plants flower continuously over many weeks between late June and September, and remain very compact for years.

Lythrum 'Pritchard's Variety' is said to be of salicarian lineage, yet this I have for long doubted. In good soils it grows to 4½ ft (1·3 m), yet the growth is so compact and erect that it suggests the habit of *L. virgatum*. This is a magnificent plant, floriferous and always reliable. The long pink spires are a delight from early July to late September, and after flowering the leaves redden to be fired with golden hues by the autumn sun. Even the sere stems of seeded spires look attractive through the winter, either in the garden or in a dried flower arrangement. All these plants give a wealth of cut flowers in summer. The roots of mature plants call for surgical division, and sharp secateurs to sever portions bearing both fibre and red-eyed buds are often easier to use than a knife. Lythrum thrives, when in moist soil, in sun or partial shade and remains one of the best perennials to grow in clay loams.

Macleaya (Plume Poppy)   *Papaveraceae*

Macleaya cordifolia has both fleshy and fibrous wandering roots that are best confined to rather dry, light soils, and curbed by an annual spading if planted in large borders. This is a handsome plant growing to 5½ ft (1·6 m). Growth is erect and no staking is required. The stems rise above the large ornamental leaves to bear spikes of very small pendant ivory flowers between July and September. The older spikes give remarkably delicate and long-lasting cut flowers. Plants look fine from head to foot, the larger basal leaves, lobed and silvered beneath, giving a nice balance to the tapered growth above.

  Macleaya microcarpa is also an impressive perennial with large handsome leaves and tall feathery spikes of tiny, pendant tubular flowers. In *M. m.* 'Kelway's Coral Plume' the flower buds are flushed with coral-pink. Plants can grow from 7 to 10 ft (2–3 m) according to their situation. The wandering roots are sufficiently vigorous to make it unsuitable for inclusion in the border, yet it is a valuable screen plant or one to fill a sunny or partially shaded corner with indifferent soil, as long as it is adequately drained. The leaves of both species may also be used in floral arrangements if the stems are first dipped in hot water.

Meconopsis (Blue Poppy)   *Papaveraceae*

Meconopsis betonicifolia is still better known as *M. baileyi*, the famous Himalayan blue poppy collected by Captain F. M. Bailey in 1914. Apart from raising plants from seed, the newcomer is best advised to purchase young pot-grown stock for a spring planting in a deep, cool soil laden with humus. In medium loams an equal admixture of peat and sharp sand or grit, thoroughly incorporated to a good depth, suits the deeply probing roots well and gives the young plants a good start in the garden. Should these throw any flowering stems the first year they should be cut out forthwith. By autumn a good root system will then be established, and the plants will winter well to give those large, fragile blue poppies in the summer. Some of these may be cut, just before the blooms open, with a good length of stem. The bases should be singed or dipped in hot water without delay prior to setting in a deep vase. With timely cutting the blooms will open in the vase to reveal a shower of golden orange stamens standing out from the centre of the wafer-thin blue petals. Plants grow best in light shade and, as with all fragile flowers, out of the wind. Moisture, shade and shelter are the three basic requirements for this popular 3-ft (90-cm) poppy, which resents any disturbance once established.

Mertensia (Virginian Cowslip) *Boraginaceae*

Mertensia virginica likes to have its dark fleshy roots in the same conditions as those of meconopsis. This little known plant is the virginian cowslip, a charming and choice subject which revels in cool shade. Plants give a graceful growth of lance-shaped leaves, and stems up to 2 ft (60 cm) long daintily arched at the tips by pendant clusters of little blue bell-flowers between mid-April and June. *M. virginica* requires careful siting in a border, as the plants are dormant by the beginning of summer. The roots are best left undisturbed, and although they can be divided with a surgeon's skill, new stock can also be raised from saved seed. These are among the most charming cut flower subjects of late spring. As with the related pulmonaria, the flowers should not be cut until at least half the cluster is open, and should then be put into deep water immediately. The fragile blooms are easily knocked off by careless handling. *M. ciliata* is similarly reliable and attractive, and conveniently flowers some three or four weeks later.

Mimulus (Monkey Flower)   *Scrophulariaceae*

Mimulus, too, will flourish in the same conditions as meconopsis, and the moister the soil is in summer the better. The fibrous roots are shallow and surface-feeding and more responsive to a gritty soil than to a clay loam. Not only is it a very floriferous perennial, colourful over a long season, between May and September, and fine at the front of a border, but it is an excellent subject to grow in well tended tubs in town courtyards. Plants form mats of fresh green leaves on self-rooting stems. The most vigorously perennial and reliable is the hybrid *M.* 'A. T. Johnson'. This produces a profusion of stems up to 1 ft (30 cm) high crowded with red-splashed yellow trumpet flowers that are sometimes lightly

Mimulus

fragrant. Flowering lasts longer than with other mimulus, May to the end of September being normal in my garden.

Mimulus burnetii grows to about 9 in (22·5 cm) and bears a wealth of fine orange blooms between June and September. This, too, is prolific and reliable. *M. cupreus* is an inch or so shorter and the trumpet blooms are coppery and delightfully speckled. The cultivar *M. c.* 'Red Emperor' is more reliably perennial than the somewhat temperamental 'Whitecroft Scarlet' in my experience, but both these 6-in (15-cm) dwarfs are delightfully generous. Plants respond to mulching and are readily divided in spring. Those trimmed over after a thrashing from a summer's storm recover quickly to flower anew. All these mimulus give the flower arranger cheerful subjects for small bowls and vases, even if their life span is brief.

Monarda (Bergamot) *Labiatae*

Monarda forms a thick mat of fibrous roots in humus-rich, well flocculated soils. They are a joy to handle and divide, being strongly aromatic of thyme and citrus fruits. Good drainage is essential for longevity, but although plants are tolerant of fairly dry light soils and partial shade, they revel in summer moisture and sun. Plants often take a season to settle down, after which growth is leafily erect to $3\frac{1}{2}$ ft (105 cm). The leaves are also aromatic, and the curious honeysuckle-like flowers top the squared stems in profusion between late June and September. These are available in a small range of reds, pinks and purples. 'Cambridge Scarlet', 'Croftway Pink' and the light purple 'Prairie Night' are all good, colourful and heavily aromatic perennials giving a generous supply of cut flowers for the house. A leaf added to the (Indian or China) teapot is deliciously refreshing.

Morina (Whorl Flower) *Dipsacaceae*

Morina longifolia's fleshy roots are best in light, well drained soils in the sun. In such a site it forms a fine rosette of large, very long and narrow spiny leaves. From the centre of this distinctive and prickly foliage rise sturdy erect stems to 30 in (75 cm) bearing attractive whorls of small white and rosy blooms between June and August. Flowering is intermittent and seldom profuse, but one may often cut a few stems very late in the summer. The seed heads dry very well and make unusually fine winter decoration.

Muscari (Grape Hyacinth, Tassel Hyacinth)   *Liliaceae*

Muscari armeniacum is most widely known in *M.* 'Heavenly Blue'. This easy and free-flowering grape hyacinth produces its clear gentian-blue spikes on 6-in (15-cm) stems in late March and April. These give most welcome and fragrant cut flowers for small bowls. *M. botryoides* is a less vigorous and more dwarf species with fine china-blue blooms. The white *M. b.* 'Albus' is particularly attractive.

One of the most useful muscari is *M. comosum*, growing to just over 1 ft (30 cm) and giving first-class cut flowers for the house in May. *M. c.* 'Plumosum' has fine feathery violet plumes which give this the common name of the tassel hyacinth.

The green-purple blooms, later turning to yellow, of *M. moschatum*, borne on stems just under 1 ft (30 cm) high in April, may not be to everyone's liking, but these are the most fragrant of all. The larger *M. m.* 'Major' is taller at 1 ft (30 cm) and a little more vigorous.

Muscari shares most bulbous plants' need for a well drained soil, and these early and valuable grape hyacinths are undoubted sun lovers. In good soils increase is rapid, making division of the offsets elementary after three years.

Narcissus (Daffodil, Jonquil)   *Amaryllidaceae*

Narcissus is a vast genus giving a wealth of cut blooms which last well in a vase after being given a long, deep drink. Many are rightly popular for their lasting qualities, and some have a purity and simplicity that is deeply appealing. The host of daffodils contains a number with a sweet fragrance that is doubly precious in spring, and these alone will be briefly considered and recommended here.

The jonquils, *N. jonquilla*, with deep green rushy leaves and short-cupped golden blooms are the most sweetly fragrant of all. The smallest of these is the 3–6-in (7·5–15-cm) *N. juncifolius*, whose little yellow blooms of March and April last very well in a miniature vase shared with some blue sprays of pulmonaria. It is a mistake to plant the bulbs of any narcissus carelessly or too shallow, and even the diminutive bulbs of this species require a minimum depth of 3 in (7·5 cm).

Among the hybrid jonquils 'Trevithian' gives two or three pale yellow blooms, of great sweetness, to a stem, and these are very good for cutting. 'Buttercup', the very late 'Gracilis', and the creamy 'Nirvana' all grow to between 12 and 18 in (30 and 45 cm) high. The trio of *N. odorus* 'Campernelli', 'Campernelli Plenus' and 'Rugulosus', of similar stature, add some charming and distinctive flowers to the choice.

Among the Tazetta narcissi the white and yellow 'Compressus' and 'Odoratus' are both sweet-scented one-footers (30 cm) appearing in late March.

Narcissus poeticus has three fine representatives growing up to 18 in (45 cm) high, the double pheasant's-eye 'Flore Pleno', the earlier 'Praecox', and the very heavily fragrant 'Recurvus'.

For courtyard tubs the trumpet daffodils of 'Louise de Coligny' are excellent. The white perianth and fluted apricot-pink trumpet blooms borne up to 15 in (37·5 cm) are sweetly scented in April.

From the point of view of the cutter in spring, it is best to plant bulbs in well prepared ground in late summer rather than autumn. The roots respond well to bonemeal, sulphate of potash, or hoof and horn meal, but manures should not be considered. Daffodils grown for cut flowers should be given a sunny site and be protected from the harrying winds. Lifting and dividing should be undertaken every third or fourth year but not until the foliage has died right back. The smaller daffodils may be induced to flower earlier by the use of cloches. The little *N. juncifolius* is more than worthy of a place in a rock garden. For the general run, a small bed set aside in the kitchen garden affords a good means of rearing clean stock.

Nepeta (Catmint) *Labiatae*

Nepeta × faassenii is often erroneously sold as *N. mussinii*, of which this is a hybrid. This is a valuable hardy perennial with fibrous roots best in poor, light, sharply drained soil in the full sun. The 1-ft (30-cm) spikes of lavender-blue flowers are often available for six months of the year. More useful for cutting is the 3-ft (90-cm) 'Six Hills' form. This, too, is very floriferous, between June and September, with pungently aromatic leaves. Although both forms tend to drop their blooms, these are so numerous as to make this of little account. These are subjects for spring planting and division, and while plants benefit from cutting the remaining stems should not be cut back in autumn. Nepeta looks well beside a sunny path. The most shapely plants come from basal cuttings taken in spring about every third year.

Nepeta 'Souvenir d'André Chaudron', known in the U.S.A. as 'Blue Beauty', is quite distinct. The brittle and more fleshy roots are slowly invasive and deeply probing even in the heavier loams. The leaves are longer, narrower, and more green, and the leafy stems are very upright to 18 in (45 cm) when grown in light soil, and topped with much larger, elongated, tubular flowers of a fine bright lavender-blue from June until late August. These give the best cut flowers of all nepeta, and make a charming contribution to an informal vase.

Nerine *Amaryllidaceae*

Nerine bowdenii is hardy enough in the south if the bulbs are planted some 6 in (15 cm) deep in well drained light soil in a sunny and sheltered site. In such a favourable situation this most valuable plant will give up to half a dozen flowers to a stem. These are held in large, loose umbels on stems up to nearly 2 ft (60 cm) long. The rosy pink blooms are a precious delight from September to the end of October, and they are resistant to the lighter frosts usually experienced at this time. The almost rushy leaves first appear in spring and last until the end of summer, but by the time the flowers appear they emerge almost unaccompanied. The cut blooms are among the finest of all cut flowers, taking on an added brilliance in a vase and lasting a good two weeks. The bulbs are best planted in very early spring and left undisturbed until overcrowding occurs. In cold gardens a straw quilt for winter protection is more than worthwhile for these late pink beauties of the large lily family. Bulbs often take a season or two to settle down, and while good winter soil drainage is vital they should never be allowed to dry out during the summer months.

Onopordon (Scotch Thistle) *Compositae*

Onopordon acanthium is a giant silvery thistle growing to a ghostly majestic 8 ft (2·4 m). The massive, winged stems, with their huge, silvered, deeply cut, spiny leaves, are topped by striking heads of silver and purple fluffy flowers between July and September. The deeply probing fleshy roots are adaptable to many soils where good drainage is assured. While onopordon will tolerate partial shade well, plants do better in a sunny position and look very imposing where aptly sited. They look very fine against a wall or some other plain background where their sculptured, silvery sharpness shows up most tellingly. Both leaves and flower heads are popular with arrangers of large floral displays. Onopordon is readily raised from seed sown in early spring, and good-sized flowering plants are thereby obtained within two seasons. Some gardeners seem to think onopordon is an annual or biennial. The huge specimen in a friend's nursery makes a mockery of this assertion. Following a laborious transplanting in its third year to a more open site, it drooped at first but then recovered and flowered yet again.

Origanum (Marjoram, Oregano) *Labiatae*

Origanum majorana is the sweet marjoram, which gives leafy, aromatic 1-ft (30-cm) bushes of pretty pink blooms throughout the summer. These make charming subjects for informal arrangements. As with most herbs, neatness and longevity are greatly encouraged by plantings in light spartan soils in full sun, and sharp drainage is

vital to all origanums. The fibrous roots are readily divided in
spring, which is also the best time for new plantings, either in the
kitchen garden or beside a sunny path.

Origanum laevigatum, with its profusion of 15-in (37·5-cm)
stems crowded with spikes of flowers, is a beautiful haze of purple
between August and October, and fully worthy of a border planting.

Also worthy of a front row border planting, or a raised alpine
bed, is the little *O. rotundifolia*. This is sufficiently choice to merit
a careful planting in a gritty soil bearing just the right balance of
humus for the deeper-feeding roots. In late spring the low mounds
of little round leaves and apple-green bracts are a delight, and in
July a succession of small hop-like blooms pours out from the
centre in a pink profusion of great beauty which lasts until September. I can never steel myself to cut either these or the bracts, but
both make charming displays in a small table bowl and last very
well if the cutting is timely. This 6-in (15-cm) gem is propagated
from cuttings taken early in the season and inserted in a sandy
mix kept humid.

Paeonia (Peony)   *Paeniaceae*

Peonies give some of the best and longest-lasting cut blooms, but
a degree of patience is required to reap the richest rewards from
these hardy and exceedingly long-lived plants. The curious, fleshy
and brittle roots, which become woody with age, are remarkably
unfussy as to soil, though probably at their best in heavier loams
with good winter drainage. Light soils will also give excellent results, however, if they are not shallow and have been deeply enriched with humus forming material. A deeply worked soil is
essential to give good long-term results via the large roots, and a
good level of soil fertility should always be maintained.

Peonies should be planted in autumn, October being a good
month, with the crowns not more than 2 in (5 cm) beneath the
surface. In the heavier loams 1 in (2·5 cm) is quite sufficient.
Deeper plantings will do nothing but harm, and flowering will be
greatly delayed or inhibited. The roots should be naturally spaced
out in the ample planting station and, if dry, watered in and firmed.

These are subjects for a permanent planting, deeply resentful of disturbance, so plants should be stationed 3 ft (90 cm) apart from the very outset. Any tendency of peonies to sink into the ground may be countered by carefully raising them, using a deeply driven fork for leverage. A little bonemeal in the planting station will be of great benefit to the plants in their first season, and giving an annual mulch of this combined with some well rotted manure, or any other form of potash, very lightly worked into the topsoil around the plants, is a good practice to acquire. Healthy young roots with a trio of well formed eyes, or buds, give a better start than any transplanted larger plant. Growers usually offer two-year-old stock and this is superior in every way to divisions of old plants.

None of this means that peonies are difficult subjects to culti-vate. Provided the soil is adequately drained and fed, and the initial planting is precise, they are easy perennials improving with age. As long as the roots and crowns are not carelessly forked in autumn mulchings, they are remarkably healthy and tenacious of life, and a flowering span of fifty years is by no means unduly re-markable. Some of the choicest peonies may cost two or three pounds apiece, yet even this is but a small price for half a century's worth of beautiful blooms. Some of the peony species are decidedly choice, and many of these come readily from seed if one is not too impatient for flowering results.

Peonies are very hardy perennials suitable for cultivation in even the coldest gardens. Indeed, some of the best flowering plants are those in cold districts where a prolonged period of dormancy in autumn and winter seems to induce improved flowering in spring and early summer. Some peonies are suitable for the larger herba-ceous borders where there is ample room for their bushy width, especially those renowned for their beautiful foliage, and delight-fully colourful, particularly in spring and autumn. Peonies may also be grown in groups between shrubs if planted away from their greedier roots. The early-flowering forms are best planted where the opening buds are least likely to be prematurely marred by spring frosts. Obviously, those catching the early morning sun will be more liable to such unsightly singeing of the blooms. Plants

in the sun will not bloom for so long as those in light shade, where
the paler-bloomed varieties will not be bleached by the hot June
sun. Those grown specifically for cut flowers are admirable subjects for planting in twin rows in a separate bed, or in the kitchen
garden, where their needs may be conveniently and fully met. I
have also seen some mature and floriferous peonies flourishing in
the dappled shade of a cherry orchard.

The flowering season of peonies is brief in comparison with
many other perennials, but by selection this may be eked out to
cover May and June and a little of July.

The selection here is confined to those with outstandingly beautiful blooms or especial fragrance. Among the earliest-flowering
species *P. mlokosewitschii* has beautiful leaves, fine single yellow
blooms and black and coral seed heads. Another rather expensive
beauty is the yellow 'Claire de Lune', with large blooms of great
substance. Among the *P. officinalis* forms 'Mutabilis' is at first
coral-pink, becoming white and the blooms of 'J. C. R. Weguelin'
are a glowing crimson of huge proportions, up to 8 in (20 cm)
across.

Among the single-flowered June beauties, Kelway's 3½-ft (105-
cm) 'Beersheba' is very fine with her fragrant rosy blooms, and
'Chocolate Soldier' is strikingly dark and shining, free-flowering
and fragrant. Of similar height, 'Red Flag', with its golden stamens
and dark stems, is also very fragrant with fine autumn leaves.

Nearly all the double-flowered forms are scented to some degree,
and all the following are very fragrant and have splendid blooms.
The 3½-ft (105-cm) 'Alice Harding', whose large white blooms are
fused with amber tints, also has beautiful autumn foliage. 'Kelway's Supreme', at 3 ft (90 cm), bears fine clusters of large flushed
white flowers into early July, and mature plants are incredibly
prolific. 'La Lorraine' bears clusters of beautiful creamy white
blooms of a wonderful delicacy. 'Madame Calot' is renowned for
her pink and white blooms of great size and refinement, and
'Shimmering Velvet' is a splendid dark crimson of considerable
substance. There are many others.

The Imperial peonies have a wonderfully refined beauty. The
blooms have a wide saucer of petals half filled with narrow peta-

loids tightly packed and ruffled in a rosette. Some of these recall the rarer forms of water-lily, so subtle are the colours and so rare the substance. 'Bowl of Beauty', 'Crimson Glory', 'Evening World', 'Kelway's Majestic' and 'Queen Alexandra' give a choice of rare and beautiful colour combinations. All are magnificent and deliciously fragrant perennials.

Cutting opened blooms from the garden is wasteful. The longest-lasting cut flowers are those taken when the tight round buds have just split to reveal their colour. Buds will open in a vase and the flowers last a full two weeks.

Young peonies should be left unmolested by the scissors for the first two or three years, and although the leaves of some are irresistibly attractive the cutting of these should always be severely restrained. The leaves perform the usual functions of life for the plants, and they also serve a vital part in the formation of new eye-buds on the crowns of maturing plants.

Propagation by division calls for a surgeon's eye and skill to select the best portions of the root with a few good eyes, and to cut these out deftly from the mass presented by an old and woody plant. These are then grown on for a full season in well prepared and enriched soil. Mere division of old plants is seldom satisfactory. This skilful propagation requires a strong and very sharp knife and considerable care, October being the most propitious time.

Papaver (Poppy) *Papaveraceae*

Papavers may not be among the most reliable or long-lived perennials, but they have a fleeting, fragile beauty and a colour range varying from the most delicate to the most vividly flamboyant which make them very telling in a flower arrangement. Poppies have a brief vase life, which can be as little as one day if certain precautions are not observed. Cutting is best done in the early morning or evening on a calm day, open blooms being left in favour of buds just about to open. The lower leaves should be removed and the base of the stems either singed over a flame or dipped in boiling water for up to half a minute. They should then be stood in deep water for several hours prior to setting in a vase.

Poppies demand sharp drainage and are best suited to lighter soils in the sun, but a little humus for the roots should always be assured. *P. alpinum* raised from seed brings a delightful array of yellow, white, salmon-pink and orange blooms, stamened in gold and borne on 6–9 in (15–22·5-cm) stems throughout most of the summer.

Papaver nudicaule is the biennial Icelandic poppy. It has a brief life, but is perhaps the most charming of all in a vase. The 1-ft (30-cm) stems bear flowers between May and September. Readily raised from seed, a range of colour embracing many breathtakingly subtle shades is available. The Kelmscott strain is particularly fine, full of beautiful colours and large blooms. Like their alpine relations, these poppies have wafer-thin, fragile petals and the colours assume a transparent clarity that is particularly appealing. Not only do the cut blooms require careful handling, but plants should be found a site well out of the wind.

Returning to perennial forms after a forgivable lapse, *P. orientale* confines its flowering mostly to May and June. Of these 'Colonel Bowles' is upright to 2 ft (60 cm) and brightly red, while 'Hewitt's Old Rose' is 1 ft (30 cm) taller. 'Marcus Perry' is a vivid orange-scarlet with black markings and grows to 30 in (75 cm). 'Perry's White' has a slightly guilty blush but is more upright at 3 ft (90 cm). These are raised from root cuttings, whereas the more intricate-flowered cerise-pink 'Princess Victoria Louise' and the orange double 'Olympia' readily come true from seed. All these are more suited to the kitchen garden than the border, but richness of soil will produce lax and untidy habits. The dried seed heads may be gilded and used for winter decoration.

Penstemon   *Scrophulariaceae*

Penstemon has several forms of hardy perennials giving cut flowers reminiscent of the foxglove with their pendant tubular bells speckled within. All these demand a well drained, preferably light soil, and while a little shade is well tolerated, sun is relished. A little humus for the roots is a simple requirement, and where this is met flowering is prolonged and the blooms less readily drop when cut for the house. Good soil drainage allied to a little humus is more desirable than richness of diet to any penstemon.

Penstemon barbatus is still known to many as *Chelone barbata*. This grows leafily upright with slender stems to almost 3 ft (90 cm). The flower spikes are crowded with a host of tubular flowers of a fine scarlet between June and September. This graceful perennial should not be deprived of summer moisture, and division every fourth year is always best undertaken in the spring. Plants raised from seed give a wide variation of colour by no means as attractive as the honest scarlet.

Penstemon 'Garnet' is a hybrid of considerable merit. Unlike many other forms this is reliably hardy and fully perennial following a mid-spring planting. Plants grow bushily upright to 18 in (45 cm), the stems being densely packed with pendant tubular flowers of a deep but bright garnet-red speckled with gold within. Flowering is very profuse and prolonged between June and September, giving the arranger some valuable red blooms to counter the wealth of summer yellows. Division is often something of a problem if the parent plant is not to suffer unduly, but this is an acceptable risk as basal cuttings taken in late spring or early summer root readily, and a little self-layering sometimes makes even this unnecessary.

Penstemon pinifolius is a delightful alpine form of easy cultivation in a light, well drained soil open to the sun. This forms a dense lowly bush of semi-prostrate twiggy stems clothed with pine-like leaves. In established plants growth mounds up to just over 6 in (15 cm) and is brightly covered with little scarlet tubular flowers, golden within, from late June into September. The cut flowers make a charming and colourful contribution to small arrangements. Propagation is by taking heeled cuttings in spring. This, too, is fully hardy and reliably perennial, and very telling at the front of the border or in a raised alpine bed.

Phlox   *Polemoniaceae*

Phlox brings a richness of colour and fragrance to the garden not exceeded by any other group of plants. By thoughtful selection this beautiful bounty may be made to extend from June until October with a reassuring reliability. Border phlox, contrary to many dutiful echoings, are best in light shade. The summer sun will bleach out the colour from some varieties making the reds less intense and the pinks decidedly washy.

Border phlox revel in a well worked, well fed and humus-rich soil to feed their mass of fine, fibrous roots, which mostly confine their activities to the top foot (30 cm) of soil. Clay loams lightened with generous amounts of fine grit or sharp sand and sedge peat give excellent and long-lasting results, but light sandy soils must be bulked up by a deep incorporation of organic matter on a lavish scale. Mulching is a good annual practice and summer droughts should be countered by copious watering. It is equally, or even more, important to keep the plants moist in spring and early summer. If plants are deprived of moisture in May the foliage and flowers will be the poorer by July. Thus humus is vital to produce the best phlox.

Phlox are notoriously stubborn to raise from seed, and division of old plants is not a good practice, nor is increasing stock from tip cuttings. The best plants come from root cuttings bedded out in late spring, or from digging up outlying new shoots with roots attached. Such plants are not hosts to the stem-abiding eelworms that once plagued growers.

Timing is the essence of gaining good cut flowers. Phlox cut too late and in the heat of the day will soon drop their petals in a shower on the floor. Stems bearing well formed trusses should be cut when the head is fully developed in the cool of the evening. Those cut early and late in the season last longer, while the smaller spikes taken in autumn from new stock planted in the spring last longest of all. Cut flowers of plants grown in shade also last longer than those taken from phlox grown in the sun—as is the case with quite a number of hardy perennials. And spring and autumn flowers in general have a longer vase life than those blooming in mid-summer. The cut blooms should be given an immediate long, deep drink overnight before setting in a vase. The bases of the stems should be slit and the lower leaves carefully removed. The lowest leaves of all cut flowers should be removed, as these will quickly foul the vase water.

Two of the most valuable border phlox for cutting are white. 'Mia Ruys' grows to barely 2 ft (60 cm) and is probably the earliest to flower. In my garden this blooms in late May or early June. 'Everest' is aptly named, growing to a full 4¾ ft (1·4 m) to bear huge trusses of red-eyed white blooms very late in the season—between late August and October. Both these give excellent, fragrant cut flowers.

Both 'Mother of Pearl' and 'White Admiral' grow to 30 in (75 cm). The latter is pure white with blooms of fine substance, while the former's white blooms are beautifully and lightly suffused with pink. Both these are very fine plants. Slightly more dwarf, 'Prince of Orange' is outstanding for its sturdy and reliable growth giving a wealth of magnificent orange trusses. This 2-footer (60 cm) is the most heavily fragrant of all phlox, filling the garden with its rich perfume on a warm evening, and those in a vase soon scent a room.

The 3½-ft (105-cm) 'Eventide' is a reliable and valuable late-flowerer—one needs to see it in the evening to appreciate its lavender-mauve blooms—and for bluer tones one must grow the 3-ft (90-cm) 'Skylight' and 'Hampton Court'. Among the purples the old 'Border Gem' at 3½ ft (105 cm) remains unexcelled, and the 3-ft (90-cm) 'Le Mahdi' is also excellent, as is the much newer 30-in (75-cm) 'Otley Purple'.

Among the reds the 3-ft (90-cm) 'Starfire' with its dark foliage is outstandingly bright, and the older 'Leo Schlageter' has wonderful scarlet blooms. 'Windsor' is a very fine carmine-rose with a magenta eye, and 'Othello' has a sombre beauty in his deep claret-red flowers. Among the pinks 'Dodo Hanbury Forbes', 'Elizabeth Arden', 'Mies Copijn' and 'Sandringham' are very good. The dark-eyed pale mulberry 'Fairy's Petticoat' and the purple-violet 'Harlequin' with its variegated foliage are also distinctive. All these are of paniculata and hybrid origins.

Phlox maculata may have sired some of the above, but this is a distinct species with two fine cultivars in the full 3-ft (90-cm) range. These also have fibrous roots which relish humus-rich and summer-moist soils. The vernal leaves are distinctly narrow, and stems rise erectly to bear splendid spires of blooms, pink in *P. m.* 'Alpha' and white, tinged with violet, in 'Omega'. Both cultivars flower profusely for eight weeks or more between June and September and, like the *P. paniculata* kinds, are fully hardy and perennial and worthy to grace the most select of herbaceous borders.

Phygelius (Cape Fuchsia)   *Scrophulariaceae*

Phygelius aequalis and *P. capensis* are sub-shrubby perennials requiring a well-drained, medium soil in the sun. *P. capensis* grows up to 3 ft (90 cm) in poorer soils. While its habit is not distinctive or particularly pleasing, the bright red, waxy, tubular flowers borne in candelabras about the stems, which give it its name of Cape fuchsia, are fine from July until late October. A few stems of these late in the season make a distinctive contribution to any vase. *P. capensis* grown in a warm and sheltered site against a southerly wall will grow to a height of 6 ft (1·8 m). Frosts may sere back some stems, and these may be trimmed back in late spring to maintain shapeliness, but plants are fully hardy and perennial. In richer soils *P. capensis* will become widely bushy, giving a means of securing basal cuttings without difficulty to increase stocks.

Phygelius aequalis is very similar of habit, but the tubular flowers are a salmon-pink on the outside, and orange within the throat. This, too, is fully hardy in the south when planted in a light, well drained soil, and flowers over a similarly long period. Again, this will grow in quite poor soils and remain more compact for a spartan diet. A planting in full sun encourages flowering in both species, and if this is seldom profuse, it often covers four months until the sharper autumn frosts scythe down the blooms. Both plants are best regarded as subjects for a spring planting.

Physalis (Cape Gooseberry, Chinese Lantern)   *Solanaceae*

Physalis franchetii is known to many as the Cape gooseberry or the Chinese lantern plant, but it is known to me only as a fearful rampager with brittle white roots only too reminiscent of couch

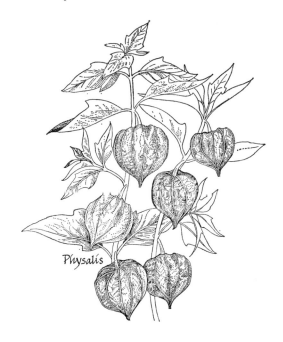

Physalis

grass. To plant this in a border is an act of lunacy. In kitchen gardens physalis may be kept in check by a ruthless annual spading, but plants are safest well confined in a separate bed or a large terrace tub. To obtain the best results physalis should be planted in a fairly rich soil, and here the roots will run amok unless relentlessly curbed. Any piece of root left in the ground will soon sprout anew. Thus physalis is most easily raised in a well nurtured tub or a polythene-lined trench. Plants grow very leafily to 30 in (75 cm). In midsummer small clusters of tiny buff flowers are mostly hidden by the wealth of leaves. By autumn plants look a sorry sight until the fruits and their air-bags colour up to a fine orange-red. These may be cut and used fresh, or dried to provide valuable and cheerful winter decoration.

Physostegia (Obedient Plant)   *Labiatae*

Physostegia virginiana is the obedient plant, whose hinged blooms
stay put a while after being lightly moved. The fibrous roots are
adaptable to most soils except those that are dry in summer.
Plants are very upright and shapely. In 'Summer Snow' the
tapered spikes of pure white flowers come in profusion between
early July and September, borne up to 30 in (75 cm). In the 2-ft
(60-cm) cultivar 'Vivid' the spikes are a bright rose-pink and
come in good numbers between August and October.

Physostegia speciosa 'Rose Bouquet' is fully worthy of a border
planting. This grows very erectly to 30 in (75 cm) with fine, dark
green, lightly toothed, narrow leaves clothing the square stems,
topped by beautiful spires of densely packed shell-pink flowers
between late August and October. In my experience this is less of
a spreader than *P. virginiana*, yet all are very distinctive perennials.
P. s. 'Rose Bouquet' always stands out in early autumn as a welcome pink beacon to relieve the wealth of yellow blooms given by
the rudbeckias and solidagos. All are of easy growth where not
deprived of summer moisture. Division of the fibrous roots in
spring is elementary, as is any necessary curbing of excess growth.
All three give very fine cut flowers for the house, the autumn
blooms being especially valuable.

Platycodon (Chinese Balloon-flower)   *Campanulaceae*

Platycodon grandiflorus mariesii has brittle, fleshy roots. These
penetrate to a good depth and demand a deeply worked, freely
draining soil in the sun. The pale purple shoots are tardy to
appear, being rightly wary of late spring frosts. In a suitable site
this platycodon is fully hardy and long-lived. Plants grow up to
just 1 ft (30 cm), but the sparsely leaved stems are often lax until
plants are fully established and allowed to remain undisturbed. In
July the round buds at the top of the stems swell to become air-
filled bags, making the common name of Chinese balloon-flowers
perfectly apt. These open into large saucers, up to $2\frac{1}{2}$ in (6 cm)

across, of a beautiful violet-blue, which is variable in plants raised from seed—though this means of raising stock is probably better than spoiling established plants by even a skilled surgical division in spring. Flowering extends from July to September, and a group at the front of a sunny border will remain troublefree for many years following a spring planting. Cutting should be restrained for the good of the plants, and this calls for discretion as not all the 'balloons' in a cluster on the stem open together.

Polygonatum (Solomon's Seal) *Liliaceae*

Polygonatum multiflorum revels in shade as long as the soil is moist. The fleshy, rhizomatous roots expand steadily. Long leaves clothe the arching stems, which rise to a good 30 in (75 cm). The top half of these is daintily hung with clusters of little pendant, creamy, green-tinged flowers that give the flower arranger some charming subjects in May and June. This easy-growing perennial is fully hardy, and propagation is by division in autumn. The plants' rate of expansion makes it unsuitable for inclusion in a border, but it is a most useful plant for shady places.

Polygonum *Polygonaceae*

Polygonum is so free-flowering that one mature plant will give the flower arranger a wealth of blooms for the house. Certainly this is the case with *P. amplexicaule*. This has both fleshy and fibrous roots, which revel in humus-laden soils in sun or partial shade. It will form a dense mound of stem-clinging, dock-like leaves set with branching stems of red bottle-brush spikes of blooms between July and late October. In *P. a.* 'Atrosanguineum' the flowers are a deep red, but in the newer 'Firetail' the spikes are very much thinner. Where ample room is allowed these make splendid border subjects, pleasing of foliage and flower, generous, reliable, fully hardy and troublefree. In autumn the foliage turns to beautiful shades of red, orange and flame, and cut flowers last well. In *P. bistorta* 'Superbum' the habit is more compact, up to 18 in (45 cm), and the heads of flowers are a bright pink and floriferous between July

F

and October. Division in spring is easier if a sharp knife is used, but plants may remain down for years.

Primula (Primrose, Cowslip, Polyanthus)   *Primulaceae*

Primula vulgaris mostly consists of primroses, cowslips and the resultant and popular polyanthus. All three are readily raised from seed or increased by division. Plants revel in light shade and summer-moist soils, and heavier loams give excellent results. In moist clays the cowslip will flourish in full sun, but the others are always the better for a little shade. The modern strains of polyanthus contain a wide range of colours, and Blackmore and Langdon's Blue, Pink, Gold, Crimson, White and Red are outstanding. These are obtainable in separate colours or in a mixture as mature plants or seedlings. The coloured cowslips of Cunnington's Strain are now available from seedsmen, and these embrace a fine choice of red, orange, yellow, amber and light brown. The key to success with these early-flowering primulas is moist soil and a site sheltered from the wind. Bunches of blooms, together with some leaves, always make fine table bowls.

Pulmonaria (Lungwort)   *Boraginaceae*

Pulmonaria is a genus of small hardy perennials that brave the chill of early spring with an endearing reliability. *P. saccharata* has both fleshy and fibrous roots that thrive in moist shade or sun. It gives a mound of green heart-shaped leaves attractively mottled in white, and a mass of 6–9-in (15–22·5-cm) stems bearing clusters of nodding pink and sky-blue flowers in March and April. These make charming bowl companions to the above primulas. In *P. angustifolia* the leaves are narrower and plain deep green, and the sprays of bright gentian-blue little bell-flowers come between March and May. *P. rubra* is regaled with bright deep red flowers whereas *P. alba* is white with attractive leaves. All these early-flowering subjects are of the easiest cultivation in almost any soil that is not bone dry. *P. saccharata* is the most vigorous and spreading, and in good soils will need some annual curbing, whereas *P.*

angustifolia remains compact. All are readily propagated by division.

Pulmonaria

Pulsatilla (Pasque Flower) *Ranunculaceae*

Pulsatilla vulgaris, the Pasque flower, with its ferny foliage and silken 8-in (20-cm) stems of large lavender-purple flowers adorned with a shower of golden stamens in April and May, is a fine hardy perennial. Good soil drainage and a sunny sheltered site are the main requirements for this plant of fragile blooms. Division is best not attempted as plants are readily raised from seed, and by this means one may obtain blooms of pale purple or blue, red, pink, and even white. These silken beauties make charming subjects for small bowls,

Pyrethrum *Compositae*

Pyrethrum has a widespread popularity as a cut flower perennial of easy cultivation in most gardens. The finely fibrous roots give the best results in a deeply worked and highly fertile soil. A generous amount of compost, peat or well rotted manure should be thoroughly incorporated into the lighter soils. Heavy soils are unfavourable unless they are lightened with fine grit or sharp sand.

The roots will revel in the gritty mixture and this will do much to ensure that the winter drainage is adequate. Pyrethrums are fine subjects for the kitchen garden, where they may receive copious waterings when in bud and during spells of drought. Although plants are of the simplest cultivation, the most rewarding are those which are well nurtured and guarded against attacks from slugs. These pests find pyrethrums irresistible, and coarse ashes should be sprinkled over and around plants in autumn. Greenfly, too, can be a despoiling nuisance unless plants are sprayed.

Pyrethrums should never be planted in autumn. Plants set out in March and April soon become established in a nicely flocculated soil if the roots are well spread out, a simple injunction that is vital to success with pyrethrums. Spacing, too, is important, as plants crowded together tend to produce a mass of tangled stems, and any form of support by way of pea-sticks should be supplied before the stems begin to rise. The first crop of flowers from a spring planting will be inferior. Flowering is chiefly confined to May and June and, following a cutting of all stems, a second valuable crop may be reaped in September and October. Established plants may be induced to flower in April if cloched over the winter, and by a judicious stopping and thinning out the season may be extended into July. Perhaps the best time to plant new stock is in July so that one may reap a good crop the following spring.

Propagation is by elementary division in March or April, or after flowering at the end of June. The woodier central parts are best discarded entirely in favour of the new and outlying growth.

Good cultivation is necessary with pyrethrums to produce cut blooms of the sort of quality that is always desired and demanded by florists. For cut flower purposes plants should be stationed 18 in (45 cm) apart to encourage a free circulation of air. This is of prime importance in the production of sturdy and upright growth. A pre-flowering mulch is always worthwhile, as this enhances the flowering. The blooms of pyrethrum are not bleached by the sun or unduly spoiled by rain, two vital assets that make these most valuable subjects. Plants detest winter wetness about their roots, and plantings in clay loams usually result in heavy losses of stock. Plants grown in dry, mean soils, on the other hand, cannot be expected to produce blooms of any size or substance. While a good level of fertility is always desirable, nitrogenous manures or fertilizers are probably best avoided in favour of those containing potash. Some varieties are more prone to a nitrogen-induced laxity than others, and thereby lose their natural erectness of stem. This should be borne well in mind, as a bed of pyrethrums with twisted and tangled stems is a disheartening abomination. Well grown plants should have straight stems to $2\frac{1}{2}$ or 3 ft (75 or 90 cm). Regular cutting is good for the plants' roots. Blooms should be cut with the longest stem possible and when the blooms are three parts open. The single-flowering cultivars give the longest-lasting blooms, but the less vigorous double cultivars also have a good vase life. Most of the best pyrethrums are the work of Kelway's of Langport, and many of those recommended below emanate from this old nursery.

Among the single cultivars, the white-centred pink 'Charming' grows sturdily upright to 30 in (75 cm), 'Comet' is a bright and early carmine, while 'Evenglow' is a deep rich salmon-pink of strong growth. 'Kelway's Lovely' is a very fine light pink, and 'Silver Challenge' is very large and regaled with a double row of petals of lightly flushed white. 'Scarlet Glow' is sturdy of stem and late with its glowing blooms. 'Kelway's Glorious' is sturdy and reliable, and its splendid scarlet blooms come very early. From Norfolk the newer 'Bressingham Red' is also an excellent plant for cutting with very large crimson flowers. Other good singles for cutting include the bright cerise 'Brenda' and 'Salmon Beauty'.

Among the double-flowered cultivars the pure white 'Aphrodite' and 'Lady R. Churchill' are both equally good plants raised by Kelway's. 'Madeleine' is lilac-pink, floriferous and pretty, as is her sister 'White Madeleine', and 'Profusion' is a good and large-flowered pink. Both the light-centred lilac-pink 'Beauty of Stapleford' and the crimson 'Duke of York' are very attractive with their anemone-centred blooms of fine substance. The soft light green feathery foliage is also very decorative, forming a perfect foil to these harbingers of summer.

Ranunculus

Ranunculus asiaticus grows from curious claw-like tubers. These are planted with the claws pointing downwards at a depth of just 2 in (5 cm) and about 6 in (15 cm) apart. Plants should be given a warm and sunny site, preferably in a specially prepared and slightly raised bed. Sharp drainage is of prime importance, and lighter soils are far more favourable than heavy loams. Ideally, the light soil should be bulked up with a mixture of leafmould, well rotted manure or compost, and fine grit or sharp sand. Plants of the buttercup family relish summer moisture, and this is no exception. Where this nice balance of winter drainage and summer moisture obtains, the tubers may be left down in southern gardens if given a little winter protection, but more often they are lifted in July and dried and stored for the winter. Planting of the giant French strains should be undertaken in spring, from late February onwards, and flowering covers most of May and June. This period may be extended by successional plantings during the season. Plants grow to give wiry stems from 9–12 in (22·5–30 cm) long crowned with semi or fully double flowers. Not only are plants floriferous, with blooms up to 3 in (7·5 cm) across, but the cut flowers are among those with the longest vase life. Kelway's New Improved strain remains remarkable, giving a wealth of colour from blooms up to 5 in (12·5 cm) across. Spring plantings should be guarded against desiccating winds as tubers will not sprout in dry conditions. Other forms have such densely wrapped petals that they are known as the turban ranunculus. While these are a little hardier, and often taller, the French strains give a better choice of colour. The turbans are usually planted in winter, but any time between November and March will do if the weather is open and the ground has been thoroughly prepared well in advance. These tuberous ranunculus give a diversity of colour ranging from the most vivid red, pink and yellow to creamy white and soft pastel shades. An initial purchase should be confined to one of the proven strains offered by growers.

Reineckia *Liliaceae*

Reineckia carnea is a solitary species and a little known hardy perennial giving a basal clump of broad grassy leaves from which the flowering stems rise to a little over 1 ft (30 cm). These are topped with loose spikes of small, tubular, lightly pink and fragrant flowers in April. Much later in the season comes a bonus of little red berries. The cut blooms make a graceful contribution to a spring vase. The rhizomatous roots are remarkably unfussy as to soil, and their steady expansion makes division elementary.

Rudbeckia (Black–eyed Susan) *Compositae*

Rudbeckia is the gold of the late summer and early autumn garden. Where the drainage is adequate many of these fibrous-rooted hardy perennials will grow well in the heavier loams yet give equally good results in lighter soils with some humus. Starting with the tallest, *R.* 'Herbstsonne' grows leafily erect and strongly to 6 ft (1·8 m). In sheltered sites where the soil is not too rich it will stand unaided, but where support is necessary it should be both timely and substantial to take the sheer weight of the tough stems. The individual blooms of wide drooping rays with the prominent central green cone measure up to 3 in (7·5 cm) across. Flowering is profuse and continuous between August and late October. Cut flowers, with the base of the stems slit, last very well in a vase, drinking prodigious quantities of water.

Rudbeckia laciniata 'Golden Glow' is another 6-footer (1·8 m). I once grew this in good border soil where it proved so lax that I gave the plants to a neighbour. He promptly planted them in some of the heaviest Essex clay where they later grew bolt upright and withstood all the summer winds with utter disdain. Such humbling lessons stand one in good stead! The blooms of 'Golden Glow' are quite large and fully double, and do indeed add a golden glow to the early autumn months. These have a briefer but very cheerful vase life. *R.* 'Goldquelle' grows bushily to about 3 ft (90 cm) to bear a wealth of fine double lemon-yellow blooms in early autumn.

Rudbeckia fulgida speciosa is more of a black-eyed susan with its large golden blooms with distinct black centres. This grows to 30 in (75 cm). *R. subtomentosa*, at 3 ft (90 cm), is much laxer, with softer leaves, but the golden-yellow blooms are large, delightful, and good subjects for a vase. Flowering is very profuse from August onwards, but it demands sharper drainage than most rudbeckias to enhance longevity for its rather meagre fibrous roots, and while the other forms are best divided this is safest raised from seed, which is quick to germinate and grow away.

The best rudbeckia in my experience is *R. fulgida deamii*, which gives a profusion of nicely proportioned black-eyed, fine-rayed, golden blooms from the first days of August until the harder frosts of November put an end to the plant's flowering for the season. Plants form a slowly spreading mat of leaves and flowering stems upright to about the 2-ft (60-cm) mark. The German 'Autumn Sun' ('Herbstsonne') remains the most amiable of giants. Cut blooms will mean sacrificing buds but plants are sufficiently free-flowering to make this loss tolerable.

Ruta (Rue, Herb–of–grace) *Rutaceae*

Ruta graveolens is a refined form of the herb rue. This has compact, partly fleshy and partly fibrous roots admirably suited to sharply drained soils in the sun, even poor and stony soil. Plants form 2-ft (60-cm) evergreen bushes of delicately lobed foliage. In *R. g.* 'Jackman's Blue' this is remarkably fine; it must be among the bluest foliage of all hardy perennials. Plants are long-lived following a spring planting in light soil, remaining blue until the severer frosts of winter damage some of the leaves. This is of little moment as plants are better for a light trim back in late spring to maintain neatness of habit. Firm cuttings inserted in a sandy soil root readily in spring or autumn, which is preferable to a destructive division. In July the pungent foliage (many people find its scent unpleasant) is topped with small heads of tiny mustard-yellow flowers that make an apt contrast to the blue leaves, and flowering continues until November. The cut flowers have an exceedingly long vase life, as have the leaves, which complement delightfully the cut blooms of other late-flowering perennials, such as *Polygonum amplexicaule* with its little claret bottle-brush spikes and *Geranium wallichianum* with its open saucers of violet and white. 'Jackman's Blue' is worthy of a border planting, where it may form a distinctive foil to other sun loving perennials.

Sanguisorba (Burnet) *Rosaceae*

Sanguisorba is a hardy perennial with bottle-brush spikes of flowers. In *S. obtusa* these are attractively curved and drooping, and a rosy pink. Plants grow up to 3 ft (90 cm) and flower between July and September. *S. canadensis* grows slenderly to 5 ft (1·5 m) to be topped by long white pokers of flowers above deeply cut and attractive leaves. In *S. sitchense* the leaves are similarly fine, and the slender stems, up to 5 ft (1·5 m) high, are topped with shorter spikes of a deep rosy red, between early July and September. All are fully worthy of border cultivation where there is summer moisture for the tough fibrous roots, and none requires staking. *S. sitchense* is almost too good to cut, being a fine plant from early spring until autumn. Division in spring will need a hefty, sharp knife. Sanguisorba has suffered a change of genus, once being classed under poterium, and I still cling to the old name in my own garden with an affectionate defiance, though for the sake of readers I have given the latest name preference here.

Santolina (Cotton Lavender) *Compositae*

Santolina chamaecyparissus 'Nana' (or *S. c. corsica*) relishes the same spartan conditions as ruta, but whereas the herb-of-grace has, for me an unpleasant pungency this has pleasantly aromatic foliage. *S. c.* 'Nana' grows to just over 1 ft (30 cm) to form a compact evergreen bush reminiscent of a dwarf conifer lightly silvered all over. This is one of the finest silver-white-foliaged perennials yet raised, fully worthy of growing near the front of the sunny herbaceous border where the soil is light and sharply drained. The fibrous roots then remain compact and long-lived. Division, again, is too destructive, but stock is readily increased from trimmed cuttings taken during the growing season. Like ruta, it also bears little heads of yellow flowers, but they are more button-like and golden and come during July and August. Cut flowers look and last well in small informal arrangements, and the foliage forms a fine and valuable contrast to a wide range of subjects. Some growers still list this little cotton lavender as *S. incana* 'Nana', but while this is more mellifluous the botanists' change is more apt, and more commendable, in its description of this diminutive plant as the false cypress.

Saxifraga (Saxifrage, London Pride)   *Saxifragaceae*
Saxifraga is a very large genus too often overlooked by the flower arranger. The selection here is brief yet it gives a choice of perennials with flowering stems from 4–12 in (10–30 cm) or more, and plants suitable for both sunny and shady sites. All are of easy cultivation when grown in the conditions indicated.

   The following saxifrages are for spring planting in well drained, gritty soils in the full eye of the sun. A little lime or chalk in the soil is particularly favoured by *S. aizoon*. In such a soil it will produce small rosettes of finely toothed, narrow leaves that become so encrusted with excrescences of lime as to appear silver. From the centre of these attractive and lowly small rosettes the slender wiry stems rise to a somewhat incongruous height of 1 ft (30 cm) to bear small clusters of little open white blooms in late spring. *S. a.* 'Rosea' is more pink than rose and *S. a.* 'Lutea' is an attractive pale yellow. The hybrid *S.* × 'Kathleen Pinsent' is a very fine plant bearing graceful sprays of clear pink flowers on 1-ft (30-cm) stems above small rosettes. Another excellent hybrid flowering in the late spring is the distinctive *S.* 'Southside Seedling', which gives a mass of little pink-spotted white blooms on branching stems over fine rosettes. Plants attain a height of just over 1 ft (30 cm). All are fully hardy and reliably perennial where the drainage is good.

   Leaving the Encrusted section we turn to a trio of shade dwellers. The finest of these is *S. fortunei*. This grows well in a light soil bulked up with peat and grit, and in a site sheltered from the worst frosts. The leaves are red beneath and very attractive from spring to autumn. In September and October the 1-ft (30-cm) stems bear spikes of white star-like blooms in graceful profusion. Plants require a nice balance of good drainage and adequate moisture. *S.* × *urbium* is the true London pride, giving an airy shower of tiny pink and white speckled blooms of 1-ft (30-cm) stems between April and June. This is a valuable and charming plant for moist shade giving a wealth of dainty cut flowers. The little Mossy hybrids form the third part of the trio and, with their bright evergreen mats of mossy foliage, revel in moist shade or sun. Flowering is profuse and prolonged between March and June, giving simple little flowers in shades of red, rose and pink on stems from 4–7 in (10–17·5 cm). The red 'Triumph', the carmine 'Carnival' and the pink 'Winston Churchill' are only three of the cultivars that give fine cut flowers for little table bowls. These are of the easiest cultivation, and delightful in wide crevices in paving.

Scabiosa (Scabious, Pincushion Flower) *Dipsacaceae*

Scabiosa caucasica remains one of the most popular cut flower perennials. Vast numbers of these are sold each year, a fact attributable more to faulty plantings than to any increase in popularity. Scabious is a plant that requires attention to its cultivation if longevity and quality of bloom are to be given priority. It should be planted in spring in a light soil bearing lime. Plantings in autumn and in the heavier loams are fraught with serious risks. Late April sees the emergence of strong new growth, and this remains the best time to plant these fibrous-rooted perennials. A deeply worked soil with good drainage and a sunny aspect are also fundamental requirements for success. An initial purchase of young stock from a reputable grower is a good beginning, whereas the division of old plants whose roots have become woody is never propitious. Division of established stock should also always be done in spring and calls for a total rejection of all except the outermost parts bearing fibrous roots. These small pieces should be firmly planted and nurtured in a sandy soil and kept moist until they are ready for transplanting in mid-summer to crop the following year. Plants are best kept vigorous and floriferous by

Scabiosa

division every second or third year, backed up by the annual
raising of a few young plants to make good any losses sustained
from plantings in less favourable soils.

Flowering extends from late June until the end of September,
and regular cutting of the stems, a few at a time, is good for the
roots. This continuous cutting obviates the need for any dead-
heading, and this in turn greatly prolongs the flowering season.

Some growers plant scabious closely, later taking out every other
plant to raise new stock, while others use a much wider spacing of
1½–2 ft (45–60 cm). Gross feeding with rich manures is best
avoided altogether, but bonemeal or some other form of potash is
helpful if incorporated into the prepared ground some months

prior to planting. The deeply probing roots resent disturbance and call for correct siting at the outset.

It is wise to take sound local advice in selecting cultivars if one is contemplating growing any quantity. Among the most popular the deep blue 'Clive Greaves', the light blue 'Moonstone' and the white 'Miss Willmott' all grow to about 30 in (75 cm). Early morning cutting of blooms just fully open gives the best vase subjects. Plants are suitable for either border or kitchen garden cultivation.

Schizostylis (Kaffir Lily) *Iridaceae*

Schizostylis, with its bright red blooms, very like the more dwarf forms of gladiolus, is a most valuable plant. More bulbous than rhizomatous, the fibrous roots require a deeply worked soil where the drainage is good. These, however, are not plants for dry, light soils, though with a liberal incorporation of grit and peat these will give good results. Schizostylis is best planted in spring but, as plants take a season or two to settle down, autumn plantings may be undertaken. The bulbous rhizomes are planted some 3 in (7·5 cm) deep, and it is important to ensure the soil does not dry out in summer.

Schizostylis coccinea has 20-in (50-cm) stems each bearing up to nearly a dozen brilliant scarlet, six-petalled, star-like blooms up to 2 in (5 cm) across in September and October, above and amid clumps of narrow iris-like leaves. *S. c.* 'Major' grows to a full 30 in (75 cm), and its larger vivid blooms give the flower arranger first-class material for the autumn. Both the type and its larger form are fully hardy in the south when grown in good conditions in the full sun or a little light shade. Plantings in cold sites and clay loams are seldom rewarding. *S. c.* 'Major' is probably the most vigorous and hardy of the several cultivars available and should be the first choice of those new to these perennials.

In *S.* 'Mrs Hegarty' the flowers are a beautiful pink. They have a fine satin-like substance and are borne on 20-in (50-cm) stems a few weeks later than those of the type. Both this and *S.* 'Viscountess Byng' are well worth covering with large cloches to protect the blooms from the mutilating wastage of autumn frosts. The Viscountess in particular is certainly worth cultivating for her fine silvery pink blooms of great substance. By cloching, her charms may be preserved from the sharper winter frosts, and by this means it is possible to cut schizostylis from September until well after Christmas. *S.* 'Viscountess Byng', the last to flower, is therefore fully worthy of a warm and sheltered site and a roomy tent of double polythene sheeting erected in autumn.

As with many late-flowering plants, hardiness is enhanced by letting established clumps remain undisturbed for as long as possible, and those from spring plantings have the edge here, especially if the ensuing summer is wet. Spring is also the best time to lift and divide. Plants may be raised in large pots on a sunny terrace or in a cold conservatory.

Sedum   *Crassulaceae*

Sedum spectabile, with its handsome succulent leaves, jade-green and compact in early spring, rounding out in summer, and by autumn forming a fine mound up to 18 in (45 cm) high, is set with large heads or plates of little pink blooms that are beloved and visited by peacocks, red admirals, and any other butterflies that have escaped the menace of chemical sprays applied by short-sighted gardeners. Plants develop a deeply probing mass of fibrous roots from a fleshy crown when planted in well worked soils. They are remarkably adaptable to many soils where the drainage is good, and are valuable plants for poor, stony soils in full sun or a little shade. A little lime deters the slug, and some potash improves the colour of the blooms of these very hardy and long-lived perennials. Mature plants may be divided in spring or, more easily, new stock can be raised from cuttings. *S. s.* 'Brilliant' is a bright deep rose, while the hybrid 'Autumn Joy' is first rose-salmon before becoming bronzed. These September- and October-flowering plants give a wealth of heads on short stems. They may be cut at will and used with telling effect in table bowls, though vases tend to make the flower heads look strangely clumsy.

Senecio (Ragwort)   *Compositae*

Senecio doronicum is a ragwort of easy growth in sun or partial shade. While no claims are made that this is among the best of hardy perennials, the plant is very generous with its growth of deep green leaves and showers of bright orange-gold rayed flowers on 1-ft (30-cm) stems throughout May and June. The cultivar *S. d.* 'Sunburst' is now the only form commonly offered. Well grown in a kitchen garden this gives an incredible profusion of stems growing to just over 1 ft (30 cm) and bearing quite large open-rayed golden blooms with deeper central disks above a wealth of dark green narrow leaves. Plants are best grown in a well worked soil to facilitate winter drainage, though the soil must not be allowed to dry out in summer.

Senecio tanguticus is the giant Chinese ragwort growing to an imposing 6 ft (1·8 m) in moist soils. The stems are topped by fine spikes of small, star-like yellow blooms above attractive, deeply cut foliage in September, while the heads of fluffy seeds remain as a secondary attraction on uncut stems. The spreading roots are best curbed in the kitchen garden rather than in the herbaceous border.

Both plants are propagated by division in spring. The cut flowers should be given an immediate and deep drink before setting in an informal arrangement.

Sidalcea (Greek Mallow)   *Malvaceae*

Sidalcea is a fine hybrid of the generous mallow family. It is a sun loving perennial that makes a fine contribution to the border where the soil has been deeply worked and contains some humus. Here the partly fleshy and partly fibrous roots may probe deeply to give a good anchor for the wealth of stems, leaves and flowers above. In some of the taller cultivars the sheer weight of the growth may require some early support in the form of stout pea-sticks, especially after a shower of rain, but generally these delightful Greek mallows require no staking whatever.

In the 5-ft (1·5-m) range the old 'Rose Queen' bears long spikes of clear rose blooms. The growth is bushy and robust. More desirable is the 'Rev. Page Roberts' with his more open habit, finely cut leaves, and sturdy stems with very fine shell-pink salvers running up the spikes. Neither of these 5-footers (1·5 m) requires staking, but the 4-ft (1·2-m) 'Wensleydale' sometimes does require support for its very compact and bolt upright slender stems. These are beautifully clothed with two types of leaves, some rounded and others so deeply lobed as to resemble Maltese crosses. The spikes are densely packed with rosy red blooms of goodly size. 'William Smith' is a very fine 3-footer (90 cm) with a profusion of salmon-red blooms, and the 30-in (75-cm) 'Loveliness' is altogether charming with its abundance of soft shell-pink flowers and very graceful habit.

The flowering of these sidalceas often verges on the incredible between late June and September. It is a good and sound practice to cut plants well back very soon after flowering to promote root vigour. This small service enables one to claim full hardiness and longevity for these perennials. Winter wetness is the main enemy, readily countered by good soil drainage. The cutting of stems and thinning out of overcrowded plants prolong the period of flowering to cover nearly three months. Plants are propagated by division or from basal cuttings taken in spring.

Sisyrinchium (Satin Flower) *Iridaceae*

Sisyrinchium striatum when not in flower may be readily mistaken for a clump of irises. From these sword-like clumps rise stems to 2 ft (60 cm) bearing spikes of fine primrose-yellow blooms. Flowering is profuse and prolonged from plants kept young, tidy and vigorous by a very simple and frequent division of the meagre fleshy and fibrous roots. By this means flowering covers many weeks from early June until the end of August. Where there is some humus this sisyrinchium will flower equally well in partial shade or sun.

Solidago (Goldenrod) *Compositae*

Solidagos were once thought of as the tall goldenrods that flowered briefly in autumn, and whose roots required an annual curbing to keep them within bounds. *S. canadensis* is one of these, but the cultivar 'Golden Wings' is worth growing for the reliability of its late flowers. The hybrid *S.* 'Ballardii' grows 1 ft (30 cm) taller, to 6 ft (1·8 m), and in September this is an imposing sight with its sturdy stems bearing fine spikes of blooms.

The late E. Walkden devoted much of his life to improving the solidago as a garden-worthy plant, and succeeded gloriously in his aim by producing a number of exceptionally fine plants with well behaved roots and attractive foliage and habit of flowering. More recently some fine German-raised hybrids have been introduced. Thus we may now choose plants ranging from as little as 1 ft (30 cm) right up to the giant *S.* 'Ballardii'.

The very erect and attractively golden-leaved 'Golden Gate', together with the desirable 'Golden Shower' and 'Golden Falls', make a fine trio in the 30-in (75-cm) range for the August to October period. The 3-ft (90-cm) 'Goldenmosa', with its mimosa-like blooms, and the beautiful 2-ft (60-cm) 'Crown of Rays', bearing its golden spikes horizontally, are also very fine garden plants. Smaller still, at 18 in (45 cm), the strongly growing 'Cloth of Gold' is admirable in September. The 27-in (67·5-cm) 'Lemore' is another very good plant, bearing masses of primrose-yellow blooms in early autumn. Of the most dwarf kind the 1-ft (30-cm) 'Golden Thumb' (or 'Queenie') is very neat and reliable with its bright yellow flowers.

Most of these are worthy of inclusion in the border, but the older and more robust forms are better raised in the kitchen garden. Plants grow well in most soils, but humus is always relished by the fibrous roots, which can be divided in spring. Solidagos are best cut as soon as the plants colour up.

Solidaster   *Compositae*

Solidaster luteus is a hybrid which has an aster as one parent and a
solidago as the other. Established plants grow easily to give
narrow-leaved bushes up to 2 ft (60 cm) high bearing showers of
bright yellow, small Michaelmas daisies between August and
October. Young plants, and those in too rich soils, tend to be un-
desirably lax in habit, but solidaster has been popular as a cut
flower perennial for the last fifty years. This incredibly prolific
plant is readily divided in spring, and while plants relish the full
sun partial shade is well tolerated as long as the soil is not too dry.
A few plants of this are always worth growing if only to counter the
predominance of red and pink Michaelmas daisies. Cut when the
blooms are just opening, it lasts very well in vases.

Stachys (Lamb's-tongue, Donkey's-ear, Sow's-ear)

Labiatae

Stachys lanata (or *S. olympica*) has such silky soft leaves as to be
affectionately known to some as Lambs'-tongues or Donkeys'-
ears, while the more down-to-earth think of Sows'-ears. The roots
are partly fleshy and partly fibrous, and it is essential that these be
planted in sharply drained, even gritty soil. This is not a plant for
clay-bound gardens or wet districts—remarks that apply to nearly
all perennials with soft or silvery foliage. *S. lanata* tolerates some
shade, but plants are better in the full sun. The growth is spreading
to form a silver-grey carpet of woolly or felty leaves that are best
mulched about with grit to prevent spoiling by rain-splashed soil.
In light, dry soils *S. lanata* is of the easiest cultivation. In such a
soil it will throw up a profusion of silver-white stems topped with
pokers of lilac-pink flowers through which some diminutive leaves
curiously peer. Well kept groups of stachys look very attractive
and make fine foils to darker subjects. A simple lifting and dividing
of the plants should be undertaken in late spring every other year.
By this means one may often have spikes of flowers from mid-June
to late August, and both these and the leaves give the flower
arranger some softly attractive material.

Stachys

Stokesia (Stokes' Aster) *Compositae*

Stokesia laevis 'Blue Star' is still not widely grown and is seldom seen in floral arrangements, yet it is a first-class hardy perennial giving attractive and long-lasting cut flowers over nearly four months of the season. The deeply probing roots are both fleshy and fibrous and somewhat fragile. They must have a deep and sharply drained soil. Where this is not assured winter losses are to be expected. Thus stokesia is better in light soils, and while plants tolerate partial shade they are more content in the full sun. The leaves are deep green, long and narrow, forming an evergreen rosette. Stems grow to about 15 in (37·5 cm) to bear clusters of large blue cornflowers similar to, but finer than, those of the better known *Centaurea montana*. Flowering is prolonged between July and late October, but cutting the short stems sometimes means sacrificing some buds as the blooms do not all open at the same time. Nevertheless, these are finely chiselled and gloriously blue subjects for the vase, and plants are sufficiently choice to grace the herbaceous border for many troublefree years. Spring division calls for some surgical skill, but plants may be raised from seed, even though this may well give variations in colours calling for a later culling.

Tellima   *Saxifragaceae*

Tellima grandiflora's fibrous roots are fully hardy and perennial in a wide range of soils in shade or sun. Such an adaptable plant is valuable as it is also attractive of leaf, habit and flower. *T. grandiflora* forms a clump of rounded, golden-green leaves that are attractive for most of the year, in autumn taking on beautiful hues of orange and red. The slender red flowering stems rise gracefully to some 21 in (52·5 cm), the leaves ascending to halfway. The top 9 in (22·5 cm) of the stems are hung, on one side only, with little pendant, light green bell-flowers in early May. The blooms turn to pink as they mature, and flowering extends well into June. Cut flowers should have the bases of the stems slit and should be given an immediate and deep drink. *T. grandiflora* is a delightful vase subject, and a fine plant for poorish soils in the shade, yet it is curiously neglected or unknown to many flower arrangers and gardeners alike. Division is elementary in autumn.

Thalictrum (Meadow Rue)   *Ranunculaceae*

Thalictrum dipterocarpum is a species containing a trio of beauties that are fine garden plants and give the flower arranger some distinctive and dainty subjects. *T. dipterocarpum* itself is a very fine perennial, with its handsome ferny foliage and delicate haze of much branched stems up to 5 ft (1·5 m) bearing showers of mauve blooms centred with prominent anthers for many weeks between July and early September. *T. d.* 'Album', with its sprays of white airy blooms borne up to about 3½ ft (105 cm), is a beautiful sight for several weeks in July and August, and gives a wealth of very good cut flowers for the house. Both plants grow well in good border soil bearing sufficient humus to retain ample summer moisture. A few pea-sticks should be used early to give the plants some light support.

In *T. d.* 'Hewitt's Double' the brittle fleshy roots radiate from a small central crown in a manner very similar to eremurus. Planted several inches deep on a saddle, these must have a deeply worked, well nourished and humus-laden soil if one expects a new root system to form above the old. The purple shoots appear tardily in late spring, and a slender pea-stick should then be firmly inserted a few inches away. Plants grow rapidly in June, the much branched stems embracing and hiding the stick in a delicate wealth of beautiful foliage and clouds of tiny, but fully double mauve flowers between July and mid-September. This is a superb 5-footer (1·5 m) for a little shade.

Tiarella (Foam Flower) *Saxifragaceae*

Tiarella also has a trio of shade dwellers that revel in light soils retaining some moisture, and these, too, have attractive leaves and delicately charming flowers.

Tiarella cordifolia has such an abundance of blooms between May and July as to be commonly known as the foam flower. The fibrous roots are remarkably adaptable to a wide range of soils, as long as these are not too dry in summer, and plants seem most content in shade rather than sun. The leaves of all three are maple-like, and those of *T. cordifolia* are tinged with bronze. The wiry stems rise in profusion to a little under 1 ft (30 cm), bearing spikes of densely crowded little fluffy white flowers. In rich soils plants steadily expand to make division of the fibrous roots a simple task. This is best undertaken after flowering. *T. polyphylla* is similar, but the spikes of white starry flowers are flushed with light pink above light green leaves.

Tiarella wherryi is the star of the trio, a delightful hardy perennial for the front of the border where there is some shade. The leaves are the most beautiful golden-green from spring onwards, until autumn adds its hues of buff and gold, orange and red. The perfectly proportioned stems rise to 9 in (22·5 cm), and these are topped with delicate spikes of starry white blooms very lightly touched within with pink. In moist soils flowering often extends from earliest May until September, while plants remain more compact than those of *T. cordifolia* and *T. polyphylla*. These two may be divided after two or three years, yet one may have to wait twice as long before *T. wherryi* has produced sufficient growth to justify such propagation. Plants thrive in peaty and leafmould-rich soils.

All these little perennials give the flower arranger charming subjects, with most material being given by the more vigorous *T. cordifolia*.

Tolmiea (Pickaback Plant)   *Saxifragaceae*

Tolmiea menziesii is related to tiarella, as is evident from the leaves. This, too, has fibrous and adaptable roots, but it lacks the choiceness that makes tiarella such a good border plant. Nevertheless, this is a useful plant for poor soils in shade, and an unusual subject for the flower arranger. The leaves carry their young in such a manner as to make this known as the pickaback plant. The flowering stems rise to nearly 2 ft (60 cm) to bear loose spikes of greenish purple, tiny tubular flowers between April and June. Both the leaves and the flower spikes make surprisingly attractive floral arrangements. Plants are of the easiest growth and readily divide after flowering.

Tradescantia (Spiderwort, Trinity Flower, Moses-in-the-Bullrushes)   *Commelinaceae*

Tradescantia × *andersoniana* will grow and flower well in sun or partial shade where the fleshy and fibrous roots have access to some summer moisture. The attractive clumps of rushy leaves suggest moisture, and where this is assured plants will flower right through the summer from June until September. Height varies between 2 and 3 ft (60 and 90 cm) according to soil and moisture. The flowers are borne in clusters amid the light green leaves, and flowering is very profuse in July and August. Well grown plants have blooms of fine substance. The three-petalled satiny blooms with their golden stamens are known as Trinity flowers or Moses-in-the-bullrushes.

Tradescantia 'Caerulea' is a bright blue, and double in 'Caerulea Plena'. 'James Stratton' is a beautiful rosy blue, whereas the larger-flowered 'J. C. Weguelin' is azure. 'Purple Dome', too, has large blooms of fine substance and 'Iris Prichard' is a good rosy mauve. 'Rubra' has smaller deep rosy red blooms, but is very reliable and free-flowering, and 'Osprey' has large white blooms with fluffy blue centres. All these give delightful cut flowers, especially as some leaves sheathe the flowering stems. The time to cut is when one or two blooms of a cluster are just open, as those in bud open well in a vase. Propagation is by division in autumn every third year.

Trollius (Globe Flower) *Ranunculaceae*

Trollius cultorum embraces a number of hybrid globe flowers, and these are the gold of the early summer garden. Trollius is a sun lover and grows well in most soils so long as these are kept just moist throughout the summer. Plantings on dry, light soils should not be entertained. The best plants are those grown in well fed, humus-rich loams, and here the plants' response more than compensates for any initial work with the spade. Not only are plants then extremely generous in May and June, but the long stems and large colourful blooms make these very good cut flower perennials. They also have attractively glossy leaves. The time to cut is when the buds are coloured, but before they are fully open. The cut flowers may also be dried if they are cut while the buds are still tight, and the leaves removed, before being hung up to dry slowly in an airy and darkened outhouse.

Trollius 'Earliest of All' begins flowering in late April, with its lemon-yellow blooms on 18-in (45-cm) stems, closely followed by the splendid 30-in (75 cm) 'Orange Princess', then by the 30-in (75-cm) bright yellow 'Goldquelle'. All three give excellent cut flowers, and cutting back in late June will induce a late second crop.

Trollius

Verbascum (Mullein)   *Scrophulariaceae*

Verbascum is a sun lover with both fleshy and fibrous roots which probe profoundly to provide an anchor for its beautiful summer spires. Deeply worked, free-draining soils are essential to its longevity, and winter wetness rather than cold is its chief enemy. A little lime in the soil is relished, and heavy loams must be thoroughly lightened. These remarks apply to the hardy and perennial forms we may consider here. The common and splendid great mullein is, alas, beyond my brief in this book. In my search for a perennial counterpart *V. vernale* (or *chaixii*) now takes pride of place in the garden. I grow this in a clay loam improved with grit, and plants grow strongly erect to a full 5 ft (1·5 m) unaided. The evergreen rosette of huge green spear leaves attractively balances the spires of purple-centred blooms that stand out like buttery beacons in the garden between July and September. The principal spires remain uncut, but the smaller secondary spikes will grace a large vase for well over a week, if the cutting is timely and the stems are first quickly plunged into deep water overnight. So profuse is the flowering that such cutting is barely noticeable in the garden.

The 3½-ft (105-cm) pale bronze and lilac 'Cotswold Beauty', the 3-ft (90-cm) 'Pink Domino', and the biscuit-yellow and plum *V. hartleyi* may all be similarly used for cut flowers. These demand sharp drainage and sun, and propagation is by root cuttings taken in spring.

The Phoeniceum Hybrids are probably the best verbascums to grow for cut flowers. They are lighter and more graceful subjects growing from 2½-3 ft (75-90 cm). As with the genus generally, they are readily (and best) raised from seed. They flower in their second year to give fine spikes of red, pink, lilac, purple and occasionally white blooms. Cut when a few of the lower blooms are open these make charming subjects for floral displays. Full sun and deep, light soil suit these dwarfs best. Flowering is profuse and covers many weeks between late June and the end of August.

Vernonia   *Compositae*

Vernonia crinita is a valuable plant for its late flowers and trouble-free habit. The fibrous roots are content in most good loams and remain remarkably compact, fully hardy and perennial. The leafy stems grow strongly erect to nearly 6 ft (1·8 m) and staking is seldom necessary. The fluffy purple flowers are individually small but borne in clustered heads between September and November. Short stems of these give the arranger some precious late blooms just before the scything frosts of winter arrive.

Veronica   *Scrophulariaceae*

Veronica, in the five species considered here, gives very good cut flowers if the cutting is timely on all counts. Cut when in full bloom, or in the sun, these veronicas are of little value as vase subjects. With one exception, they hold their blooms in slender spires. Cut in the cool of the evening, when the bases of the spires only are in bloom, and given an immediate long, deep drink, they last very well in a vase. The fibrous roots of these perennials are content in most well worked soils in sun or a little shade.

The tallest is *V. virginica* 'Alba', whose roots are best in good loams rather than in thin soils lacking humus. The slender stems, bearing fine whorls of narrow leaves, rise erectly to 5 ft (1·5 m) and gracefully scorn the need for any support. In late July they bear the most slender of spires of white blooms. Flowering continues until September with a rare grace. This is one of the very finest of tall plants for the herbaceous border, remaining compact, fully hardy, long-lived and full of garden merit.

Veronica exaltata is more bushy, yet this too has slenderly upright leafy stems rising to a full 4 ft (1·2 m). The roots here are more finely fibrous and best in soils bearing some humus. Too rich soils and close plantings tend to produce an undesirable laxity of habit, but where content this is another very fine plant, giving a wealth of blue spires between early July and September. Timely cut flowers have a very long vase life. Shorter by at least a foot (30 cm) is *V. longifolia*. This also has blue spires and is best where not crowded in by other plants. The blooms are deeper than those of *V. exaltata* but equally good in a vase.

Veronica spicata is the shortest of the blue-spired forms. The fibrous roots expand steadily to give a mat of leaves from which rise graceful 15-in (37·5-cm) stems. Flowering is profuse in lighter soils with a little humus, and covers many weeks between June and late August. It is easy to grow and very rewarding at the front of the border. Cut flowers have a long vase life.

Lastly, *V. gentianoides* is valuable for its flower spikes of May and June. From mats of glossy green leaves rise stems to about 18 in (45 cm) bearing beautiful light blue blooms larger than those of the other species mentioned. *V. g.* 'Nana' is half the height and very charming and easy. Both give the flower arranger some delightful subjects. Plants relish humus-rich soils. All these valuable hardy perennials are richly rewarding to both gardener and flower arranger, especially the tallest pair. Plants are readily propagated by division.

Vinca (Periwinkle)   *Apocynaceae*

Vinca major and *V. minor* have several cultivars valuable for their simple blooms and attractive evergreen leaves. The periwinkles are useful trailing perennials to grace inhospitable places such as beneath trees and hedges and sites in heavy shade. *V. major* is a rampager with self-rooting prostrate stems capable of scrambling over old tree stumps, and bearing showers of quite large mauve flowers amid and over the dark green leathery leaves between mid-April and September. The variegated form, with its cream-splashed leaves, is not so vigorous, and is a more garden-worthy plant.

Vinca minor is rightly much shorter at 6 in (15 cm), and although vigorous of growth it is never troublesome where aptly planted. In mild springs it will often bear its first charming open bright blue flowers in early March, and flower intermittently throughout the summer. 'Bowles' Variety', with its larger sky-blue flowers, is especially commendable for its comparatively compact growth. 'Atropurpurea' has pretty purple blooms between July and September. In 'Aureo-variegata' the leaves are blotched with gold, which shows up the blue blooms to advantage, whereas in 'Aureo-variegata Alba' the mottled leaves tend to detract from the tender white flowers.

All these are fine plants for shade, even heavy shade. Vinca is best planted out from pot-grown stock, the fine fibrous roots being kept just moist until establishment is certain. Stems bearing leaves and flowers make charming subjects for arrangements in bowls and dishes.

Viola (Violet)   *Violaceae*

Viola odorata is the sweet violet, parent of many of the florists' strains of violets. This viola is best grown in cool shade where the medium to heavy loam has been improved with a deep incorporation of sharp sand and liberal quantities of leafmould or peat and well rotted farmyard manure. Humus is vital, as is the assurance of a free circulation of clean air about the plants. Dry soil and

Viola

lack of air greatly increase the risk of incurring the unwelcome
attentions of the red spider, and in such situations flowering will
be brief and meagre. In a moist site sheltered from frost and rattling
winds, *V. odorata* will begin flowering in February and continue
with a flourish into May, bearing its blooms on stems up to 6 in
(15 cm) high. Flowering on a much lesser scale occurs intermittently throughout the summer, and autumn sees a brief re-
newed flush of blooms. These late blooms are curious in that they
are smaller and never open. It is these autumn flowers which bear
most seed. Plants raised from seed will give a proportion bearing
blue, purple and plum-red blooms, and occasionally a few with
flowers of soft yellow or even white.

The spreading fleshy-rooted runners are readily divided to increase stocks so long as pieces bearing two or three good crowns
are selected. These are planted with the crowns just proud of the
soil and watered in. Firm planting 1 ft (30 cm) apart in March or
April will produce a crop of blooms the following season.

The evergreen leaves of *V. odorata* are lightly green and roundly
heart-shaped, and the violets nestle amid and above these in a

sweetly fragrant carpet. Violas should be grown in generous patches of well prepared ground, then their scent will be most readily appreciated by those who pass by. *V. o. praecox* will flower from autumn through to the spring. These very valuable little flowers are well worth cloching in September to protect them against damaging rains and frosts. *V. o.* 'Czar' has been widely popular with growers of cut flower perennials for over a century. The very large single blue flowers are sweetly fragrant and borne on good long stems of 6 or 7 in (15 or 17·5 cm). The richly blue 6-in (15-cm) 'Princess of Wales' is another old favourite, which gives very good crops of large and fragrant cut blooms for the house. 'Governor Herrick' has very fine ruby-purple flowers between March and May, with stems up to 8 or 9 in (20 or 22·5 cm) long. Although these have no fragrance the plants are notably resistant to the red spider, and give the arranger a wealth of cut flowers that are among the best of the genus. *V. o.* 'Sulphurea' retains the parental fragrance in its soft yellow blooms, borne on 6-in (15-cm) stems, and this is decidedly useful and attractive for a mixed table bowl of violets.

Among the double-flowered forms of violet, 'Marie Louise' is generous with her scented mauve blooms, as is the paler and perfumed 'Duchesse de Parma', and the double white 'Comte de Brazza'.

Violas are fleeting little beauties to be cut in the cool of the evening or in the morning when wet with dew. Their vase life may be eked out by dipping the bunches directly head down into a large bowl of water and allowing them a long soak before setting. A fine mist spray of water is also appreciated by those in a vase.

Those who have grown lilies-of-the-valley will find these violas flourish in the same conditions of soil and partial shade.

Alphabetical List of Selected Hardy Perennial Grasses

These are of value to both gardener and flower arranger for the same vital purpose. Used with discretion, these ornamental and hardy grasses afford a fine relief to bushy and round-leaved subjects. While round-leaved subjects and spire plants effectively counter the bushier subjects, so these narrow-leaved grasses, with their graceful habit, add a telling influence both in the garden and in a vase of mixed subjects. Most of these grasses are herbaceous in habit, but a few that retain their leaves through the winter have been specially included for their obvious value during a time of natural shortage. The selection includes a range of height, habit and flower, some for sun and others for partial shade, for soils varying from light loam to heavy mud. Some are rapid growers while others may remain undisturbed for a number of years following an apt planting. Propagation is by division in spring, and this is generally also the most favourable planting season.

Avena candida, now horribly renamed *Helictotrichon semper-virens*, produces attractive clumps of narrow glaucous leaves which persist throughout the winter. The large flower sprays are borne on arching stems in early summer to about the 2-ft (60-cm) mark in good border soil and sun. They should be removed when flowering finishes.

Carex pendula and *C. stricta* 'Aurea' are fine sedges for moist soil in sun or a little shade. The 3-ft (90-cm) *C. pendula* is striking for its splendid arching stems of pendulous green flower spikes out of a wealth of narrow leaves in May and June. *C. stricta* 'Aurea' is more dwarf at just 2 ft (60 cm), with beautiful narrow golden leaves finely edged in light green, and fluffy little spikes of brown pokers. This is a beautiful golden sedge for moist shade, a memorable neighbour to the blue-leaved *Hosta sieboldiana*.

Cortaderia selloana (syn *C. argentea*) is the well known pampas grass, whose silvery plumes towering above a mass of arching leaves to a height of 6–8 ft (1·84–2·4 m) look best in the splendid isolation of a lawn. It is best established from pot-grown stock and planted in well drained soil open to the sun. Spring planting is to be favoured for this giant grass, and new stock is raised from seed rather than from divisions.

Festuca glauca forms a delightful hummock of densely crowded, very narrow blue leaves from which a shower of graceful golden flower spikes rise to just under 1 ft (30 cm) in early summer. These are better removed from the plant and used in a vase to leave the hummock compact and blue for the rest of the summer. The blue grass is very useful and attractive at the front of the herbaceous border, or used as an edging to paths where the soil is well drained but not too rich, either in sun or a little shade. A rather spartan diet aids compactness and intensifies the blueness of the leaves.

Glyceria maxima 'Variegata' is best grown in mud, and the advent of polythene sheeting makes this a simple undertaking. Here it will reach up to 5 ft (1·5 m) with arching, narrow striped leaves, pink in spring and turning golden and green through the summer, when its pendulous sprays of golden-bronze flowers emerge. This is a rampant plant in mud but easily confined in a lined trench or hole. In summer-moist garden soil the height is reduced to 3 ft (90 cm). Glyceria will flower equally well in full sun or quite heavy shade as long as there is ample moisture for the roots.

Lasiogrostis splendens is a good-natured grass with green leaves and 3-ft (10-cm) wiry stems bearing large pendant plumes of attractive creamy flowers which come between June and August. These are valuable to flower arrangers, while the gardener will be pleased to know that this grass has compact roots which readily divide in the spring.

Miscanthus sinensis has several very striking and garden-worthy cultivars. *M. s.* 'Variegata' is exceptionally fine and graceful to 4 ft (1·2 m). Its finely striped narrow leaves are very upright but gracefully arched at the tips. For flowers one must turn to *M. s.* 'Silver Fern' with its wealth of silvery plumes emerging from their brown-purple buds. This grows to an imposing 6 ft (1·8 m) and is valuable for its late flowers, which come in September and October. *M. s.* 'Zebrinus' is also capable of growing to 6 ft (1·8 m), but this is more remarkable for its leaves, which bear horizontal bands of gold. All three should be planted in spring in good border soils where they may remain for years to be troublefree and distinctive perennials.

Molinia altissima grows erectly to a little over 3 ft (90 cm) to bear fine plumes of flowers, but the leaves of autumn are even more attractive and valuable for their many buff hues. *M. caerulea* 'Variegata' is doubly valuable, having equally attractive flowers and leaves. This is a neat and delightful grass in good summer-moist soils. It grows to just 18 in (45 cm) amd responds best to a spring planting. The slender smoky-purple flower spikes appear between mid-August and October. Both forms grow well in sun or a little shade.

Pennisetum orientale is very attractive between July and September with its generous and dainty array of feathery spikes of pale purple borne on stems growing to just over 1 ft (30 cm). These make excellent vase subjects. *P. alopecuroides* is much more robust, growing to a good 3 ft (90 cm) and bearing its feathery 6-in (15-cm) purple pokers above bright green leaves a few weeks later. Both species flower reliably in partial shade or full sun.

Phalaris arundinacea 'Picta' is the well known, and often much regretted, but very attractive gardener's garters, growing to a full 3 ft (90 cm) or more. In rich summer-moist soils this is a terrible rampager, growing to an impressive 4½ ft (1·3 m), and even in poor soils the roots invade steadily. The gold and green striped narrow leaves are just as attractive as those of that other rampager, glyceria. This is best grown in a confined area in the kitchen garden, where an annual inspection and spading of its fleshy and fibrous roots may be thoroughly carried out with a minimum of disturbance to other plants.

Phleum phleiodes, much better behaved and 18 in (45 cm) high, gives neat tufts of leaves and a reliable show of small flowering pokers over many weeks between July and September, whether planted in sun or a little shade.

Stipa gives a trio of attractive and useful grasses. *S. calamagrostis*, with its arching plumes of July and August, grows erectly to 3 ft (90 cm), as does the evergreen *S. gigantea*, which gives golden showers of feathery spikes. The more dwarf *S. pennata* is more erect of habit and bears large feather grass plumes that are most valuable to the flower arranger between June and August. All three make excellent vase subjects.

G

Selective Lists of Perennials for Cutting

In the Border: In Allotments and Kitchen Gardens: In Raised Beds and Tubs in Courtyards and Patios: Raised from Seed: In Heavy Soils: In Light Soils: For Shady Positions: With Yellow and Gold Flowers: With Pink, Red and Orange Flowers: With Blue and Purple Flowers: With White, Cream and Green Flowers: With a Long Flowering Season: With Early (E) or Late (L) Flowers: With Fragrant or Aromatic (A) Flowers: With Fine Foliage: With Long-lasting Cut Flowers: For Drying: For Small Bowls and very Small Vases: Cut Flowers that are Good Travellers.

In the Border

Achillea filipendulina
Aconitum
Agapanthus
Alchemilla mollis
Allium
Anaphalis
Anthericum liliago
Armeria maritima
Artemisia lactiflora
Aruncus
Asphodelus
Aster amellus and hybrids
A. novi-belgii, dwarf forms
Astilbe
Astrantia

Bergenia
Brunnera macrophylla

Campanula, dwarf species
C. lactiflora
C. latifolia
C. persicifolia
Catananche caerulea
Cimicifuga
Crinum × powellii
Crocosmia masonorum

Dianthus
Dicentra
Dictamnus
Dierama
Digitalis

Echinacea
Eremurus
Erigeron
Eryngium
Euphorbia

Foeniculum vulgare

Galtonia candicans
Gentiana
Geranium
Geum borisii
Gypsophila

Helenium
Helianthus
Heliopsis
Hemerocallis
Heuchera
Heucherella
Hosta

Iris

Kniphofia

Liatris
Ligularia clivorum
L. przewalskii
Limonium
Linaria 'Canon J. Went'
Lychnis
Lysimachia
Lythrum

Mimulus
Monarda

Nepeta

Origanum

Penstemon
Phlox
Platycodon
Polygonum

Sanguisorba

Santolina
Sedum 'Ruby Glow'
S. spectabile
Sidalcea
Stokesia

Tiarella

Veronica

some ferns and grasses

In Allotments and Kitchen Gardens

ALLOTMENT

Acanthus mollis
A. spinosus
Achillea ptarmica
A. filipendulina
Aconitum
Alchemilla mollis
Anemone × *hybrida*   (syn   *A. japonica*)
Anthemis tinctoria
Aster, Michaelmas daisies
A. ericoides
A. yunnanensis

Brunnera

Centaurea
Chrysanthemum maximum
C. uliginosum
Coreopsis grandiflora
Crambe

Digitalis
Doronicum

Echinops
Erigeron
Eryngium
Eupatorium

Foeniculum

Gaillardia
Galega
Geum

Gypsophila
Helenium
Helianthus
Heliopsis
Hesperis

Inula
Iris

Lathyrus
Lavatera olbia rosea
Linaria purpurea

Macleaya

Nepeta

Onopordon
Origanum majorana

Physostegia
Pyrethrum

Rudbeckia gloriosa
Ruta graveolens

Solidago

Tellima
Tolmiea menziesii

KITCHEN GARDEN

all those under allotment
and also:

Allium
Alstroemeria
Anaphalis
Aquilegia

Bellis
Bergenia

Caltha
Camassia
Campanula lactiflora
C. latifolia
Cedronella
Cheiranthus
Convallaria majalis
Crinitaria

Delphinium
Dianthus

Euphorbia

Galtonia

Lamium maculatum
Lavandula
Lupinus

Muscari

Narcissus

Paeonia
Papaver
Physalis
Polygonatum
Primula
Pulmonaria

Ranunculus

Sanguisorba
Scabiosa
Sedum spectabile
Sisyrinchium striatum

Thalictrum
Trollius
Tulipa

Vernonia crinita
Viola

ornamental grasses and selected ferns

In Raised Beds and Tubs in Courtyards and Patios

Alchemilla mollis
Allium
Anaphalis
Aquilegia
Armeria maritima
Aster, dwarf forms
Astrantia

Bellis
Bergenia

Camassia
Campanula carpatica
C. portenschlagiana
C. rotundifolia
Catananche
Convallaria

Dianthus

Euphorbia polychroma

Fritillaria meleagris

Gentiana

Helleborus
Hosta

Iris, more dwarf kinds
Ixia

Lamium maculatum
Linaria

Mimulus
Muscari

Narcissus
Nepeta

Origanum

Papaver
Physalis
Physostegia
Platycodon
Primula
Pulmonaria
Pulsatilla

Santolina
Saxifraga, Mossy hybrids
S. × urbium
Sisyrinchium

selected ferns and ornamental grasses

Raised from Seed

Alstroemeria
Aquilegia

Campanula carpatica
C. lactiflora
C. persicifolia
C. rotundifolia
Cheiranthus
Coreopsis grandiflora

Delphinium
Dianthus
Dictamnus
Digitalis

Echinacea purpurea
Eremurus

Foeniculum

Gaillardia
Galega
Gentiana septemfida
Geranium wallichianum
Geum

Hesperis

Lathyrus
Linaria
Lunaria
Lupinus
Lychnis

Meconopsis
Mimulus

Onopordon

Papaver
Primula
Pulsatilla vulgaris

Rudbeckia gloriosa

Scabiosa

In Heavy Soils

Achillea ptarmica
Alchemilla mollis
Aconitum
Artemisia lactiflora
Aster, Michaelmas daisies
Astilbe
Astrantia

Brunnera

Caltha
Camassia
Campanula lactiflora
C. latifolia
Cimicifuga

Digitalis
Doronicum

Echinops
Eupatorium

Helenium
Heliopsis
Hemerocallis
Hosta

Inula
Iris ochroleuca
I. sibirica

Ligularia
Lythrum

Macleaya

Physostegia
Polygonum
Primula
Pulmonaria

Ranunculus

Tradescantia

Trollius

grasses, e.g. Carex and Scirpus

In Light Soils

Acanthus
Agapanthus
Allium
Anaphalis
Anthemis
Armeria maritima
Aster amellus

Campanula carpatica
C. portenschlagiana
C. rotundifolia
Catananche
Cheiranthus
Coreopsis
Crocosmia

Dianthus
Dictamnus

Erigeron
Eryngium

Geum
Gypsophila

Heuchera
Heucherella

Lavandula
Lavatera
Limonium

Linaria
Lunaria

Nepeta

Origanum

Papaver
Penstemon
Phygelius
Pyrethrum

Ruta graveolens

Santolina
Scabiosa
Stachys lanata

For Shady Positions

Aconitum
Alchemilla mollis
Anaphalis
Aquilegia
Artemisia lactiflora
Astilbe
Astrantia

Bellis
Bergenia
Brunnera macrophylla

Campanula
Cimicifuga
Convallaria majalis

Dicentra
Digitalis

Gentiana
Geranium
Geum borisii

Helleborus
Hemerocallis
Heucherella
Hosta

Lamium maculatum

Macleaya
Meconopsis
Mimulus

Phlox

Polygonatum
Polygonum
Primula
Pulmonaria

Saxifraga, Mossy hybrids
S. × *urbium*

Tellima grandiflora
Thalictrum
Tiarella
Tolmiea

Viola

ferns

With Yellow and Gold Flowers

Achillea filipendulina
Adonis
Alchemilla
Allium flavum
A. moly
Anthemis
Asphodelus

Aster ericoides 'Brimstone'

Caltha
Cheiranthus 'Harpur Crewe'
Coreopsis
Crinitaria linosyris

Delphinium 'Sungleam'
D. zalil
Digitalis
Doronicum

Foeniculum vulgare

Geum 'Lady Stratheden'

Helenium
Helianthus
Heliopsis
Hemerocallis

Inula
Iris

Ligularia clivorum
L. przewalskii

Mimulus luteus

Oenothera

Primula

Ranunculus
Rudbeckia

Santolina

Sisyrinchium
Solidago

Trollius

With Red, Pink and Orange Flowers

Allium pulchellum
Alstroemeria, Ligtu Hybrids
Anemone × *hybrida* 'Queen Charlotte'
Armeria maritima
Aster
Astilbe

Bellis perennis
Bergenia

Centaurea dealbata
Crinum × *powellii*
Crocosmia masonorum

Dianthus
Dicentra
Dictamnus fraxinella (*D. albus*)
Dierama

Echinacea purpurea
Eremurus
Erigeron

Gaillardia (flame)
Geum borisii
G. 'Mrs. Bradshaw'

Helenium (flame)
Helleborus orientalis
Hemerocallis
Heuchera
Heucherella

Incarvillea
Iris

Kniphofia

Lavatera olbia rosea
Liatris
Linaria 'Canon J. Went'
Lupinus
Lychnis
Lythrum

Mimulus
Monarda

Nerine bowdenii

Origanum

Paeonia
Papaver
Penstemon
Phlox
Phygelius
Physalis (seed cases)
Physostegia 'Rose Bouquet'
Polygonum amplexicaule
Primula
Pulmonaria rubra
Pyrethrum

Sanguisorba
Saxifraga, Mossy hybrids
S. × *urbium*
Schizostylis coccinea
Sidalcea

Tradescantia

With Blue and Purple Flowers

Acanthus (bicolour)
Aconitum
Agapanthus

Allium azureum
A. cyaneum
Aquilegia (bicolour)
Aster alpinus
A. amellus
A. novi-belgii
A. yunnanensis

Brunnera macrophylla

Camassia
Campanula
Cedronella foeniculum

Delphinium

Echinacea purpurea
Echinops
Erigeron
Eryngium
Eupatorium

Galega
Gentiana
Geranium 'Johnson's Blue'
G. wallichianum

Hosta lancifolia (flowers)
H. sieboldiana (leaves)

Iris foetidissima
I. pallida
I. sibirica

Lavandula
Limonium
Linaria purpurea
Lunaria rediviva
Lupinus

Meconopsis

Monarda 'Prairie Night'
Muscari

Nepeta

Onopordon

Phlox
Platycodon
Primula
Pulmonaria angustifolia

Scabiosa caucasica
Stokesia laevis

Thalictrum dipterocarpum
Tradescantia

Veronica exaltata
V. longifolia
V. spicata
Viola

With White, Cream and Green Flowers

Achillea ptarmica
Allium pulchellum 'Album'
Anaphalis
Anemone × *hybrida*   'Louise
   Uhink'
Artemisia lactiflora
Aruncus
Aster novi-belgii and dwarfs
Astilbe
Astrantia carniolica
A. involucrata

Bellis perennis

Campanula carpatica

C. persicifolia
Chrysanthemum
Cimicifuga
Convallaria majalis
Crambe

Dianthus
Dictamnus fraxinella (*D. albus*)

Eremurus

Galtonia
Gypsophila

Helleborus niger
Heuchera

Iris

Kniphofia 'Maid of Orleans'

Lysimachia

Macleaya cordifolia

Papaver
Phlox 'Everest'
P. 'White Admiral'
Polygonatum multiflorum
Physostegia 'Summer Snow'

Tiarella

Veronica virginica 'Alba'

With a Long Flowering Season
(eight weeks or more)

Achillea filipendulina
A. ptarmica
Aconitum 'Spark's Variety'
Allium cyaneum

A. pulchellum
Anaphalis nubigena
Armeria maritima 'Vindictive'
Artemisia lactiflora
Aster amellus and related hybrids
Astilbe, e.g. 'Gertrude Brix'
Astrantia carniolica
A. involucrata

Bellis

Campanula carpatica
C. lactiflora 'Pouffe'
C. l. 'Prichard's Variety'
C. persicifolia
C. portenschlagiana
C. rotundifolia
Catananche caerulea
Cheiranthus

Dianthus allwoodii

Erigeron 'Quakeress'

Gaillardia
Gentiana septemfida
Geranium 'Johnson's Blue'
G. wallichianum
Geum

Gypsophila paniculata

Helianthus decapetalus
Hemerocallis fulva
Heuchera
Heucherella

Lavatera
Limonium latifolium
Linaria purpurea
Lythrum

Macleaya cordifolia
Mimulus
Monarda

Nepeta × *faassenii*
N. 'Six Hills'

Origanum rotundifolia
O. vulgare

Polygonum amplexicaule
Pulmonaria

Scabiosa
Sidalcea
Stokesia laevis

Thalictrum dipterocarpum 'He-
    witt's Double'
Tiarella wherryi

Veronica (especially *V. exaltata*)
Viola

With Early (E) or Late (L) Flowers

Aconitum (L)

Bellis (E and L)
Bergenia (E)
Brunnera (E)

Caltha (E)
Campanula portenschlagiana (L)
Cheiranthus (E and L)
Cimicifuga (L)
Echinacea (L)
Euphorbia polychroma (E)

Gentiana (L)

Helleborus (E and L)

Iris (E and L)

Nerine bowdenii (L)

Phlox, some (L)
Polygonum amplexicaule (L)
Primula (E)
Pulmonaria (E)

Schizostylis coccinea (L)
Sedum spectabile (L)
Solidago (L)

Tellima (leaves, E and L)
Tiarella (leaves, E and L)
Trollius (E)

Vernonia crinita (L)
Vinca (E)
Viola (E)

With Fragrant or Aromatic (A) Flowers

Achillea filipendulina (A)
Anthemis tinctoria (A)
Aquilegia pyrenaica (white
    flowers only)
Artemisia lactiflora
Asphodelus luteus

Bergenia cordifolia

Cheiranthus
Cimicifuga 'White Pearl'
Convallaria majalis
Crambe cordifolia

Dianthus
Dictamnus (A)

Foeniculum vulgare (A)

Hemerocallis dumortieri
Hesperis matronalis

Iris, Spanish
Iris, bearded, some

Lavandula
Ligularia przewalskii
Lilium, some

Melioon (A)
Mimulus luteus
Monarda

Narcissus
Nepeta (A)

Origanum (A)

Paeonia
Phlox

Reineckia carnea

Santolina (A)

Viola odorata

With Fine Foliage

Acanthus
Achillea
Aconitum
Alchemilla mollis
Anaphalis nubigena
Artemisia lactiflora
Astilbe
Astrantia

Bergenia

Brunnera macrophylla
Cimicifuga
Convallaria majalis
Crocosmia masonorum

Delphinium belladonna
Dicentra
Dictamnus

Eryngium

Foeniculum vulgare and bronze
form

Galega

Heuchera
Heucherella
Hosta

Ligularia clivorum
L. przewalskii

Monarda

Paeonia
Papaver

Polygonum amplexicaule
Pulmonaria saccharata

Ruta graveolens

Santolina
Stachys lanata

Tellima grandiflora
Thalictrum
Tiarella wherryi

grasses and ferns

With Long–lasting Cut Flowers

Achillea filipendulina
Allium
Alstroemeria
Anaphalis
Anthemis tinctoria
Artemisia lactiflora
Astrantia
Aster amellus and hybrids
A. novi-belgii

Catananche
Chrysanthemum
Cimicifuga
Convallaria
Crocosmia

Dianthus
Doronicum

Echinops
Erigeron
Eryngium

Foeniculum vulgare

Geum
Gypsophila

Heuchera
Heucherella

Macleaya cordifolia
Monarda

Nepeta
Nerine bowdenii

Origanum

Paeonia

Physostegia
Polygonum amplexicaule
Pyrethrum

Rudbeckia

Saxifraga × *urbium*
Scabiosa
Schizostylis coccinea
Sedum spectabile

some grasses

For Drying

(leaves (L), flowers (F),
seed vessels (S))

Acanthus (F)
Achillea filipendulina (F)
Agapanthus (S)
Alchemilla (F)
Allium (S)
Anaphalis (F)
Artemisia lactiflora (F)
Aster ericoides (F)
Astrantia (F)

Catananche (F)
Cedronella foeniculum (F)
Centaurea macrocephala (S)
Cimicifuga (F and S)

Dictamnus (S)

Echinops (F)
Eryngium (F)

Foeniculum vulgare (F and S)

Hosta (L)

Iris, variegated (L)
I. foetidissima (S)

Lavandula (F)
Limonium (F and S)
Lythrum (S)

Morina longifolia

Paeonia (L)
Papaver (S)
Physalis (S)
Polygonum (F)

Ruta graveolens (L)

Salvia superba (S)
Santolina (L)

Tellima (L)
Thalictrum (L)
Tolmiea (L)

Vernonia crinita (F)

grasses and ferns, together with many leaves, may be pressed

For Small Bowls and Very Small Vases

((C) = cuttings from laterals etc.)

Achillea × 'King Edward'
A. ptarmica (C)
Allium beesianum
A. cyaneum
Armeria maritima
Artemisia lactiflora (C)
Aster alpinus

Aster ericoides

Bellis 'Dresden China'
B. perennis
B. 'Rob Roy'
Brunnera (C)

Campanula carpatica
C. portenschlagiana
C. rotundifolia
Convallaria majalis
Corydalis lutea
C. ochroleuca
Crambe cordifolia (C)

Dianthus, alpine forms
Dicentra (C)

Erodium, alpine forms

Foeniculum (C)
Fritillaria

Galega (C)
Gentiana
Geranium dalmaticum
Geum borisii
Gypsophila (C)

Helleborus niger
Heuchera (C)
Heucherella (C)

Iris, miniature forms

Lamium maculatum

Narcissus juncifolius

Origanum rotundifolia

Papaver, alpine forms

Saxifraga, Mossy hybrids
Scabiosa graminifolia

Viola
Vinca

Good Travellers

(when correctly harvested,
steeped, bunched and boxed)

Achillea filipendulina
A. ptarmica
A. × 'Moonshine'
Alstroemeria
Anaphalis
Anemone × *hybrida*
Aster novi-belgii

Catananche caerulea 'Major'
Chrysanthemum maximum, e.g.
    'Everest'
C. Otley Koreans
Coreopsis grandiflora
Crocosmia masonorum

Dianthus
Doronicum

Echinacea purpurea
Echinops
Erigeron
Eryngium variifolium
E. 'Violetta'

Gaillardia grandiflora
Gypsophila paniculata

Helenium
Helianthus
Heliopsis
Heuchera

Incarvillea

Limonium latifolium

Paeonia
Physalis
Pyrethrum

Scabiosa caucasica
Schizostylis
Solidago
Stokesia laevis

Trollius

grasses and ferns generally

Some Sources of Supply

Due to space requirements, the following list of nurserymen is necessarily brief, but, to the best of the author's knowledge, it is representative of plant and seed sources throughout the country. It should be remembered that nurserymen do not necessarily include all their available plants in their catalogues or lists, and some discreet persistence will occasionally unearth a much wanted but elusive plant. Those who are determined to obtain a particular named variety should not forget the specialist societies concerned with violas, irises, delphiniums, daffodils and so on.

J. CUNNINGTON
VERULAM HARDY PLANT
  GARDENS
VERULAM ROAD
ST ALBANS
HERTS AL3 4DH

a discerning range of herbaceous and alpine subjects including some neglected species and varieties, and those raised here

GAYBORDER NURSERIES LTD
MELBOURNE
DERBYSHIRE

especially gaillardias and some lesser known border phlox

BLACKMORE & LANGDON LTD
STANTON NURSERY
PENSFORD
NR. BRISTOL

delphiniums, aquilegia and some phlox
  (mainly postal service)

BRESSINGHAM GARDENS
DISS
NORFOLK IP22 2AB

a wide range of lesser known herbaceous and alpine plants and grasses
  (postal service only)

W. CUNNINGHAM & SONS   especially lavender, solidago and
DEWDROP NURSERY   helianthus
HEACHAM   (postal service only)
NORFOLK

VAN TUBERGEN LTD   bulbous subjects, including rare
WILLOW BANK WHARF   items
RANELAGH GARDENS   (postal service only)
LONDON SW6

F. TOYNBEE LTD   a good selection of herbaceous
BARNHAM   and alpine plants
WEST SUSSEX PO22 OBH

LYE END NURSERY   a limited but valuable selection
WOKING   of herbaceous subjects, includ-
SURREY   ing those raised here

BROADLEIGH GARDENS   bulbous subjects, narcissi
BARR HOUSE   specialists
BISHOPS HULL
TAUNTON
SOMERSET

KELWAYS NURSERIES   especially irises, peonies and
LANGPORT   pyrethrums
SOMERSET TA10 9SL   (mainly postal service)

PERRY'S HARDY PLANT FARM   ferns in particular
ENFIELD
MIDDLESEX EN2 9BG

TREASURES OF TENBURY LTD   many unusual subjects, includ-
TENBURY WELLS   ing sedges (carex)
WORCESTERSHIRE

THOMAS CARLILE LTD   a wide range of herbaceous sub-
LODDON NURSERY   jects, including those raised
CARLILE'S CORNER   here
TWYFORD RG10 9PU

R. V. ROGER LTD
THE NURSERIES
PICKERING
YORKSHIRE

a fine range of herbaceous and alpine subjects

HILLIER & SONS
WEST HILL NURSERY
ROMSEY ROAD
WINCHESTER
HAMPSHIRE

a wide range of herbaceous and alpine subjects, ferns and grasses

THOMPSON & MORGAN LTD
LONDON ROAD
IPSWICH
SUFFOLK IP2 OBA

a good range of herbaceous and alpine seeds
        (postal service only)

ALLWOOD BROS.
HASSOCKS
SUSSEX

dianthus (pinks) raisers and specialists
        (postal service only)

General Index

acid soils, 27, 88
allotments, 21–2
aphids, 30
autumn planting, 68, 91, 150

Bailey, Captain F. M., 142
Benlate, 31
bindweed, eradicating, 31
Blackmore and Langdon, 90
bleach, 35
Bloom, Alan, 93, 103
boggy soils, 68, 126, 191
bonemeal fertilizer, 87, 91, 94, 104, 109, 126, 151, 172

centipedes, 30
chafer-grubs, 29, 30
chalk, 113, 126, 133
chlorosis, 27, 29
clay and heavy soils, 27–8, 42, 51, 58, 60, 67, 68, 115, 142, 164, 167
climbing plants, 24, 25, 129
cloches, 25–6, 61, 77, 118, 173, 174
compost, 28, 48, 52, 97, 133, 138
containers, cut flowers outside in, 22–3; planting in, 22
courtyards, 22–3, 140
crane flies, 30
cutting flowers, 15–16, 33–6
cutworms, 30

diseases, 29–31; chlorosis, 27, 29; mildew, 31, 60, 61; rust, 49; virus, 31
docks, eradicating, 31
dry-stone walls, 94

earthworms, 27, 29

earwigs, 30

Fish, Margery, 57
Foerster, Karl, 103
foliage, for decoration, 24–5, 35, 205
froghoppers, 30

garlic, to prevent slugs, 21
gilding, decorative, 106
grit, to improve soil, 28, 58, 74, 97, 102, 115, 163–4, 184

hedgehogs, 21, 30
herbs, 24, 107, 149, 168
hover-flies, 30
humus, 27, 29, 51, 52, 111, 132

John Innes Institute, 99

Kelway's, 165
kitchen gardens, 20–1

lacewings, 30
ladybirds, 30
leafmould, 52, 98, 118, 133, 166
leather-jackets, 30
Lemoine, Victor, 87
lime, lime-hating plants, 52, 88, 97, 98, 125, 133; uses and abuses of 27–8, 29, 113, 126, 134

manure, 61, 163, 172
mildew, 31, 60, 61
millipedes, 30
mulching, 28, 55, 156, 164

Palmer, Lewis, 43
patios, 22–3

peat, sedge, 28, 52, 67, 156
pests, 29–30; *see also individual pests,*
  e.g. earwigs, slugs
planting schemes, large gardens,
  18–21; small gardens, 16–18; *17;*
  terraces and courtyards, 22–3
polythene sheeting, 26, 61
pot-grown stock, 48, 72, 97, 142
potash, 41, 48, 61, 74, 80, 87, 91, 104,
  165, 172, 174

rainwater, 28, 34
raised beds, 22
red spider, 188
roots, and second flowering, 26;
  invasive, 19, 41, 48, 142, 158, 159,
  175; vigour improved by cutting
  flowers, 15–16
Russell, George, 137, 138
rust disease, 49

scented flowers, 24, 204–5
secateurs, 33
sedge peat, 28, 52, 67, 156
sharp sand, to improve soil, 28, 58,
  74, 97, 102, 115, 163, 164, 184
slugs, 21, 29, 30, 94, 103, 111, 114,
  164
snails, 29, 30

soils, acid, 27; boggy, 68, 126, 191;
  clay, 27–8, 42, 51, 58, 60, 67, 68,
  115, 142, 164, 167; light loams,
  28–9; liming, 27–8, 29; preparation, 27–9
soot, 94
spittle bugs, 30
staking cradles, 88
stems, cut flowers, 34, 35–6, 49
Stern, Sir Frederick, 102
straw, to improve soil, 28; straw
  quilt, 102, 103, 149

terraces, 22–3
thistles, eradicating, 31
toads, 21, 30

van Tubergen, 51, 127
vegetables, for decoration, 20–1
virus diseases, 31

Walkden, E., 177
weeds, 31–2
wind hating plants 88, 118, 143, 154,
  162, 163
wind resistant plants 42, 56, 81, 141,
  186, 188
wireworms, 29

Index of Plants

Only the more generally used common names have been included in the index.

Page numbers in *italic* refer to illustrations.

Acanthus, 39–40, 199, 201, 205, 206; *A. mollis*, 39, 195; *A. m. latifolius*, 39; *A. spinosus*, 39, 195

Achillea, 18, 20, 33, 40–1, 205; *A.* 'Clypeolata', 40–1; *A.* × 'King Edward', 40, 207; *A.* × 'Moonshine', 41, 208; *A.* 'Taygetea', 40; *A. decolorans* 'W. B. Child', 41; *A. eupatorium*, 40; *A. filipendulina*, 16, 21, 40, 41, 194, 195, 200, 204, 206, 208; *A. f.* 'Coronation Gold', 40; *A. f.* 'Gold Plate', 40; *A. f.* 'Parker's Variety', 40; *A. millefolium* 'Cerise Queen', 41; *A. ptarmica*, 195, 198, 202, 207, 208; *A. p.* 'The Pearl', 41; *A. p.* 'Perry's White', 41; *A. tomentosa*, 40

Aconitum, 23, 41–3, 194, 195, 198, 199, 201, 204, 205; *A.* 'Arendsii', 42–3; *A.* × *cammarum*, 41–2; *A.* × *c.* 'Bicolor', 42; *A.* × *c.* 'Blue Sceptre', 42; *A. c.* 'Bressingham Spire', 42–3; *17*; *A.* × *c.* 'Spark's Variety', 42; *A. orientale*, 43; *A. septentrionale* 'Ivorine', 42; *A. volubile*, 43

Adonis, 200

Agapanthus, 43–4, 194, 199, 201, 206; Headbourne Hybrids, 43; *A. campanulatus* 'Albus', 43; *A. c.* 'Isis', 43–4; *A. patens*, 44; *A. praecox*, 44

Alchemilla, 44–5, 200, 206; *A. alpina*, 45; *A. mollis*, 44-5, 194, 195, 197, 198, 199, 205

Allium, 45–7, 194, 196, 197, 199, 206; *A. albopilosum*, 46, 47; *A. azureum*, 202; *A. beesianum*, 46, 47, 207; *A. caeruleum*, 46, 47; *A. cernuum*, 46, 47; *A. cyaneum*, 45–6, 47, 202, 207; *A. flavum*, 200; *A. karataviense*, 47; *A. moly*, 200; *A. narcissiflorum*, 46; *A. neapolitanum grandiflorum*, 47; *A. pulchellum*, 46, 47, 201; *A. p.* 'Album', 46, 202

Alpines, 23, 25, 40

Alstroemeria, 47–8, 196, 197, 206, 208; Ligtu Hybrids, 48, 201; *A. aurantiaca*, 48

Althaea, 34, 48–9; *A. rosea*, 48-9

Alyssum, alpine, 25

Anaphalis, 49–50, 194, 196, 197, 199, 202, 206, 208; *A. cinnamomea*, 49, 50; *A. margaritacea*, 49, 50; *A. nubigena*, 49, 50, 205; *A. yedoensis*, 49

Anchusa myosotidiflora, 66

Anemone, 50–2; *A.* × *hybrida*, 50–1, 195, 208; *A.* × *h.* 'Bressingham Glow', 51; *A.* × *h.* 'Lady Gilmour', 51; *A.* × *h.* 'Louise Uhink', 51, 202; *A.* × *h.* 'Profusion', 51; *A.* × *h.* 'Queen Charlotte', 51, 201; *A.* × *h.* 'White Queen', 51; *A. fulgens* de Caen, 52; *A. f.* St Bavo, 51–2; *A. f.* St Brigid, 52;

Anemone—*cont.*
A. f. annulata grandiflora, 51–2;
 A. hupehensis japonica (Japanese
 anemone), 50; *A. h. j.* 'Splendens',
 50; *A. japonica*, 195; *A. lesseri*, 51;
 A. ranunculoides, 52
Anthemis, 20, 52–3, 199, 200; *A.
 tinctoria*, 52, 195, 204, 206; *A. t.*
 'Grallagh Gold', 52; *A. t.* 'Mrs
 E. C. Buxton', 52
Anthericum, 53; *A. liliago*, 53; 194; *17*
Aquilegia, 33, 53–5, 196, 197, 199,
 202; *54*; *A.* 'Copper Queen', 55;
 A. 'Crimson Star', 55; *A.* 'Drag-
onfly', 55; *A.* 'Hensol Harebell',
 53–4; *A.* McKana Hybrids, 54;
 A. 'Mrs Nicholls', 55; *A.* Mrs
 Scott Elliott's Long-spurred
 Hybrids, 54; *A.* 'Snow Queen',
 55; *A. alpina*, 53–4; *A. flabellata*,
 53–4; *A. glandulosa*, 53–4; *A.
 longissima*, 55; *A. pyrenaica*, 55,
 204; *A. p.* Langdon's Rainbow
 Strain, 55
Arabis, alpine, 25
Armeria, 33, 55–6; *A.* Giant Hybrids,
 56; *A. corsica*, 56; *A. latifolia*
 'Bees' Ruby', 56; *A. l.* 'Ruby
 Glow', 56; *A. maritima*, 16, 17,
 55–6, 194, 197, 199, 201, 207;
 A. m. 'Alba', 56; *A. m.* 'Blood-
stone', 56; *A. m.* 'Laucheana',
 55–6; *A. m.* 'Vindictive', 56; *17*
Artemisia, 56–7; *A. absinthium* 'Lam-
brook Silver', 57; *A. lactiflora*, 18,
 23, 56–7, 194, 198, 199, 202, 204,
 205, 206, 207; *17*; *A. maritima*
 'Nutans', 57; *A. m.* 'Silver Queen',
 57; *A. schmidtiana* 'Nana', 57
Artichokes, 20, 22
Aruncus, 194, 202
Asparagus, 20
Asphodel, *see* Asphodelus
Asphodeline liburnica, 58; *A. lutea*, 57
Asphodelus, 57–8, 194, 200; *A.
 albus*, 58; *A. cerasiferus*, 58; *A.
 liburnicus*, 58; *A. luteus*, 57–8, 204;
 A. ramosus, 58
Aster, 58–61, 195, 198, 201; dwarf,

17–18, 25–6, 197; *A. x frikartii*, 59;
 A. acris, 59; *A. a.* 'Nanus', 59; *A.
 alpinus*, 25, 202, 207; *A. amellus*,
 18, 59, 194, 199, 202, 206; *A. a.*
 'Jacqueline Genebrier', 59; *A. a.*
 'King George', 59; *A. a.* 'Violet
 Queen', 59; *A. ericoides*, 59–60,
 195, 206, 207; *A. e.* 'Brimstone',
 60, 200; *A. e.* 'Cinderella', 60; *A.
 linosyris*, 83; *A. novae-angliae*, 60;
 A. n. a. 'Harrington's Pink', 60
A. novi-belgii, 60–1, 194, 202, 206,
 208; *A. n-b.* 'Blue Bouquet', 61;
 A. n-b. 'Choristers', 60; *A. n-b.*
 'Crimson Brocade', 60; *A. n-b.*
 'Eventide', 60; *A. n-b.* 'Fellowship', 60; *A. n-b.* 'Freda Ballard',
 60; *A. n-b.* 'Lady in Blue', 61;
 A. n-b. 'Little Boy Blue', 60; *A.
 n-b.* 'Little Pink Beauty', 61; *A.
 n-b.* 'Little Red Boy', 61; *A. n-b.*
 'Marie Ballard', 60; *A. n-b.* 'Rose
 Bonnet', 61; *A. n-b.* 'Royal Velvet',
 60; *A. n-b.* 'Snowsprite', 61; *A.
 subcoeruleus* 'Wendy', 59; *A.
 thomsonii*, 59; *A. t. nanus*, 59; *A.
 tongolensis* 'Berggarten', 58; *A.
 yunnanensis*, 195, 202; *A. y.*
 'Napsbury', 58–9
Astilbe, 20, 21, 22, 62–3, 79, 80, 194,
 198, 199, 201, 202, 205; *A.*
 'Bressingham Beauty', 62; *A.*
 'Federsee', 62; *A.* 'Gertrude Brix',
 62; *A.* 'Granat', 62; *A.* 'Irrlicht',
 62
Astrantia, 63–4, 194, 197, 198, 199,
 205, 206; *64*; *A.* 'Major', 63; *A.*
 'Maxima', 63; *A. carniolica*, 63,
 202; *A. c.* 'Rosea', 63; *A. c.* 'Rubra',
 63; *A. involucrata*, 63–4, 202
Aubretia, 30
Avena candida, 190

Beans, dwarf, 21; runner, 22
Bellis, 64–5, 196, 197, 199, 204; *B.
 perennis*, 64–5, 201, 202, 207; *B. p.*
 'Dresden China', 65, 207; *B. p.*
 'The Pearl', 65; *B. p.* 'Rob Roy',
 65, 207

Bergamot, *see* Monarda

Bergenia, 65–6, 194, 196, 197, 199, 201, 204, 205; *B.* 'Abendgut', 66; *B.* 'Ballawley', 66; *B.* 'Bressingham Bountiful', 66; *B.* 'Margery Fish', 66; *B.* 'Pugsley's Pink', 66; *B.* 'Silberlicht', 66; *B. cordifolia*, 65, 206; *B. c.* 'Purpurea', 65; *B. delavayi*, 65–6; *B. schmidtii*, 65

Black-eyed susan, *see* Rudbeckia

Border carnation, *see* Dianthus

Brunnera, 66–7, 195, 198, 204, 207; *B. macrophylla*, 66–7, 194, 199, 202, 205; *B. m.* 'Variegata', 66

Burning bush, *see* Dictamnus

Calamintha, 67; *C. nepetoides*, 67

Caltha, 25, 67–8, 196, 198, 200, 204; *C. palustris*, 67–8; *C. p.* 'Plena', 68

Camassia, 68–9, 196, 197, 198, 202; *C. cusickii*, 68; *C. esculenta*, 68; *C. howellii*, 69; *C. leichtlinii*, 68–9; *C. l.* 'Album', 69; *C. l.* 'Atroviolacea', 69; *C. l.* 'Plena', 69; *C. quamash*, 68, 69; *C. scilliodes*, 69

Campanula, 30, 33, 69–72, 199, 202; alpine, 18, 25; dwarf, 194; *C. alliariifolia*, 69; *C. a.* 'Ivory Bells', 69; *C. burghaltii*, 69, 71; *C. carpatica*, 16, 69, 71, 197, 198, 199, 202, 207; *C. c.* 'Blue Moonlight', 69; *C. c.* 'Bressingham White', 69; *C. c.* 'Wheatley Violet', 69; *C. glomerata*, 70; *C. g.* 'Joan Elliott', 70; *C. g.* 'Nana Alba', 70; *C. g.* 'Superba', 70; *C. lactiflora*, 70, 71, 194, 196, 198; *C. l.* 'Alba', 70; *C. l.* 'Loddon Anna', 70; *C. l.* 'Pouffe', 70; *17*; *C. l.* 'Prichard's Variety', 70; *C. latifolia*, 70–1, 194, 196, 198; *C. l.* 'Brantwood', 70–1; *C. l.* 'Gloaming', 70–1; *C. latiloba*, 71; *C. l.* 'Percy Piper', 71; *C. muralis*, 71; *C. persicifolia*, 71, 194, 198, 203; *C. p.* 'Fleur de Neige', 71; *C. p.* 'Pride of Exmouth', 71; *C. p.* 'Snowdrift', 71; *C. p.* 'Telham Beauty', 71; *C. p.* 'Wirral Belle', 71; *C. portenschlagiana*, 16, 23, 71–2, 197, 199, 204, 207; *C. poscharskyana*, 72; *C. p.* 'Alba', 72; *C. rotundifolia*, 16, 72, 197, 198, 199, 207; *C. r.* 'Olympica', 72

Cape gooseberry, *see* Physalis

Carex, 199; *C. pendula*, 190–1; *C. stricta* 'Aurea', 190–1

Carrots, 21

Catananche, 16, 33, 72–3, 197, 199, 206; *C. caerulea*, 72–3, 194; *C. c.* 'Major', 73, 208

Catmint, *see* Nepeta

Cedronella, 73–4, 196; *C. foeniculum*, 73–4, 202, 206

Centaurea, 74, 195; *C. dealbata*, 74, 201; *C. d.* 'John Coutts', 74; *C. d.* 'Steenbergii', 74; *C. macrocephala*, 206; *C. montana*, 74, 179; *C. pulchra* 'Major', 74; *C. simplicicaulis*, 74

Centranthas, *see* Kentranthus

Cephalaria, 75; *C. gigantea*, 75

Cheiranthus, 75–6, 196, 198, 199, 204, 206; *C.* 'Constant Cheer', 76; *C.* 'Harpur Crewe', 76, 200; *C.* 'Rufus', 76; *C. linifolius*, 76

Chelone barbata, 155

Chinese lantern, *see* Physalis

Christmas rose, *see* Helleborus

Chrysanthemum, 35, 76–9, 203, 206; dwarf, 26; *C. maximum*, 76–7, 195, 208; *C. m.* 'Cobham Gold', 76, 77; *C. m.* 'Esther Read', 76; *C. m.* 'Everest', 77; *C. m.* 'Horace Read', 76; *C. m.* 'Jennifer Read', 76; *C. m.* 'John Murray', 76–7; *C. m.* 'Major', 208; *C. m.* 'T. Killin', 76; *C. m.* 'Wirral Pride', 76; *C. m.* 'Wirral Supreme', 76; *C. parthenium*, 77; *C. p.* 'White Bonnet', 77; *C. rubellum*, 77–8; *C. r.* 'Clara Curtis', 77; *C. uliginosum*, 77, 195; *C. vulgare*, 77

Chrysanthemums, Korean, 78; 'Autumn Day', 78; 'Carlene', 78; 'Charles Nye', 78; 'Coral Mist', 78; 'Lilac Time', 78; 'Margaret Simpson', 78; 'Polly Peachum', 78; 'St George's Day', 78; 'Wed-

Chrysanthemums—*cont.*
ding Day', 78; 'Yellow Maize', 78
Chrysanthemums, Otley Koreans,
26, 78–9, 208; 'Amber Glory', 78;
'Cheerfulness', 79; 'Copper Nob',
78; 'Dandy', 79; 'Firestone', 78;
'Gloria', 78; 'Gold Dust', 79;
'Pirate', 78; 'Powder River', 79;
'Rapture', 78; 'Shining Light',
78
Cimicifuga, 23, 79–80, 194, 198, 199,
203, 204, 205, 206; *C. cordifolia*, 79,
80; *C. foetida intermedia* 'White
Pearl', 79–80, 204; *C. japonica
acerina*, 79; *C. racemosa*, 80; *C.
ramosa*, 80
Columbine, *see* Aquilegia
Convallaria, 80–1, 197, 206; *C.
majalis*, 80–1, 196, 199, 203, 204,
205, 207; *C. m.* 'Fortin's Giant',
81; *C. m.* 'Rosea', 81
Coreopsis, 81–2, 199, 200; *C.* 'Gold-
fink', *17*; *C. grandiflora*, 81–2, 195,
198, 208; *C. g.* 'Badengold', 82;
C. g. 'Mayfield Giant', 81; *C. g.*
'Perry's Variety', 81–2; *C. g.* 'Sunburst', 81; *C. lanceolata*, 82; *C.
verticillata*, 81; *17*
Cortaderia argentea, 191; *C. selloana*,
191
Corydalis, 82; *C. lutea*, 82, 207; *C.
ochroleuca*, 82, 207
Cotton lavender, *see* Santolina
Cowslip, *see* Primula
Crambe, 83, 195, 203; *C. cordifolia*,
83, 204, 207
Crinitaria, 83–4, 196; *C. linosyris*,
83–4, 200
Crinum, 84; *C.* × *powellii*, 84, 194,
201; *C. bulbispermum*, 84
Crocosmia, 84–8, 199, 206; *86*; *C.*
'Citronella', 87; *C.* Earlham Hy-
brids, 87; *C.* 'Fire King', 87; *C.*
'His Majesty', 87; *C.* 'Kathleen',
87; *C.* 'Marjorie', 87; *C.* × *crocos-
miiflora*, 87; *C. aurea*, 87; *C.
masonorum*, 85, 194, 201, 205, 208;
C. pottsii, 85, 87
Curtonus, 84–7; *C. paniculata*, 85

Daffodil, *see* Narcissus
Daisy, *see* Bellis
Dead nettle, *see* Lamium
Delphinium, 30, 33, 34, 88–91, 102,
196, 198, 202; *D.* 'Alice Artindale',
88; *D.* 'Artist', 88; *D.* 'Betty
Baseley', 90; *D.* 'Betty Hay', 89;
D. 'Blue Nile', 89; *D.* 'Blue Tit',
90; *D.* 'Cinderella', 90; *D.* 'Cristella', 89; *D.* 'Cupid', 90; *D.*
'Evenglow', 88; *D.* 'Great Scott',
88; Pacific Hybrids, 89; *D.* 'Pageboy', 90; *D.* 'Purple Ruffles', 89;
D. 'Silver Moon', 89; *D.* 'Strawberry Fair', 89; *D.* 'Sungleam', 89,
200; *D.* 'White Nylon', 88; *D.
belladonna*, 205; *D. grandiflorum*
(chinense) 'Blue Butterfly', 90–1;
D. nudicaule, 90; *D. ruysii* 'Pink
Sensation', 90; *D. zalil*, 91, 200
Delphiniums, Belladonna Hybrids,
89–90; 'Blue Bees', 89–90; 'Lamartine', 90; 'Moerheimii', 90;
'Wendy', 89, 90
Dianthus, 24, 27, 29, 30, 91–4, 194,
196, 197, 198, 199, 201, 203, 204,
206, 208; *D.* 'Beauty of Cambridge', 92; *D.* 'Dad's Favourite',
92; *D.* 'Excelsior', 92; *D.* 'Fiery
Cross', 92; *D.* 'The Grenadier',
92; *D.* 'Imperial Clove', 92; *D.*
'Madonna', 92; *D.* 'Mrs Sinkins',
92; *D.* 'The Rifleman', 92; *D.*
'Robin Thain', 92; *D.* 'Salmon
Clove', 92; *D.* 'Scarlet Fragrance',
92; *D.* 'White Ladies', 92; *D.
allwoodii*, 92–3; *D. a.* 'Diane', 93;
D. a. 'Doris', 93; *D. a.* 'Helen', 93;
D. a. 'Ian', 93; *D. a.* 'Lilian', 93;
D. a. 'London Poppet', 93; *D. a.*
'Robin', 93; *D. deltoides*, 93; *D. d.*
'Albus', 93; *D. d.* 'Brilliant', 93;
D. d. 'Erectus', 93; *D. d.* 'Hansen's
Red', 93; *D. gratianopolitanus*, 93;
D. g. 'Baker's Variety', 93; *D. g.*
'Flore Pleno', 93; *D. plumarius*, 93
Dianthus, alpine, 18, 25, 93–4, 207;
'Little Jock', 93; 'Mrs (Nellie)
Clark', 93; 'Oakington Hybrid', 93

Dicentra, 94–6, 194, 199, 201, 205, 207; *95*; *D. eximea* 'Adrian Bloom', 95, 96; *D. e.* 'Alba', 95; *D. formosa* 'Bountiful', 95; *D. spectabilis*, 94–5, 96

Dictamnus, 96–7, 194, 198, 199, 204, 205, 206; *D. alba*, 96, 201, 203; *D. fraxinella*, 96, 201, 203

Dierama, 97–8, 194, 201; *D. pulcherrima*, 97–8

Digitalis, 98–9, 194, 195, 198, 199, 200; Excelsior Hybrids, 98; *D. ambigua*, 98–9; *D. ferruginea*, 99; *D. grandiflora*, 98; *D. mertonensis*, 99

Doronicum, 99–100, 195, 198, 200, 206, 208; *D. caucasicum*, 100; *D. plantagineum*, 100; *D. p.* 'Harpur Crewe', 99–100; *D. p.* 'Miss Mason', 100; *D. p.* 'Spring Beauty', 100

Echinacea, 23, 100–1, 194, 204; *E. purpurea*, 100–1, 198, 201, 202, 208; *E. p.* 'The King', 101; *E. p.* 'Robert Bloom', 101; *E. p.* 'White Lustre', 101

Echinops, 101, 105, 106, 196, 198, 202, 206, 208; *E. humilis* 'Taplow Blue', 101; *E. ritro*, 101

Eremurus, 102–3, 194, 198, 201, 203; Highdown Hybrids, 102; *E. bungei*, 102; *E. himalaicus*, 102; *E. olgae*, 102; *E. robustus*, 102; *E. stenophyllus*, 102

Erigeron, 16, 33, 103–4, 194, 196, 199, 201, 202, 206, 208; *E.* 'Darkest of All', 103; *E.* 'Dignity', 103; *E.* 'Dimity', 103; *E.* 'Foerster's Liebling', 103; *E.* 'Gaiety', 104; *E.* 'Merstham Glory', 103; *E.* 'Prosperity', 103–4; *E.* 'Quakeress', 103; *E.* 'Rose Triumph', 103; *E.* 'Serenity', 104; *E.* 'Sincerity', 104; *E.* 'Wupperthal', 103; *E. simplex*, 103

Erodium, alpine, 25, 207

Eryngium, 105–6, 194, 196, 199, 202,

205, 206; *104*; *E.* 'Violetta', 105, 208; *E. alpinum*, 105; *E. bourgatii*, 105; *E. planum*, 105; *E. tripartitum*, 105; *E. variifolium*, 105–6, 208

Erysimum linifolium, 76

Eupatorium, 106, 196, 198, 202; *E. ageratoides*, 106; *E. purpureum*, 106

Euphorbia, 23, 106–7, 194, 196; *E. characias*, 107; *E. polychroma*, 106, 197, 204; *E. veneta*, 107; *E. wulfenii*, 107

Fennel, *see* Foeniculum

Ferns, 200, 205, 207, 208

Festuca glauca, 191

Foeniculum, 107, 196, 198, 207; *F. vulgare*, 21, 24, 107, 195, 200, 205, 206

Foxglove, *see* Digitalis

Fritillaria, 108–9, 207; *108*; *F. meleagris*, 108–9, 197; *F. persica*, 108–9

Gaillardia, 20, 109–10, 196, 198, 201; *G. aristata*, 109; *G. a.* 'Dazzler', 109; *G. a.* 'Golden Giant', 110; *G. a.* 'Mrs Harold Longster', 110; *G. a.* 'Ipswich Beauty', 110; *G. a.* 'Mandarin', 110; *G. a.* 'Wirral Flame', 110; *G. a.* 'Wirral Pride', 109; *G. grandiflora*, 109, 208

Galega, 110, 196, 198, 202, 205, 207; *G. officinalis*, 110; *G. o.* 'Alba', 110; *G. o.* 'Her Majesty', 110; *G. o.* 'Lady Wilson', 110; *G. orientalis*, 110

Galtonia, 110–11, 196, 203; *G. candicans*, 110–11, 195

Gentian, *see* Gentiana

Gentiana, 25, 111–12, 195, 197, 199, 202, 204, 207; *111*; *G. septemfida*, 18, 111–12, 198

Geranium, 112, 195, 199; *G.* 'Johnson's Blue', 112, 202; *G. armenum*, 112; *G. dalmaticum*, 207; *G. psilostemon*, 112; *G. wallichianum*, 169, 198, 202; *G. w.* 'Buxton's Blue', 112

Geum, 33, 113, 196, 198, 199, 206; *G.* 'Dolly North', 113; *G.* 'Lady Stratheden', 113, 200; *G.* 'Mrs Bradshaw', 113, 201; *G. borisii*, 113, 195, 199, 201, 207; *17*
Giant scabious, *see* Cephalaria
Glyceria, 193; *G. maxima* 'Variegata', 191
Goldenrod, *see* Solidago
Grape hyacinth, *see* Narcissus
Grasses, 190–3, 195, 197, 199, 205, 206, 207, 208
Gypsophila, 113–14, 195, 196, 199, 203, 206, 207; *G. paniculata*, 113–14, 208; *G. p.* 'Bristol Fairy', 114; *G. p.* 'Flamingo', 114; *G. p.* 'Rosy Veil', 114

Harebell, *see* Campanula
Heaths, 26
Hedera, 24–5; *H. helix*, 24
Helenium, 114–15, 195, 196, 198, 200, 201, 208; *H.* 'Baudirektor Linne', 114; *H.* 'Bressingham Gold', 114; *H.* 'Bruno', 115; *H.* 'Butterpat', 114; *H.* 'Chipperfield Orange', 114, 115; *H.* 'Coppelia', 114; *H.* 'Gold Fox', 114; *H.* 'Golden Youth', 114; *H.* 'Mahogany', 114; *H.* 'Moerheim Beauty', 114, 115; *H.* 'Pumilum Magnificum', 114, 115; *H.* 'Wyndley', 114, 115
Helianthus, 115–16, 195, 196, 200, 208; *H. atrorubens*, 115–16; *H. a.* 'Capenoch Star', 116; *H. a.* 'Capenoch Supreme', 116; *H. a.* 'Monarch', 115–16; *H. a.* 'Soleil d'Or', 116; *H. a.* 'Triomph de Gand', 116; *H. decapetalus*, 115; *H. d.* 'Loddon Gold', 115; *H. d.* 'Maximus', 115; *H. rigidus*, 116; *H. r.* 'Miss Mellish', 116
Helictotrichon sempervirens, 190
Heliopsis, 116–17, 195, 196, 198, 200, 208; *H.* 'Golden Plume', 117; *H.* 'Goldgreenheart', 117; *H.* 'Incomparabilis', 117; *H. patula*, 117

Helleborus, 117–18, 197, 200, 204; *H. antiquorum*, 118; *H. lividus corsicus*, 118; *H. niger*, 25, 117–18, 203, 207; *H. orientalis*, 118, 201
Hemerocallis, 18, 119–20, 195, 198, 200, 201; *H.* 'Black Falcon', 119; *H.* 'Fandango', 119; *H.* 'Halo Light', 119; *H.* 'Hyperion', 119; *H.* 'Imperator', 119; *H.* 'Pink Prelude', 119; *H.* 'Stafford', 119; *H.* 'Whichford', 119; *H. dumortieri*, 119, 205; *H. flava*, 119; *H. fulva*, 119
Herbs, 24
Hesperis, 120, 196, 198; *H. matronalis*, 120, 205
Heuchera, 33, 120–1, 195, 199, 201, 203, 205, 206, 207, 208; *H.* × *brizoides*, 120–1; *H.* × *b.* 'The Huntsman', 121; *H. sanguinea*, 120–1
Heuchera, Bressingham Hybrids, 121; 'Coral Cloud', 121; 'Greenfinch', 121; 'Pearl Drops', 121; 'Red Spangles', 121; 'Scintillation', 121; 'Snowflakes', 121
Heucherella, 195, 199, 200, 201, 203, 205, 206, 207; *H.* 'Bridget Bloom', 121
Hollyhock, *see* Althacea
Hosta, 35, 122–3, 195, 197, 198, 200, 205, 206; *122*; *H.* 'Honeybells', 123; *H. fortunei* 'Albo-picta', 123; *H. f.* 'Aurea', 123; *H. f. aureomarginata*, 123; *H. lancifolia*, 123, 202; *H. minor* 'Alba', 123; *H. plantaginia* 'Grandiflora', 123; *H. sieboldiana*, 123, 191, 202; *H. s.* 'Elegans', 123; *H. tardiflora*, 123; *H. ventricosa*, 123

Incarvillea, 124, 201, 208; *I. delavayi*, 124; *I. grandiflora*, 124
Inula, 124–5, 196, 198, 200; *I. ensifolia*, 125; *I. oculis-christi*, 100, 125; *I. orientalis*, 124–5
Iris, 125–7, 195, 196, 197, 200, 201, 204, 207; *I.* 'Blue Valley', 126; *I.* 'Cliffs of Dover', 126; *I.* 'Gold Flake', 126; *I.* 'Golden Fare', 126;

Iris—*cont.*
I. 'Gudrun', 126; *I.* 'Helen McGregor', 126; *I.* 'Ola Kala', 126; *I.* 'Paradise Pink', 126; *I.* 'Sable', 126; *I.* 'Senlac', 126; bearded, 125–6, 205; Dutch, 125; English, 125; Spanish, 125, 205; *I. chrysographes*, 125, 126; *I. c.* 'Black Knight', 126; *I. delavayi*, 125, 126–7; *I. foetidissima*, 127, 202, 207; *I. f.* 'Lutea ', 127; *I. f.* 'Variegata', 127; *I. ochroleuca*, 125, 127, 198; *I. pallida*, 202; *I. p. variegata*, *17*; *I. pseudacorus*, 125, 126; *I. sibirica*, 125, 126, 198, 202; *I. s.* 'Caesar', 126; *I. s.* 'Perry's Blue', 126; *I. s.* 'Snow Queen', 126; *I. stylosa*, 125; *I. unguicularis*, 125
Ixia, 197
Ixiolirion, 127; *I. ledebourii*, 127; *I. montanum*, 127
Ivy, *see* Hedera

Jonquil, *see* Narcissus

Kaffir lily, *see* Schizostylis
Kale, dwarf curly, 21
Kentranthus, 127–8; *K.* 'Albus', 128; *K. ruber*, 128; *K. r.* 'Atrococ-cineus', 128
Kingcup, *see* Caltha
Kniphofia, 128–9, 132, 195, 201; *K.* 'Samuel's Sensation', 129; Stark's Hybrids, 129; *K. galpinii*, 129

Lady's mantle, *see* Alchemilla
Lamb's-tongue, *see* Stachys
Lamium, 129; *L. galeobdolon* 'Varie-gatum', 129; *L. maculatum*, 129, 196, 197, 200, 207; *L. m.* 'Roseum', 129
Lasiogrostis splendens, 191–2
Lathyrus, 129–30, 196, 198; *L. lati-folius*, 129–30; *L. l.* 'Pink Beauty', 130; *L. l.* 'Pink Pearl', 130; *L. l.* 'Rose Queen', 130; *L. vernus*, 130
Lavandula, 130–1, 196, 199, 202, 205, 207; *L. officinalis*, 130; *L. spica*, 130–1; *L. s.* 'Backhouse Variety', 131; *L. s.* 'Folgate Blue', 131; *L. s.* 'Grappenhall', 130; *L. s.* 'Hidcote', 130; *L. s.* 'Munstead Blue', 130; *L. s.* 'Nana Alba', 131; *L. s.* 'Nana Atropurpurea', 130; *L. s.* 'Nana Pink', 131
Lavatera, 131, 199, 203; *L. olbia rosea*, 131, 196, 201
Lavender, *see* Lavandula
Lenten rose, *see* Helleborus
Liatris, 131–2, 195, 201; *L. callilepsis*, 132; *L. c.* 'Kobold', 132; *L. pycnostachya*, 132
Ligularia, 132–3, 198; *L. clivorum*, 132, 195, 200, 205; *L. przewalskii*, 132–3, 195, 200, 205; *L. p.* 'The Rocket', 132–3; *17*
Lilium, 133–4, 205; *L. candidum*, 133; *L. henryi*, 134; *134*; *L. regale*, 133; *L. speciosum*, 134
Lily, *see* Lilium; African lily, *see* Agapanthus; Day lily, *see* Hemero-callis
Lily-of-the-valley, *see* Convalaria
Limonium, 135, 195, 199, 202, 207; *L. latifolium*, 135, 203, 208; *L. l.* 'Blue Cloud', 135; *L. l.* 'Violetta', 135
Linaria, 135–6, 197, 198, 199; *L. purpurea*, 135–6, 196, 202, 203; *L. p.* 'Canon J. Went', 135–6, 195, 201
Lobelia, 136–7; *L.* 'Jack McMasters', 136; *L.* 'Queen Victoria', 136; *L.* × *vedrariensis*, 136–7; *L. car-dinalis*, 136; *L. fulgens*, 136; *L. f.* 'Bees Flame', 136, 137; *L. syphi-litica*, 137
London pride, *see* Saxifraga
Loosestrife, *see* Lysimachia
Lunaria, 137, 198, 199; *L. rediviva*, 137, 202
Lungwort, *see* Pulmonaria
Lupin, *see* Lupinus
Lupinus, 137–8, 196, 198, 201, 202; *L. polyphyllus*, 137–8; *L. p.* 'Bress-ingham Sunshine', 138; *L. p.* 'Josephine', 138; *L. p.* 'Lady Fayre', 138; *L. p.* 'Lilac Time', 138; *L. p.* 'Thundercloud', 138

Lychnis, 138–9, 195, 198, 201; *L. chalcedonica*, 138–9; *L. viscaria*, 139; *L. v.* 'Albiflora', 139; *L. v.* 'Splendens Plena', 139
Lysimachia, 139–40, 195; *L. clethroides*, 139–40; *L. ephemerum*, 140; *L. nummularia*, 140
Lythrum, 18, 22, 23, 141–2, 195, 198, 201, 203, 207; *L.* 'Prichard's Variety', 141–2; *L. salicaria*, 141; *L. s.* 'The Beacon', 141; *17*; *L. s.* 'Brightness', 141; *L. s.* 'Firecandle', 141; *L. s.* 'Lady Sackville', 141; *L. s.* 'Robert', 141, *L. virga tum*, 141; *L. v.* 'The Rocket', 141; *L.v.* 'Rose Queen', 141

Macleaya, 142, 196, 198, 200; *M. cordifolia*, 142, 204, 206; *M. microcarpa*, 142; *M. m.* 'Kelway's Coral Plume', 142
Maize, 20, 21
Marjoram, *see* Origanum
Marsh marigold, *see* Caltha
Meconopsis, 142–3, 198, 200, 202; *M. baileyi*, 142; *M. betonicifolia*, 142–3
Melissa, 205; *M. officinalis*, 24
Mertensia, 143; *M. ciliata*, 143; *M. virginica*, 143
Michaelmas daisies, 31, 33, 58, 60–1, 195, 198
Mimulus, 16, 144–5, 195, 197, 198, 200, 201, 204; *144*; *M.* 'A. T. Johnson', 144–5; *M. burnettii*, 145; *M. cupreus*, 145; *M. c.* 'Red Emperor', 145; *M. c.* 'Whitecroft Scarlet', 145; *M. Luteus*, 200, 205
Miscanthus, 199; *M. sinensis*, 192; *M. s.* 'Silver Fern', 192; *M. s.* 'Variegatus', 192; *M. s.* 'Zebrinus', 192
Molinia altissima, 192; *M. caerulea* 'Variegata', 192
Monarda, 145, 195, 201, 204, 205, 206; *M.* 'Cambridge Scarlet', 145; *M.* 'Croftway Pink', 145; *M.* 'Prairie Night', 145, 202
Montbretia, *see* Crocosmia

Montbretia laxiflora, 87
Morina, 145–6; *M. longifolia*, 145–6, 207
Mullein, *see* Verbascum
Muscari, 146, 196, 197, 202; *M.* 'Heavenly Blue', 146; *M. armeniacum*, 146; *M. botryoides*, 146; *M. b.* 'Albus', 146; *M. comosum*, 146; *M. c.* 'Plumosum', 146; *M. moschatum*, 146; *M. m.* 'Major', 146

Narcissus, 25, 146–7, 196, 197, 205; *N.* 'Louise de Coligny', 147; *N. jonquilla*, 147; *N. j.* 'Buttercup', 147; *N. j.* 'Gracilis', 147; *N. j.* 'Nirvana', 147; *N. juncifolius*, 147, 207; *N. odorus* 'Campernelli', 147; *N. o.* 'Campernelli Plenus', 147; *N. o.* 'Rugulosus', 147; *N. poeticus*, 147; *N. p.* 'Flore Pleno', 147; *N. p.* 'Praecox', 147; *N. p.* 'Recurvus', 147
Narcissus, Tazetta 'Compressus', 147; 'Odoratus', 147
Nepeta, 15, 148, 195, 196, 197, 199, 202, 205, 206; *N.* 'Six Hills', 148, 204; *N.* 'Souvenir d'André Chaudron', 148; *N.* × *faassenii*, 148, 204; *N. mussinii*, 148
Nerine, 148–9; *N. bowdenii*, 148–9 201, 204, 206

Oenothera, 200
Onopordon, 149, 196, 198, 202; *O. acanthium*, 149
Orchis mascula, 113
Origanum, 149–50, 195, 196, 197, 199, 201, 205, 206; *O. laevigatum*, 150; *O. rotundifolia*, 150, 204, 207; *O. vulgare*, 24, 149–50, 204

Paeonia, 25, 33, 150–3, 196, 201, 205, 206, 207, 208; *P.* 'Alice Harding', 152; *P.* 'Beersheba', 152; *P.* 'Chocolate Soldier', 152; *P.* 'Claire de Lune', 152; *P.* 'Kelway's Supreme', 152; *P.* 'La Lorraine', 152; *P.* 'Madame Calot', 152; *P.*

Paeonia—*cont.*
  'Red Flag', 152; *P.* 'Shimmering
  Velvet', 152; *P. mlokosewitschii,*
  152; *P. officinalis* 'J. C. R. Weguelin', 152; *P. o.* 'Mutabilis', 152
Paeonia, Imperial, 152–3; 'Bowl of
  Beauty', 153; 'Crimson Glory',
  153; 'Evening World', 153; 'Kel-
  way's Majestic', 153; 'Queen
  Alexandra', 153
Papaver, 33, 34, 153–4, 196, 197,
  198, 199, 201, 205, 207; *P. alpinum,*
  154; *P. nudicaule,* 154; *P. orientale,*
  35, 154; *P. o.* 'Colonel Bowles',
  154; *P. o.* 'Hewitt's Old Rose', 154;
  P. o. 'Marcus Perry', 154; *P. o.*
  'Olympia', 154; *P. o.* 'Perry's
  White', 154; *P. o.* 'Princess Vic-
  toria Louise', 154
Paradisea liliastrum major, 53
Parsley, 21
Pasqueflower, *see* Pulsatilla
Pennisetum alopecuroides, 192; *P.
  orientale,* 192
Penstemon, 154–5, 195, 199, 201; *P.*
  'Garnet', 155; *P. barbatus,* 155;
  P. pinifolius, 155
Peony, *see* Paeonia
Periwinkle, *see* Vinca
Phalaris arundinacea 'Picta', 192–3
Phleum phleiodes, 193
Phlox, 21, 24, 33, 155–8, 195, 200,
  201, 202, 204, 205; *P.* 'Border
  Gem', 157; *P.* 'Dodo Hanbury
  Forbes', 157; *P.* 'Elizabeth Arden',
  157; *P.* 'Eventide', 157; *P.* 'Ever-
  est', 157; *P.* 'Fairy's Petticoat',
  157; *P.* 'Hampton Court', 157; *P.*
  'Harlequin', 157; *P.* 'Leo Schlag-
  eter', 157; *P.* 'Le Mahdi', 157; *P.*
  'Mia Ruys', 157; *P.* 'Mies Copijn',
  157; *P.* 'Mother of Pearl', 157; *P.*
  'Othello', 157; *P.* 'Otley Purple',
  157; *P.* 'Prince of Orange', 157;
  P. 'Sandringham', 157; *P.* 'Skylight', 157; *P.* 'Starfire', 157; *P.*
  'White Admiral', 157; *P.* 'Windsor', 157; alpine, 25; *P. maculata,*
  157–8; *P. m.* 'Alpha', 158; *P. m.*

'Omega', 158; *P. paniculata,* 158
Phygelius, 158, 199, 201; *P. aequalis,*
  158; *P. capensis,* 158
Physalis, 19, 158–9, 196, 197, 201,
  207, 208; *159; P. franchetii,* 158–9
Physostegia, 160, 196, 197, 198, 206;
  P. speciosa 'Rose Bouquet', 160,
  201; *P. virginiana,* 160; *P. v.*
  'Summer Snow', 160; *P. v.* 'Vivid',
  160
Pink carnation, *see* Dianthus
Platycodon, 160–1, 195, 197, 202;
  P. grandiflorus mariesii, 160–1
Polyanthus, *see* Primula
Polygonatum, 161, 196, 200; *P.
  multiflorum,* 161
Polygonum, 161–2, 195, 198, 200,
  207; *P. amplexicaule,* 23, 161, 169,
  201, 204, 205, 206; *P. a.* 'Atro-
  sanguineum', 161; *P. a.* 'Firetail',
  161; *P. bistorta* 'Superbum', 161–2
Poppy, *see* Papaver; Blue Poppy, *see*
  Meconopsis
Primrose, *see* Primula
Primula, 20, 22, 162, 196, 197, 198,
  200, 201, 202, 204; *P. vulgaris,* 162
Pulmonaria, 23, 147, 162–3, 196, 197,
  198, 200, 204; *163; P. alba,* 162; *P.
  angustifolia,* 162, 163, 202; *P. rubra*
  162, 201; *P. saccharata,* 162, 205
Pulsatilla, 163, 197; *P. vulgaris,* 163,
  198
Pyrethrum, 20, 163–5, 196, 199, 201,
  206, 208; *P.* 'Aphrodite', 165; *P.*
  'Beauty of Stapleford', 165; *P.*
  'Brenda', 165; *P.* 'Bressingham
  Red', 165; *P.* 'Charming', 165;
  P. 'Comet', 165; *P.* 'Duke of York',
  165; *P.* 'Evenglow', 165; *P.* 'Kel-
  way's Glorious', 165; *P.* 'Kelway's
  Lovely', 165; *P.* 'Lady R. Chur-
  chill', 165; *P.* 'Madeleine', 165;
  P. 'Profusion', 165; *P.* 'Salmon
  Beauty', 165; *P.* 'Scarlet Glow',
  165; *P.* 'Silver Challenge', 165; *P.*
  'White Madeleine', 165

Ragwort, *see* Senecio
Ranunculus, 166, 197, 199, 200; *R.*

Ranunculus—*cont.*
'Kelway's New Improved', 166;
R. asiaticus, 166
Red-hot poker, *see* Kniphofia
Reineckia, 167; *R. carnea*, 167, 205
Rudbeckia, 34, 167–8, 200, 206, *R.*
'Goldquelle', 167; *R.* 'Herbst-
sonne', 167, 168; *R. fulgida deamii*,
168; *R. f. speciosa*, 168; *R. gloriosa*,
196, 198; *R. laciniata* 'Golden
Glow', 167; *R. purpurea*, 100; *R.
subtomentosa*, 168
Rue, *see* Ruta
Ruta, 168 9; *R. graveolens*, 168–9,
196, 199, 205, 207; *R. g.* 'Jack-
man's Blue', 168–9

Salsify, 21
Salvia, 29; *S. superba*, 74, 207
Sanguisorba, 169, 195, 197, 201; *S.
canadensis*, 169; *S. obtusa*, 169; *S.
sitchense*, 169
Santolina, 169–70, 195, 197, 199,
200, 205, 207; *S. chamaecyparissus*
'Nana', 169–70; *S. c. corsica*, 169;
S. incana 'Nana', 169
Saxifraga, 25, 170–1, 197; *S.* 'Southside Seedling', 170; *S.* × 'Kath-
leen Pinsent', 170; *S.* × *urbium*,
171, 197, 200, 206; *S.* × *u.* 'Carni-
val', 171; *S.* × *u.* 'Triumph', 171;
S. × *u.* 'Winston Churchill', 171;
S. aizoon, 170; *S. a.* 'Lutea', 170;
S. a. 'Rosea', 170; *S. fortunei*,
170–1; Mossy hybrids, 200, 201,
208
Saxifrage, *see* Saxifraga
Scabiosa, 27, 29, 171–3, 197, 198,
199, 204, 206; *172*; *S. caucasica*,
171–3, 202, 208; *S. c.* 'Clive
Greaves', 173; *S. c.* 'Miss Will-
mott', 173; *S. c.* 'Moonstone', 173;
S. graminifolia, 208
Scabious, *see* Scabiosa
Schizostylis, 173–4, 208; *S.* 'Mrs
Hegarty', 173–4; *S.* 'Viscountess
Byng', 173–4; *S.* × *urbium*, 201; *S.
coccinea*, 173, 201, 204, 206; *S. c.*
'Major', 173

Scirpus, 199
Sea holly, *see* Eryngium
Sea lavender, *see* Limonium
Sedum, 33, 174; *S.* 'Ruby Glow',
195; *S. spectabile*, 174, 195, 197,
204, 206; *S. s.* 'Autumn Joy', 174;
S. s. 'Brilliant', 174
Senecio, 175; *S. doronicum*, 175; *S. d.*
'Sunburst', 175; *S. tanguticus*, 175
Sidalcea, 16, 175–6, 195, 201, 204;
S. 'Loveliness', 176; *S.* 'Rev.
Page Roberts', 176, *17*; *S.* 'Rose
Queen', 175–6; *S.* 'Wensleydale',
176; *S.* 'William Smith', 176
Sisyrinchium, 176, 197, 200; *S.
striatum*, 176, 197
Solidago, 177, 196, 200, 204, 208;
S. 'Ballardii', 177; *S.* 'Cloth of
Gold', 177; *S.* 'Crown of Rays',
177; *S.* 'Golden Falls', 177; *S.*
'Golden Gate', 177; *S.* 'Golden
Shower', 177; *S.* 'Golden Thumb',
177; *17*; *S.* 'Goldenmosa', 177; *S.*
'Lemore', 177; *S.* 'Queenie', 177;
S. canadensis, 177; *S. c.* 'Golden
Wings', 177
Solidaster, 178; *S. luteus*, 178
Solomon's seal, *see* Polygonatum
Spurge, *see* Euphorbia
Stachys, 178; *179*; *S. lanata*, 178,
199, 205; *S. olympica*, 178
Stipa, 193; *S. calamagrostis*, 193;
S. gigantea, 193; *S. pennata*, 193
Stokesia, 179–80, 195; *S. laevis*, 202,
204, 208; *S. l.* 'Blue Star', 179–80
Sweetcorn, 20, 21
Sweet rocket, *see* Hesperis

Tanacetum vulgare, 77
Tellima, 23, 180, 196, 204, 207; *T.
grandiflora*, 180, 200, 205
Thalictrum, 180–1, 197, 200, 205,
207; *T. dipterocarpum*, 180–1, 202;
T. d. 'Album', 180–1; *T. d.*
'Hewitt's Double', 102, 181, 204
Thistle, globe, *see* Echinops; Scotch,
see Onopordon
Thrift, *see* Armeria
Thyme, 25

Tiarella, 23, 181–2, 195, 200, 204; *T. cordifolia*, 181, 182; *T. polyphylla*, 181, 182; *T. wherryi*, 79, 181–2, 204, 205

Toadflax, *see* Linaria

Tolmiea, 182, 200, 207; *T. menziesii*, 182, 196

Tradescantia, 182–3, 199, 201, 202; *T.* 'Caerulea', 183; *T.* 'Caerulea Plena', 183; *T.* 'Iris Prichard', 183; *T.* 'J. C. Weguelin', 183; *T.* 'James Stratton', 183; *T.* 'Osprey', 183; *T.* 'Purple Dome', 183; *T.* 'Rubra', 183; *T.* × *andersoniana*, 182–3

Trollius, 25, 183, 197, 199, 200, 204, 208; *184*; *T.* 'Earliest of All', 183; *T.* 'Goldquelle', 183; *T.* 'Orange Princess', 183; *T. cultorum*, 183

Tulipa, 197

Valerian, *see* Kentranthus

Verbascum, 184–5; *V.* 'Cotswold Beauty', 185; *V.* 'Pink Domino', 185; Phoeniceum Hybrids, 185; *V. chaixii*, 184; *V. hartleyi*, 185; *V. vernale*, 184–5

Vernonia, 185; *V. crinita*, 26, 185, 197, 204, 207

Veronica, 18, 23, 26, 185–6, 195, 204; *V. exaltata*, 186, 202, 204; *V. gentianoides*, 186; *V. g.* 'Nana', 186; *V. longifolia*, 186, 202; *V. spicata*, 186, 202; *17*; *V. virginica*, 140; *V. v.* 'Alba', 186

Vinca, 187, 204, 208; *V. major*, 187; *V. minor*, 187; *V. m.* 'Atropurpurea', 187; *V. m.* 'Aureovariegata', 187; *V. m.* 'Aureovariegata Alba', 187; *V. m.* 'Bowles Variety', 187

Viola, 187–9, 197, 200, 202, 204, 208; *188*; *V.* 'Comte de Brazza', 189; *V.* 'Duchesse de Parma', 189; *V.* 'Marie Louise', 189; *V. odorata*, 187–9, 205; *V. o.* 'Czar', 189; *V. o.* 'Governor Herrick', 189; *V. o.* 'Princess of Wales', 189; *V. o.* 'Sulphurea', 189; *V. o.* praecox, 189

Violet, *see* Viola

Wallflower, *see* Artemisia

Wormwood, *see* Cheiranthus

Yarrow, *see* Achillea